PRAISE FOR
AN AMERIKAN FAMILY

"Magnificent. . . . A uniquely intimate history of Black liberation. . . . Writing as a historian and storyteller, Holley never lets us lose sight of the complex tapestry of movements that marked the era. . . . The greatest triumph of *An Amerikan Family* is the way Holley expertly blends archival research—including court documents, congressional transcripts, FBI records and newspaper clippings—with oral history to tell human stories that are at once exceptional and recognizable. . . . Seeing the humanity in these revolutionaries can allow the next generation of activists to see themselves as capable of resilience, and of becoming new models for making change."

—*Los Angeles Times*

"Sets a standard for drama that seems impossible to sustain. But the cast of characters expands, and somehow each one the reader encounters is as compelling as the last. . . . As revealing and inclusive a portrait of the Shakurs as we have seen. . . . *An Amerikan Family* offers no romantic assurance that the Shakurs' legacy in politics or music will live on exactly as they intended. Instead, it provides readers with a visceral and unsanitized account of the Black liberation struggle as a material and often lawless battle between the American government and Black people who refuse to be trampled upon."

—*New York Times Book Review* (Editors' Choice)

"Unlike other prominent American families, the Shakurs did not have millions of dollars to establish universities and foundations in their name. But what they did create was a powerful legacy of resistance. . . . Holley's book represents the most detailed account of the Shakurs to date. . . . *An Amerikan Family* opens an important conversation about Black resistance to oppression in U.S. history."

—*The New Republic*

"[A] history of a dynasty of Black resistance. . . . Well written and richly detailed, this book is a strong contribution to the literature of Black militancy."

—*Kirkus Reviews* (starred review)

"Holley's prose is captivating, as he describes the lives of Lumumba Shakur, Afeni Shakur, and Sekou Odinga, among others, and their impact on Black nationalism as well as on modern activism. . . . Holley's riveting, detailed history is essential reading for understanding modern America and the Shakurs' enduring legacy."

—*Booklist* (starred review)

"[A] riveting group portrait. . . . Sweeping and sober, this is a vital chapter in the history of the struggle for racial justice."

—*Publishers Weekly*

"Holley presents a teeming narrative. Details may astonish readers, but the plot feels right at home in the season of Black Lives Matter and the reemergence of white nationalism."

—*Alta Journal*

"Santi Elijah Holley uncovers the truth about this family of artists and activists and tells their story in a whole new way."

—*The Root*

"This may be the book of our generation."

—Dr. Ashley Wade, ReadwithDrWade.com

"A powerful text."

—Tavis Smiley, *Tavis Smiley* podcast

"*An Amerikan Family* is a first chapter in making the world better with truth and beauty. For those of us who haven't seen their stories written as they battled the darkness around them, *An Amerikan Family* is a light helping us go forward."

—Nikki Giovanni, poet

"What COINTELPRO worked so hard at wiping out is forever chronicled in this lost chapter of Amerikan history. Funny how the history of one family can cover so much ground, unearth so many bodies, and reveal so many conspiracies and hard-borne realities—from the heart of the U.S. government's anti-Black policies to the very soul of the Black Power and liberation movements. Holley's impeccable research takes what has been handed down orally to the children of the movement and lines it up with what has been factually documented. One way or another, we have all been touched by the Shakur family, and here is a testament to the fiery spirit that has sparked the brains of generations to come."

—Saul Williams, author of *Said the Shotgun to the Head*
and *The Dead Emcee Scrolls: The Lost Teachings of Hip-Hop*

AN
AMERIKAN
FAMILY

THE SHAKURS AND
THE NATION THEY CREATED

SANTI ELIJAH HOLLEY

MARINER BOOKS
NEW YORK BOSTON

A hardcover edition of this book was published by Mariner Books in 2023.

FIRST MARINER BOOKS PAPERBACK EDITION PUBLISHED 2024

Designed by Renata DiBiase

Library of Congress Cataloging-in-Publication Data

Names: Holley, Santi Elijah, author.
Title: An Amerikan family : the Shakurs and the nation they created / Santi Elijah Holley.
Other titles: Shakurs and the nation they created
Identifiers: LCCN 2022051479 (print) | LCCN 2022051480 (ebook) | ISBN 9780358588764 (hardcover) | ISBN 9780063312647 (trade paperback) | ISBN 9780358588696 (ebook)
Subjects: LCSH: Shakur, Afeni. | Shakur family. | African American political activists—Biography. | Political activists—United States—Biography. | Black Panther Party—Biography. | Shakur, Tupac, 1971–1996. | Shakur, Lumumba Abdul, 1943-1985—Friends and associates. | Black militant organizations—New York (State)—New York. | African American families—New York (State)—New York. | New York (N.Y.)—Biography.
Classification: LCC E185.93.N56 H65 2023 (print) | LCC E185.93.N56 (ebook) | DDC 974.7/100496073—dc23/eng/20221109
LC record available at https://lccn.loc.gov/2022051479
LC ebook record available at https://lccn.loc.gov/2022051480

ISBN 978-0-06-331264-7

24 25 26 27 28 LBC 5 4 3 2 1

Dedicated to the memory of my parents,
Woodrow Holley Jr. and Susan Finley

You are appreciated

History's greatest dangers are waiting for those who fail to learn its lessons. Any oppressed people who abandon the knowledge of their own protest history, or who fail to analyze its lessons, will only perpetuate their domination by others.

—Manning Marable

CONTENTS

INTRODUCTION

ONE WARM AFTERNOON in July 2021, at a quiet café on Frederick Douglass Boulevard in Harlem, I sit down with Sekou Odinga for a cup of coffee at a sidewalk table. He's just come from an early dinner with his family, celebrating his granddaughter's college graduation. Odinga is in his late seventies, soft-spoken, with a slight lisp. His beard is long and gray, and on his head is a kufi, or skullcap, a garment traditionally worn by Muslim men. Odinga and I have spoken a few times before, but this is the first time we're meeting in Harlem, which holds special significance, as this is where, more than fifty years before, he and his close friend Lumumba Shakur co-founded the Harlem chapter of the Black Panther Party.

Harlem has seen numerous changes in the years since Black Panthers patrolled and demonstrated in these very streets. Young White parents now push baby strollers down crowded sidewalks, while college students and tourists pedal omnipresent, rent-by-the-minute, blue bicycles through traffic. On the corner of 125th and Lenox, where Marcus Garvey and Malcolm X once held court and Gil Scott-Heron once shared small talk, there is now a Whole Foods grocery store. But as Odinga and I chat, we are interrupted by Black Harlemites, young and old, who approach our table to ask about Odinga's family, to pay their respects, or just to say a quick hello. Daily life may look different than it once did, but clearly Harlem hasn't forgotten about Sekou Odinga.

It is a miracle that Odinga is free to sit here and enjoy a simple cup of coffee. He is a veteran of the Black Panther Party and its more militant offshoot, the Black Liberation Army. He is also a former fugitive from the U.S. government and was accused by authorities of orchestrating the 1979 prison escape of Assata Shakur. Odinga has been pursued by federal agents, captured, tortured by police, and incarcerated for more than thirty years. That he is alive today is nothing short of a wonder.

A week after meeting with Odinga, I return to this block on Frederick Douglass Boulevard, to another coffee shop, where I meet a young man in his midtwenties named Malik Shakur. This is the first time he and I have met, but his face looks familiar right away. It doesn't take long to register why. Malik bears an uncanny resemblance to his uncle, the rapper Tupac Shakur. Malik is about the same age as Tupac was when he was murdered in 1996. What memories he has of his late uncle are limited to a handful of photographs of Tupac holding him as an infant. But, like Tupac, Malik is also pursuing a life in art that addresses contemporary social issues. He also carries the additional burden of an instantly recognizable, eminent, and often contentious last name.

These two individuals, Sekou Odinga and Malik Shakur, act as a bridge between two distant but interrelated generations. Each of them embodies a particular moment in the history of the Shakur family. While Odinga is a survivor of the federal government's destructive pursuit of radical Black activists in the 1960s, 1970s, and 1980s, Malik is the descendant of those survivors, which makes him, too, a survivor. As survivors, each has been entrusted, in his own way, to preserve the family's remarkable but complicated legacy and to act as a voice for those who came before. As is true of any oppressed community, the survivors and descendants carry the weight, responsibility, and trauma of those who paved the way. But they also help us find perspective, direction, and courage as we navigate the challenges and atrocities of the world today.

I began working on this book in the fall of 2020. Donald Trump was president. Uprisings against police brutality were happening in numerous American cities on an almost daily basis, many of them turning violent. White supremacists clashed with antifascist activists in city centers and residential neighborhoods. COVID-19 was wreaking unspeakable havoc, taking the lives of friends and family members, and we were still months away from a vaccine being widely available. Though the nation was faced with unique, once-in-a-generation crises, these challenges were in many ways similar to the challenges the nation faced a half century earlier, when many of the events of this book take place.

Like we had in the 1960s, Americans were again taking to the streets in pursuit of racial justice and equality. Like we had been in the 1970s, we were again bullied by an authoritative president and a pervasive surveillance state. And like we had in the 1980s, we were again suffering from a drug epidemic, though opioids had replaced crack cocaine as the biggest mortal threat. All of these issues particularly affected the lives of Black Americans, who have been and continue to be profiled, incarcerated, stripped of their constitutional rights, and killed by law enforcement at higher rates than their White compatriots.

During the two years of researching and writing this book, the country not only was engaged in heated debates over its history of racial discrimination but even argued over the right to teach this history in classrooms. These debates dominated cable news television, newspapers, social media, schools, and universities, as politicians sought to use this moment to galvanize the most impressionable and aggrieved members of their base. These were not new debates. For all the supposed progress this country believes itself to have made, we tend to find ways to undo those gains. White rage replaces Black joy. Black promise is met with White dismissal. If we look at the past fifty years, a pattern emerges. The heroic fight for civil and voting rights during the Kennedy and Johnson administrations was followed by a so-called White backlash, resulting in the Nixon administration and draconian "law-and-order" policies. The rise of Black Power, feminist movements, and gay and lesbian movements was countered by Reaganomics and the devastating War on Drugs. The historic election of the nation's first Black president will forever be footnoted by the subsequent election of a president who openly sympathized with White supremacists.

Much of the events in this book take place during a time in American history when it seemed like the nation was hopelessly polarized, tearing itself apart at the seams, unable or unwilling to come to enough consensus in order to save itself from annihilation. Not only have we not learned from the mistakes of our recent history— it often feels as though we have doubled down.

When Martin Luther King Jr. was murdered in 1968, the ethos of nonviolent protest died with him. Younger Black Americans increasingly rejected what they saw as a failed strategy and instead advocated for armed self-defense, as espoused by Malcolm X, who had been murdered three years earlier. Self-defense rhetoric soon escalated into direct action and violent offensives by radical groups like the Revolutionary Action Movement (RAM), the Black Liberation Army (BLA)—which committed armed bank robberies and waged guerrilla warfare against police officers—and the Black secessionist organization called the Republic of New Afrika (RNA), whose objective was and remains the establishment of an independent Black nation in the American South. These various groups and organizations all gathered under the red, black, and green umbrella of the Black liberation movement, the original BLM.

At the center of the movement is a close-knit family, based predominantly in New York City, who each adopted the surname Shakur, following the example of the Malcolm X acolyte and Black nationalist Muslim who had changed his name at a late age to Salahdeen Shakur and become a mentor to young, politically minded activists. While not everyone who took the Shakur name was related by blood, by adopting the cognomen they became part of the family, signaling their commitment to the struggle for Black liberation. This family included two brothers, Salahdeen's sons, Lumumba and Zayd, who would become leaders in the Black Panther Party's New York chapters; a brilliant legal and housing advocate named Afeni; Mutulu, an RNA leader who would go on to become a pioneer in the field of acupuncture before becoming a fugitive; and an erudite young woman named Assata, whose writings would inspire succeeding generations, and who has the distinction of becoming the first woman on the FBI's "Most Wanted Terrorists" list.

This family would also produce the conflicted, turbulent, and

brilliant Tupac. The late rapper and actor is, of course, the most famous and recognizable member of the Shakur family, with untold
millions of fans across the globe. In his short life and brief career,
Tupac inspired, enraged, mystified, and captivated the world, as
he continues to today, more than twenty-five years after his death.
Tupac's life and lyrics have inspired documentaries, a feature film, a
Broadway play, an interactive museum exhibit in downtown Los Angeles, and academic courses at such prestigious institutions as Harvard University. His song "Changes," recorded in 1992 and released
posthumously in 1998, found renewed popularity in the summer of
2020, serving as a sort of Black Lives Matter anthem for protestors
following the murder of George Floyd, an unarmed Black man, by a
White police officer in Minneapolis.

The appearance, or reemergence, of Tupac's impassioned condemnation of police brutality, racism, and systemic poverty felt uniquely
appropriate to this particular moment in time—not because the
singer was the descendant of survivors, or because he, too, had been
targeted by the same institutional forces that pursued his family, but
because it showed how little progress we've made over the past five
decades. Tupac isn't hopeful or optimistic when he claims to "see no
changes." But he was still young and too skeptical at that point in his
life to recognize the real, profound, and enduring changes that his
own family created in this country.

The legacy of the Shakur family exists all around us—in culture,
activism, and our professional lives. When we listen to the work of
Black songwriters who express both compassion and animosity, love
and indifference, social consciousness and nihilism, we hear Tupac's
influence. When we read the work of Black poets and authors who
speak to the collective Black experience while also yearning for
home and family, we are relating to Assata. When we demand our
right to represent ourselves, whether in the courtroom or the bedroom, we are following in the path set forward by Afeni. When we
seek alternative, holistic, and non-Western forms of medical treatment, we are benefiting from the groundwork laid by Mutulu.

The Shakurs helped to magnify the beauty and possibilities of being Black in America. They were a catalyst of Black creativity, recovery, and, above all, resistance. From aboveground community organizing to clandestine armed struggle, wherever there was a fight against persecution, Shakurs were at the forefront. They fought noble battles and won important victories. They have also made critical errors and suffered devastating losses. They have been connected to shocking acts of violence, in response to the violence perpetrated against them. But through it all, they have never wavered in their commitment to the liberation of Black people in America. You can see their legacy in the streets of Ferguson, Kenosha, Minneapolis, and dozens of other American cities from coast to coast. You can hear their influence on today's top musical artists, from Beyoncé to Kendrick Lamar.

America still has a long way to go before it can honestly say it has granted its Black citizens equal protection under the law or that Black Americans are afforded the same right to life, liberty, and the pursuit of happiness as White Americans. Until that day comes, and until Black people in this country have received justice for hundreds of years of persecution, America will not know peace. This is the nation the Shakurs created.

PART I

1.
THE TRIAL

IN THE EARLY morning hours of April 2, 1969, Detective Francis Dalton, of New York City Police Department's Bureau of Special Services and Investigations, arrives at the door of apartment 9, 112 West 117th Street, in Harlem. He's accompanied by four additional officers, armed with two bulletproof vests and one shotgun. On the detective's command, the men light a rag on fire in the apartment hallway and begin shouting, "Fire! Fire!"

The two occupants of apartment 9, Lumumba Shakur and his wife, Afeni, wake to the cries and smell smoke. Lumumba jumps up, looks through the door's peephole, and sees the flames. When he opens the door, he is greeted by a shotgun pressed into his chest, while other officers, stationed outside on the fire escape, enter through the window and hold Afeni at gunpoint.

One mile away that same morning, Dhoruba bin Wahad is apprehended from his apartment; Robert Collier is taken into custody from his home on East 8th Street; and a few blocks away, Detective Joseph Coffey, accompanied by his own team, kicks open the door of Michael "Cetewayo" Tabor, holds a gun to his head, and declares, "I've got you, you Black bastard," and "If you move, I'll blow your brains out."

Before the sun rises in New York City, ten members of the Harlem chapter of the Black Panther Party are arrested and jailed, including seventeen-year-old high school student Jamal Joseph and twenty-year-old Bronx Community College nursing student Joan Bird.

Other suspects—computer analyst Sundiata Acoli, research chemist Curtis Powell, Kwando Kinshasa, Shaba Om, Lee "Mkubu" Berry, and seventeen-year-old high school student Lonnie Epps—are later apprehended or surrender. Suspects Richard Harris and Kuwasi Balagoon are already in a Newark jail, on earlier bank robbery charges. The three remaining suspects—Larry Mack, Thomas "Mshina" Berry, and Sekou Odinga—manage to get away, disappearing from sight.

From the raided homes, the NYPD Special Services teams retrieve five .38 caliber pistols, two military rifles, three shotguns, a pair of handcuffs, items that could be used as homemade explosives, a map of Bronx railroad stations, and a copy of the *Urban Guerilla Warfare* manual, written by Black Panther guerrilla team captain Kwando Kinshasa.

Twenty-one members of the Black Panther Party are indicted on conspiracy to shoot police officers and bomb police stations, railroad tracks, Manhattan department stores, and the New York Botanical Garden in the Bronx. With Joseph and Epps granted youthful offender status, Berry too ill to stand trial due to chronic epilepsy, two members already held in New Jersey on other charges, and the three escapees, only thirteen ultimately stand trial. The case is formally recorded as *The People of the State of New York v. Lumumba Abdul Shakur et al.,* but the defendants become internationally known as the Panther 21. The ensuing trial will show the world, for the first time, how desperate American law enforcement is to eliminate the Panthers and make them an example of what happens when Black people in America dare to assert their right to self-defense and self-determination.

"This has been a systematic plan by the fascist pigs to stifle the black liberation struggle in New York City," Lumumba wrote. "Now I realize the Panther 21 arrest is all part and parcel of a national conspiracy by the American government to destroy the Black Panther Party and all revolutionaries."

As the purported ringleader of the planned attacks, Lumumba Shakur was named lead defendant in the case. A dark-skinned, attractive, twenty-five-year-old man, with dark eyeglasses, mustache, and goatee, Lumumba was, at the time of his arrest, section leader of the Harlem Panthers, tasked with recruiting new members and implementing the Black Panther Party's cornerstone Ten-Point Program. He and his team claimed responsibility for installing a Black principal in a majority-Black school in Harlem, and he was deputy of the Ellsmere Tenants Council, an Office of Economic Opportunity anti-poverty program.

Under Lumumba's leadership, the Harlem Panthers were distinguished for their militancy. Lumumba's close friend and section leader of the Bronx Panthers, Bilal Sunni-Ali, called Lumumba the "leader of the most notorious chapter of the Black Panther Party," which is an accomplishment in an organization not lacking in notoriety.

The Black Panthers weren't the only ones allegedly conspiring to blow up buildings throughout the United States. In the late 1960s and through the 1970s, a wave of bombings swept the nation, in protest of America's involvement in Vietnam, police brutality, and other emblems of American hegemony. From January 1969 to October 1970, there were around 370 bombings in New York alone, roughly more than one every two days, though many of the bombings were deemed "minor." Appearing before Congress in 1970, NYPD Commissioner Howard R. Leary testified that bombings during this one-year period had achieved "gigantic proportions."

"I look for it to accelerate to a greater degree," Leary continued. "It appears that this is the only way that these extreme groups who are organized are able to find a public expression and a public platform to make known their feelings and their dissatisfactions."

The raid on the New York Panthers was spearheaded by the NYPD's surveillance team, the Bureau of Special Services and Investigations (BOSSI). Applying similar counterintelligence methods as the FBI, BOSSI had become, by 1965, "the most extensive political intelligence operation of any state, local or municipal police department in the nation's history." Throughout the late 1960s and 1970s, BOSSI infiltrated political organizations in New York City, installing undercover detectives to spy on subversive groups and individuals. The organization was touted throughout the country as "proselytizers for the cult of intelligence." Some of these agents had infiltrated the New York Panthers, became trusted members of the group, and were ultimately responsible for furnishing the intelligence that would lead to the raid on April 2.

The swift arrests came after the NYPD's undercover agents determined that the Panthers were planning to carry out the bombings of department stores, railroads, and police stations on the following day. Bail for the jailed Panthers was set at $100,000 each (more than $700,000 in today's dollars)—an amount so prohibitively high as to be considered unviable and discriminatory. Indicted on 156 counts, the defendants faced life in prison.

Unable to make the exorbitant bail, the Panthers were held separately in detention centers throughout New York City, including Rikers Island and the Queens House of Detention. Pretrial hearings began February 2, 1970, at the New York State Supreme Court. Newspaper columnist Murray Kempton remembered his impression when Lumumba, followed by the other defendants, entered the courtroom with "a pencil in his hair, his glasses gleaming, his chirrup of 'Power to the People,' his right fist half-raised and then withdrawn in a gesture that seemed less to proclaim defiance than to exchange complicities with some vast secret army that would arise whenever he chose to whisper whatever signal had been agreed upon in some smoky grove among cypresses and Spanish moss."

The Panther 21 trial attracted national attention, becoming a rallying point for young activists and leftists who connected the harassment of the Black Panther Party to the repression of other anti-imperialist movements across the country. The Panthers had captured the imagination not only of young Black Americans; affluent White college students and older White liberals were entranced by what they perceived to be a highly disciplined organization of freedom fighters and anti-racist crusaders.

Not all of the publicity surrounding the Panthers was positive. When the composer Leonard Bernstein and his wife, Felicia, hosted a fundraising party for the Panther 21 defendants at their penthouse apartment on Manhattan's Upper East Side, with the aristocracy of New York's arts society rubbing shoulders with Black Panthers, the party was condemned by the *New York Times*, which characterized it as "the sort of elegant slumming that degrades patrons and patronized alike. It might be dismissed as guilt-relieving fun spiked with social consciousness, except for its impact on those blacks and whites seriously working for complete equality and social justice. It mocked the memory of Martin Luther King Jr." The author Tom Wolfe, in a scathing article for *New York* magazine, lampooned the party as "radical chic"—a term he coined for socialites and other members of high society who take up left-wing, radical political causes.

Notwithstanding these criticisms, the fundraisers were a blessing for the jailed Panthers, who needed all the financial support they could get, from whomever they could get it. After being held for ten months at the Women's House of Detention in Manhattan, Afeni was freed on bail on January 30, 1970. Her $100,000 bond was provided by female supporters in the labor movement and members of Presbyterian and Episcopal churches, who'd raised $66,000 in cash and used church assets as collateral on the remainder. Twenty-three years old and a gifted writer, teacher, and mentor, Afeni was the first to be bailed, and she was entrusted with the responsibility of raising bail funds for as many other Panthers as possible by organizing and speaking at rallies in support of the defendants. With fashionable plaid pants, a black turtleneck, and a long black leather vest, Afeni stood on a makeshift stage before hundreds of White and Black New Yorkers, took the microphone in her hand, and called down all the fury of her ancestors—for the long history of brutality against her people, for the undue repression of her comrades, and for the indignity of being woken up early in the morning by the NYPD.

Of course, this wasn't what she'd signed up for when she joined the Black Panther Party in 1968. A headstrong young woman from the Bronx, she'd joined the Party to give her life direction and purpose—something she had been denied as the youngest daughter of a single, working mother. Now, less than two years later, she was tasked with defending not only her life but the lives of her colleagues and husband, by channeling her internal rage and indignation into speechmaking and fundraising. When Afeni set out to do something, she did it completely. There was no half stepping. This tenacity, however, wasn't always welcomed by others.

Against the advice of her Panther colleagues, Afeni chose to act as her own attorney, while the others were represented by activist attorney Gerald B. Lefcourt. Afeni had had no prior law experience, no training whatsoever, and she came to her decision only after determining that the attorney she'd been assigned, Carol H. Lefcourt, possessed "a tiny, squeaky voice" that wouldn't command respect in the courtroom. "I'm facing the same three hundred and fifty years everyone else is facing, and I am not going out like that," Afeni later recalled thinking. "With this here, Carol Leftcourt [*sic*], speaking for me? Shit."

Lumumba tried to dissuade Afeni from representing herself. He mocked her as being "too emotional" and "not educated or qualified" and said that she would "fuck everything up." This was only the beginning of the imminent and irreparable division between husband and wife.

The Shakurs were a close and devoted family, and Afeni and Lumumba could count on receiving support, including from Lumumba's father, Salahdeen Shakur, who visited courtroom proceedings with his wife, Mariyama. A stately and imposing man, Salahdeen was a respected merchant of African goods and clothing, a former associate of Malcolm X, and a mentor to young Black New Yorkers. Lumumba's older brother, Zayd, helped organize rallies and fundraisers for the Panthers, while also being assigned the difficult task of keeping the Harlem chapter afloat while most of its leaders were in jail. Zayd was often joined at these rallies by a close friend and a young newcomer to the Harlem chapter named JoAnne Chesimard, who would soon change her name and find worldwide notoriety as Assata Shakur.

Afeni and Lumumba, however, had only been married less than a year before their arrest, and if found guilty, they would never see each other again. Afeni was still a young, attractive woman, confronted with a possible life sentence. All hopes, dreams, and plans for the future were placed on hold, including nuptial commitments. So while she was out on bail in the summer of 1970, Afeni took other lovers, including a Black Panther from Jersey City named Billy Garland, whom she met while laying low in a Jersey Panther pad. But though Garland was already married with three young children of his own, when Afeni discovered she was pregnant, she decided to keep the child. If she was found guilty, her child would be the only part of herself that remained free. She didn't yet know the sex, eye color, or voice of her child, but she had a premonition he was destined for something big.

Afeni kept her pregnancy to herself at first, but as time went on, it was becoming harder to conceal. When the Panthers' defense team got wind of Afeni's infidelity and pregnancy, lead attorney Gerald Lefcourt told one of his colleagues, "Lumumba's going to look at her some morning and find out about her, and then he's going to knock me halfway across the room."

As her child continued to grow inside her, Afeni became more and more appalled by the conditions of the penitentiary. "I would like to bring to the attention of the court what I am sure the court doesn't know about," she told Justice Murtagh, "and that's the situation that exists with Miss Bird and myself and for the other women that are being held in the house of detention. The boilers are broken there. There is no hot water. The conditions are not just abominable, as they were before; they are inhuman."

There was no toilet paper, she said, and the food was spoiled. She then went on to address the prison doctors' invasive and degrading examination practices, which she and Bird were punished for refusing to undergo: "Joan and myself are being held in a lockup simply because we refuse to be examined by those doctors who are not doctors, by those doctors who care very little about the structure of the female body. So we would request to have our own physicians come in and give us any examinations we need to have in the Women's House of Detention, and we would request that some facilities be provided so we can take hot showers. The showers are dirty enough as it is, but to be subjected to cold showers in that filth is ridiculous."

When Murtagh demurred, accusing the defendants of being interested only in winning attention from the press, Afeni interrupted, finally addressing the elephant in the room: "The interest, Mr. Murtagh, is in assuring the life of my child." The court partially conceded, granting Afeni one daily glass of milk and a hard-boiled egg to contribute to the health of her child.

The journalist Kempton, observing these proceedings from the gallery, reported how Afeni rose before the judge and spoke "as though she were bearing a Prince." Despite the fact that her infidelity was now evident to all, Afeni stood in front of the court like Athena, single-handedly staring down the twin pillars of imperialism and patriarchy.

"Behind Afeni Shakur there could almost be seen the long scroll of birth and death and birth again, of pain and resurrection, the things women know," Kempton wrote, "and it could be understood that the grandness of Afeni Shakur's impudence consisted in her capacity to appreciate the special opportunities of Woman."

The trial was dragging on into its eighth month. The prosecution had introduced various dead ends into evidence, including an in-court screening of the film *The Battle of Algiers* as a Black Panther "training" film, but the case against the defendants depended almost wholly on the testimonies of the undercover detectives. In spring 1971, the BOSSI officers who had infiltrated the Panthers took the stand.

These undercover agents included Detective Eugene Roberts, who had, years earlier, infiltrated Malcolm X's Organization of Afro-American Unity (OAAU) and had risen high enough in the ranks to become Malcolm's bodyguard, until Malcolm's assassination in 1965. Roberts would later maintain that he'd tried to save Malcolm's life by applying mouth-to-mouth resuscitation after the shooting, but now, six years later, attorney Gerald Lefcourt asked Roberts: "Isn't it a fact that you helped murder Malcolm X?"

"Yes!" shouted Afeni.

The defendants were caught off guard, however, when Harlem Panther Yedwa Sudan took the stand. He had hired Lumumba and other Panthers to the Ellsmere Tenants Council, regularly smoked weed with the others, talked freely about "icing pigs," and had even gone as far as to shoot his gun erratically in the presence of others. Now he was revealed as undercover police detective Ralph White.

This was so inconceivable to Lumumba that, when asked earlier during the trial whether he'd believed Yedwa might've been an undercover officer, Lumumba replied: "Man, he *couldn't* be a cop. You should have seen the shit he *did*."

But it was precisely the shit he did that had provoked Afeni's suspicions from the beginning. Before the raid on the Panther homes, Afeni had already been speaking to other Party members, raising concerns about Yedwa. He was too erratic, she believed, too unpredictable, "a hothead," too eager to prove himself to Lumumba and the others.

Like slowly pulling at a loose thread, when Afeni cross-examined the undercover officers, she compelled each of them to admit that they had never seen her commit any of the bombings or shootings she had been charged with, unraveling the fabric on which the case was built. Her closing statement to the jury, inspired by Fidel Castro's 1953 "History Will Absolve Me" courtroom speech, was largely unprepared and improvised.

It was the statement of a woman backed against a wall, fighting not only for her life, but for the life of her unborn child:

So why are we here? Why are any of us here? I don't know. But I would appreciate it if you would end this nightmare, because I'm tired of it and I can't justify it in my mind. There's no logical reason for us to have gone through the last two years as we have . . . So do what you have to do. But please don't forget what you saw and heard in this courtroom . . . Let history record you as a jury that would not kneel to the outrageous bidding of the state. Show us that we were not wrong in assuming that you would judge us fairly and remember that that's all we're asking of you. All we ask of you is that you judge us fairly. Please judge us according to the way that you want to be judged.

On May 13, 1971, at four thirty in the afternoon, the jurors returned after forty-five minutes of deliberation with their verdict. After an eight-month trial—the longest and most expensive criminal trial in New York State history—the defendants were acquitted on all 156 counts. Spectators cheered, jumped up, and called out "Power to the People!" Still seated in her chair, Afeni sobbed to herself.

Later that day, as the lawyers and jurors celebrated with the newly freed Panthers, one of the jurors, an elderly Black man named

Benjamin Giles, approached Afeni. "Where'd you find out how to talk like that, child?" he asked.

"Fear, Mr. Giles," Afeni responded. "Plain fear."

One month after the acquittal, on June 16, Afeni gave birth to a son. She named him Parish Lesane Crooks, but one year later he was rechristened with a new name: Tupac Amaru Shakur.

2.
PATRIARCHS

FOUR YEARS BEFORE the raid on the homes of the New York Black Panthers, on the afternoon of February 21, 1965, Malcolm X was assassinated while preparing to address about four hundred supporters and spectators at the Audubon Ballroom in Washington Heights. Malcolm had planned to use this occasion to deliver the official program of the Organization of Afro-American Unity (OAAU), which he co-founded the year before. Modeled after the Organization of African Unity, the OAAU sought to unite all peoples of African descent in the West, including twenty-two million Black Americans, by encouraging communication, cooperation, and solidarity with peoples of the African continent. Malcolm advocated for greater economic and political power in Black communities, while urging Black Americans to embrace their African heritage. As well as developing a Pan-African consciousness, Malcolm and the OAAU sought to bring the plight of Black Americans to the international stage, arguing that systemic racism and racist violence in the United States were not civil rights but human rights issues, and thus the United States should be brought before the United Nations and tried for human rights violations and acts of genocide.

On June 28, 1964, Malcolm made the first public announcement of the formation of the OAAU. He had recently returned from a two-month tour of Africa and the Middle East, where he'd performed the hajj pilgrimage in Mecca, a religious requirement of all able-bodied Muslims, and visited with African leaders and officials, which inspired him to form this new organization. Speaking at the Audubon Ballroom that evening, Malcolm addressed a crowd of a thousand observers, stating that the mission of the OAAU was "to fight whoever gets in our way, to bring about the complete independence of people of African descent here in the Western Hemisphere, and first here in the United States, and bring about the freedom of these people by any means necessary. That's our motto. We want freedom by any means necessary. We want justice by any means necessary. We want equality by any means necessary."

His speech stimulated the imagination of scores of Black men and women in New York and across the nation, but it especially captivated a small and devoted family of Afrocentric New Yorkers, the Shakur family, who would adopt "by any means necessary" not only as a motto but as a call to arms.

Malcolm X had Black liberation in his blood. Born Malcolm Little on May 19, 1925, in Omaha, Nebraska, Malcolm was raised on a farm near Lansing, Michigan, by Garveyite parents. Founder of the Universal Negro Improvement Association (UNIA), the Jamaican-born Marcus Garvey arrived in Harlem in 1916, promoting Black self-determination and self-respect. By the 1920s the UNIA boasted over a million followers, with more than eight hundred chapters in the United States and abroad, becoming one of the greatest mass movements in Black history.

"We must canonize our own saints, create our own martyrs," Garvey declared, "and elevate to positions of fame and honor black men and women who have made their distinct contributions to our racial history."

Garvey's most ambitious undertaking was the Black Star Line shipping company. The Black Star Line was touted as a fleet of steamships that would transport goods to and from Africa while also relocating American Blacks to the homeland, where they would establish an independent Black nation-state. A quixotic, Exodus-style campaign, the Black Star Line was immediately beset by irresponsible or questionable business decisions, mismanaged funds, and organizational misconduct. It also attracted the attention of the young, newly appointed head of the Special Intelligence Division in the Bureau of Investigation, twenty-four-year-old John Edgar Hoover.

In an October 1919 memo to Special Agent Ridgely, Hoover described Garvey as "particularly active among the radical elements in New York City in agitating the negro movement." Hoover expressed disappointment that Garvey had not yet violated any federal laws that could lead to his deportation but asked if "there might be some proceeding against him for fraud in connection with his Black Star Line propaganda."

In a foreshadowing of the heightened surveillance tactics that would later be used against other Black leaders and organizations, the Bureau installed informants and spies in the UNIA, including the Bureau's first Black special agent, James Wormley Jones, whom Hoover appointed, according to historian Theodore Kornweibel, "to go into Harlem and to infiltrate the Garvey movement and to try and find evidence that could be used to build the legal case for ultimately getting rid of Garvey."

The federal government soon uncovered enough evidence to build a case against Garvey. On January 12, 1922, he was arrested on charges of mail fraud. The Black Star Line, already suffering devastating setbacks and losses, dissolved completely after Garvey's arrest. In December 1927, President Calvin Coolidge deported Garvey to Jamaica. After relocating to London in 1935, Garvey suffered a stroke and died on June 10, 1940, at the age of fifty-two.

Malcolm X was just fifteen years old when Garvey died, but by then, his family had already suffered its own devastating losses. When Malcolm was six, his father, Reverend Earl Little, was run over by a streetcar, nearly severing his body in two. His death was ruled as accidental by the Lansing coroner, but Malcolm wondered throughout his life if his father, an outspoken Black man and Garveyite organizer, had been murdered by racist Whites.

With the death of Malcolm's father, his mother, Louise, struggled to raise seven children on her own. Accumulating bills, discriminatory welfare agencies, and fights with the life insurance company—who brazenly judged her husband's death as suicide—took an increasing toll on Louise's mental health, until she was ruled insane and admitted to Kalamazoo State Hospital, where she remained for twenty-four years.

Drifting among Michigan, Boston, and Harlem, which he'd hailed as "Seventh Heaven," Malcolm soon reinvented himself, in the first few years of the 1940s, as "Detroit Red"—the zoot-suited, lindy-hopping, jive-talking, hair-conking, reefer-peddling street hustler and petty criminal. Malcolm's stint in the criminal underworld lasted only a few years. After a series of home burglaries throughout Boston's White and affluent neighborhoods, accompanied by his friend "Shorty" and two White women, Malcolm was apprehended by police at a pawn shop while trying to buy back a stolen watch. Subsequent searches of each of their apartments turned up more stolen goods and firearms. On February 26, 1946, Malcolm was given an eight-to-ten sentence. He was twenty years old.

While at Norfolk Prison Colony, Malcolm was introduced to the teachings of the Honorable Elijah Muhammad, the leader of a small and obscure Black separatist religious sect called the Nation of Islam (NOI). The self-ordained "Messenger of Allah," Muhammad taught a highly unorthodox form of Islam, proclaiming that the Black man was Earth's "original man," the builder of magnificent empires and civilizations in Asia and Africa, until the "devil white man" appeared, pillaging, raping, kidnapping, and enslaving millions of Black men, women, and children in the West. Black people had been cut off "from all knowledge of their own kind," Malcolm later wrote in his *Autobiography,* and "from any knowledge of their own language, religion, and past culture, until the black man in America was the earth's only race of people who had absolutely no knowledge of his true identity." Severed from their heritage and dignity, Black people had accepted their positions in the United States as second-class citizens.

As the child of Garveyites, Malcolm was naturally receptive to this message. He joined the Nation of Islam and dedicated himself to his adopted faith and his newfound life's purpose: "telling my black brother inmates about the glorious history of the black man" and also "telling the white man about himself." When he was paroled in August 1952, he emerged from prison, reinvented once more, as Malcolm X.

Appointed first as minister of the Detroit temple, Malcolm was later assigned the prominent Temple No. 7, in his beloved Harlem. Malcolm immediately set about building the NOI's ranks. Tall, handsome, charming, and already a masterful orator, Malcolm was the NOI's most zealous and successful recruiter, building it into a formidable organization, establishing new temples across the country and recruiting hundreds of new members each month; national membership swelled from just four hundred in 1952 to forty thousand members and forty-nine temples by the end of the decade.

As the public face of the NOI and Muhammad's chief spokesman, Malcolm lectured and debated on Harlem street corners, college campuses, and television news programs. The Nation of Islam's message of Black separatism, self-determination, and self-defense offered a contradistinction to the broader civil rights message of integration and nonviolent protest, as promoted by Martin Luther King Jr. and such interracial organizations as the Southern Christian Leadership Conference, the NAACP, and the Congress of Racial Equality (CORE).

The Nation of Islam was a religious group, however, and not a political organization, which put the NOI and Muhammad increasingly at odds with Malcolm, who was, by the start of the 1960s, beginning to connect the plight of Black Americans to the struggles for independence and self-determination happening across the globe, particularly in Africa and Asia.

On November 10, 1963, Malcolm was invited to speak at the first Northern Negro Grass Roots Leadership Conference, in front of a predominantly Black and non-Muslim audience, at the King Solomon Baptist Church, in Detroit, Michigan. In his speech, "Message to the Grass Roots," Malcolm distinguished the "Negro revolution" from the "Black revolution" and "house negroes" from "field negroes." Laying out what would become the foundation for the more radical and militant Black liberation groups to come, like the secessionist Republic of New Afrika, Malcolm suggested that the aim of all world revolutions, whether in China, Russia, France, or America, was the pursuit of land, and the only way to achieve land, and thus liberation, is through bloodshed:

Revolution is bloody. Revolution is hostile. Revolution knows no compromise. Revolution overturns and destroys everything that gets in its way. And you, sitting around here like a knot on the wall, saying, "I'm going to love these folks no matter how much they hate me." No, you need a revolution. Whoever heard of a revolution where they lock arms . . . singing "We Shall Overcome"? Just tell me. You don't do that in a revolution. You don't do any singing; you're too busy swinging. It's based on land. A revolutionary wants land so he can set up his own nation, an independent nation. These Negroes aren't asking for no nation; they're trying to crawl back on the plantation.

The chasm between Malcolm and the Nation of Islam, already opened by the time of his speech, widened after the revelation of Muhammad's infidelities with his secretaries, and Malcolm's offhand "chickens coming home to roost" remark following the assassination of President John F. Kennedy. Suspended "indefinitely" from the NOI in March 1964, Malcolm established a new organization, Muslim Mosque, Inc. (MMI), consisting initially of other NOI defectors, and embarked on a tour of Egypt, Liberia, Senegal, Lebanon, and Ghana. After making the hajj pilgrimage to Mecca, Malcolm received his Islamic honorific title, El-Hajj Malik El-Shabazz, embraced Sunni (Orthodox) Islam, and declared publicly that his experiences in the Holy City—praying and eating among pilgrims of all races and ethnicities—made him reevaluate his previously held beliefs about the inherent wickedness of White people.

After returning home to the United States that spring, Malcolm announced the formation of the OAAU. Though he remained popular as an orator and thinker, Malcolm struggled to attract members to his fledgling organizations. With only a couple hundred members, the OAAU couldn't reach anywhere near the membership of the Nation of Islam at its peak or Garvey's UNIA.

Regardless, authorities were still concerned about the perceived threat of Malcolm and the OAAU. The NYPD's Bureau of Special Services and Investigations (BOSSI) assigned twenty-six-year-old detective Eugene Roberts to infiltrate the OAAU, which wouldn't be revealed publicly until the Panther 21 trial. The FBI, which had been monitoring Malcolm since as early as 1953, had also become concerned about his new enterprise. In June 1964, FBI director Hoover sent a telegram to the Bureau's office in New York, directing them to "do something about Malcolm X."

Hoover, the FBI, and the NYPD weren't the only ones concerned about Malcolm. By continuing to expose the Nation of Islam's corruption and duplicity, Malcolm incensed his former spiritual father, Elijah Muhammad, as well as the leadership and rank-and-file of the NOI, who now considered Malcolm an apostate and a "hypocrite" who was "worthy of death." Threats and intimidation against Malcolm, whether coming from the NOI or the FBI, were constant.

When Malcolm was shot to death on stage at the Audubon Ballroom, police promptly arrested three men—all members of Newark's Mosque No. 25. The men were convicted and given life sentences, though two men maintained their innocence and were eventually paroled after spending two decades in prison. But questions immediately swirled about who was responsible for the assassination, who had ordered the hit, and how high the orders came from.

Malcolm's funeral was at Harlem's Faith Temple Church of God in Christ. Actor and civil rights activist Ossie Davis delivered Malcolm's eulogy: "Harlem has come to bid farewell to one of its brightest hopes," Davis began, "extinguished now, and gone from us forever." Davis concluded his eulogy on a note of praise and gratitude, calling Malcolm "our own Black, shining prince, who didn't hesitate to die, because he loved us so."

Malcolm was thirty-nine years old when he was killed. He left behind a widow, Betty Shabazz, six daughters, and thousands of followers, supporters, and disciples. One of these disciples was a New York–based businessman and associate of Malcolm. His name was James Coston Sr., but he would later change his name to reflect his Muslim faith. The name he chose for himself was Salahdeen Shakur.

New York City in the 1960s was fertile ground for Afrocentrism and Pan-Africanism. The election of Kwame Nkrumah as president of a newly independent Ghana in 1957, the first All-African Peoples' Conference in 1958, and the anti-colonialist struggles taking place across the African continent inspired many Black New Yorkers to look at the "Mother Continent" with pride and inspiration. Because of the presence of the United Nations, visiting African diplomats and heads of state could meet with the city's leaders and its large Black population. Connecting the fight against American racism with the anti-colonialist struggles happening across the Atlantic, Black New Yorkers rallied in support of Africa's anti-imperialist struggles.

These rallies boiled over on February 15, 1961. After the assassination of Patrice Lumumba—the first democratically elected, Pan-Africanist leader of the Democratic Republic of the Congo—around sixty men and women demonstrated inside the public gallery of the UN's Security Council Chamber, chanting and clashing with UN police. More than two dozen people were injured in what the *New York Times* called "the most violent demonstration inside United Nations headquarters in the world organization's history." Later that day, two hundred people continued to demonstrate outside, marching from First Avenue at 43rd Street westward across Manhattan, advancing toward Times Square before being beaten back by policemen on horseback.

The protestors at the United Nations, which included prominent activists, musicians, and writers such as LeRoi Jones (later Amiri Baraka) and Maya Angelou, represented "but a very small echo of the black discontent now abroad in the world," wrote James Baldwin in an essay published by the *New York Times* the following month. "Finally, the time is forever behind us when Negroes could be expected to 'wait,'" he continued:

> *What is demanded now is not that Negroes continue to adjust themselves to the cruel racial pressures of life in the United States, but that the United States readjust itself to the facts of life in the present world.*

One of these facts is that the American Negro can no longer, nor will he ever again, be controlled by white America's image of him. This fact has everything to do with the rise of Africa in world affairs.

Part of the readjustment of young Black Americans to their new, Afrocentric consciousness was freeing themselves of their former enslavers' surnames in favor of African- or Arabic-inspired names. Malcolm X himself had used the surname "Shabazz" interchangeably with "X," as had other NOI members. Shabazz, according to the NOI's origin myth, was an ancient African-Asian tribe that had been lost or stolen from their ancestral homeland sixty trillion years ago, before facing near extinction at the hands of the evil scientist Yakub. So-called Negroes are the descendants of this once-mighty nation. "Shakur," unlike "Shabazz," doesn't have an equivalent ancestral myth attached to it. There are no evil scientists, lost tribes, or literal White devils. Roughly translated from Arabic, "Shakur" simply means "thankful."

Salahdeen Shakur took his first name from Salah al-Din ibn Ayyub—or Saladin—the twelfth-century Kurdish sultan and military hero, famous for leading successful Islamic campaigns against European Crusaders. In addition to being a Muslim and a Pan-Africanist, Salahdeen Shakur was also an astute entrepreneur.

Recognizing a ripe business opportunity, he traveled frequently between New York and Africa, peddling colorful dashikis, *gele* headwraps, kente cloth, rugs, drums, figurines, and other African goods to young Afrocentric New Yorkers, while at the same time bringing American jeans and sneakers to sell to young Africans. As a pious Muslim, he made the hajj pilgrimage in the mid-1960s, earning himself the honorific El-Hajj Salahdeen Shakur.

Years before his conversion to Islam, the former James Coston served in the Navy and was an amateur boxer who had considered going pro. After leaving the Navy, Salahdeen worked in the Brooklyn Navy Yard. He fathered four children with his wife Aremeda, a hotel waitress in Atlantic City, New Jersey. When he and Aremeda divorced, his children all lived together with their mother in a two-bedroom apartment in Atlantic City. James Jr., born in 1940, and Anthony, born in 1942, later went on to stay with aunts and uncles in North Philadelphia and Portsmouth, Virginia. While attending school in Virginia, the two Coston brothers often fought with White students, who were caught off guard by these Northern Black boys who didn't passively accept being belittled by White people. Even the teachers and other Black students were taken aback, calling Anthony and James "crazy niggers from up North."

"My mother and father always told us, don't let anyone disrespect us regardless of who it is," Anthony reflected years later, "but if they are white, be extra hard on them, because white people have been repressing us for three hundred years; when whites abuse or disrespect us, give them pure hell."

Anthony returned to live with his father in Jamaica, Queens, to complete his last year of junior high school at Edgar D. Shimer Junior High School. His first day at the new school, Anthony was almost jumped by a crew of twenty students, but he was saved by a student named Nathaniel Burns, nicknamed "Beany," who spoke up and demanded Anthony be given a fair, one-on-one fight. Anthony and Nathaniel formed a close friendship that would last the rest of their lives, forever changing New York—and United States—history.

In the 1950s and early 1960s, street gangs were rampant throughout New York City and other metropolitan areas. Anthony Coston first got caught up in gang culture after finishing the sixth grade. He joined a gang called the Syndicate, took on his new "street name," "Shotgun," and traveled throughout Philadelphia, Atlantic City, and New York City, getting into violent and often deadly gang fights. He reflected more than a decade later, "In all three states the phenomenon was the same: the animosity and hostility of the blacks, created by hundreds of years of white repression, and created by the conditions in the white-created ghetto, were directed against each other instead of against the system that created the repression and hostilities . . . If the street-gang brothers and sisters were ever politicized to the point where they knew who their real enemy was, the American system would be in danger of collapse."

One night in the winter of 1959, Anthony and more than a dozen friends boarded a bus on their way home from a party in Jamaica, Queens, when, according to Anthony, a White man in a Navy uniform told him that "where he came from niggers didn't sit next to white people on buses." This drew a swift reaction from the teenaged Anthony, who was no stranger to fighting against racist Whites. Soon his whole crew joined in, beating and severely wounding the White man. Anthony was arrested later that night, and he was sent to Woodbourne Correctional Institution, a medium-security men's prison, for an "indefinite sentence" of up to five years.

In Woodbourne, gang violence was just as prevalent, if not more so, as on the streets of New York City, and Anthony learned the rules fast, surviving by his wits and fists. When Anthony was transferred in 1962, one year later, to the Great Meadow Correctional Institution in Comstock, New York, other inmates introduced him to the writings of Malcolm X. This was a transformative moment that would forever change the direction of his life.

Malcolm was revered by many Black inmates behind the wall. He had been one of them: a criminal and prisoner. But he had been saved in prison, reformed, and was now out in the streets, telling it like it is, giving Whitey hell, and instilling great pride in Black people. To Anthony and other Black inmates, Malcolm "was one of the greatest men on this earth."

Anthony's father came to Great Meadow to visit. The two men had been emotionally distant for years and hadn't been able to bond as father and son. They began talking casually about family matters, but both of them were hesitant to talk about what was really on their minds. Finally, Anthony's father asked his son what his opinion was of Malcolm X. When Anthony responded that he loved Brother Malcolm and was interested in Black nationalism and Islam, his father lit up, then confessed to his son that he'd become a Muslim two years earlier and had met Brother Malcolm personally. Father and son spoke for hours, connecting like they never had before.

By this time, Anthony's friend Nathaniel, who had been a member of the Sinners gang in Jamaica, Queens, had also arrived in Great Meadow, after being arrested and charged with mugging. The two old classroom buddies rekindled their friendship, bonding over their mutual love for Malcolm X. Anthony and Nathaniel pored over

Malcolm's writings, sent by Anthony's father, who by then had adopted the name Salahdeen Shakur.

Racial tensions at Great Meadow reflected the tensions of the world outside the prison walls, which had just experienced the White terrorist bombing of the 16th Street Baptist Church in Birmingham, Alabama, killing four young Black girls. Two weeks after the bombing, a large brawl broke out among around 450 White and Black inmates on the prison's handball and basketball courts. The melee was broken up after fifteen or twenty minutes, with only eighteen inmates and five guards receiving minor injuries. But Anthony was determined by corrections officials to be one of the initiators of the disturbance, and he and thirteen others were transferred to Attica Correctional Facility, where he was placed in solitary confinement for fourteen months for his alleged role in the brawl. Attica would, seven years later, become infamous for a deadly uprising by inmates protesting inhumane conditions, but Anthony remembered Attica as being, at the time, "just as racist as other New York State Prisons."

Nathaniel served a three-year sentence and was released in December 1963; Anthony followed one year later, in December 1964, a few weeks before his twenty-second birthday. Like Malcolm X before them, the two men decided to drop their "slave names" and their street names alike.

No more would they identify as Anthony Coston and Nathaniel Burns, or Shotgun and Beany. Anthony changed his name to Lumumba Abdul Shakur. He was inspired by his father and his new Islamic faith, and by the assassinated leader of the Republic of the Congo, Patrice Lumumba. Nathaniel changed his first name to Sekou, in tribute to the first president of the newly independent Republic of Guinea, Sékou Touré. He considered taking the surname Shakur for himself, in honor of Salahdeen. But ultimately he decided on Odinga, because it felt to him like a "more pure African name."

With their new names, they were now prepared to join the revolutionary struggle, to enlist in the fight for the liberation of all Black people, by any means necessary.

3.
BLACK POWER

IN THE SPRING of 1965, Lumumba got together with Sekou Odinga, lamented over the loss of Malcolm, "smoked some reefer," and made a pact: "We both agreed that we will always be activists in the struggle for [the] liberation of black people." But Malcolm's death left a void in the movement. Harlemites wandered around shell-shocked, adrift, chasing after Malcolm's ghost.

Lumumba took an apartment in Harlem, while Odinga lived between Queens and the Bronx. They continued their political and religious education with Lumumba's father, Salahdeen Shakur, who was teaching Islam to young Black men and women from his home in Jamaica, Queens. One of these acolytes was a young man who was born William Johnson but had also recently changed his name, to Bilal Sunni-Ali, and soon joined Lumumba and Odinga in their pursuit of Black liberation.

Raised in the Bronx, Sunni-Ali was a gifted young musician, and as a teenager he played flute with the Sankore Nubian Cultural Workshop, based out of the Lincoln housing projects on Harlem's 135th Street. Founded in the late 1950s by Mariamne Samad, a former member of Garvey's UNIA, Sankore hosted concerts, readings, weddings, and fashion shows, using the arts to teach African culture. The emerging trend of Black New Yorkers donning African fashion can be traced to Sankore and Samad, who sewed many of the clothes herself. "We took the African clothing that we saw and we stylised it," Samad said in an interview with *Jamaica Journal*. "We started the abbuba for the women and I created the dashiki for the men in 1958. It was like giving royalty to the black man."

Lumumba married Samad's daughter Sayeeda in October 1966. Sayeeda then introduced Lumumba to Sunni-Ali at the Sankore Nubian Cultural Workshop, and the two men bonded over their shared interest in Islam and Black nationalism. "We hit it off really well as young Muslims, as young comrades in the struggle for liberation," Sunni-Ali recalled.

Lumumba, Sunni-Ali, and others also met regularly at Salahdeen's home to continue their studies in Marxism-Leninism and the Pan-Africanist writings of Kwame Nkrumah and Patrice Lumumba. A dark-skinned, striking, intelligent, and dapper man, Salahdeen was more than a tutor to these young, enthusiastic pupils; he was a father figure. They called him "Abba." As many of these teenagers came from Garveyite households, Salahdeen's role as surrogate father was accepted and consented to by their parents. Salahdeen "adopted us as his children, even though many of us had biological parents who were present in our lives," Sunni-Ali recalled, "but our biological parents understood that we had somebody who we called Abba, because of the special relationship that they had with the struggle."

As advisor, elder, and spiritual mentor, Salahdeen provided a bridge between Garvey and Malcolm X; between the UNIA movement of the older generation and the nascent interest in Islam among younger Blacks. Sunni-Ali recalled how "a lot of young people that were in the liberation struggle, many who later joined the [Black] Panther Party, as it developed, related to Salahdeen Shakur as somebody that we could talk to about Islam, learn about Islam from."

"He was very instrumental in the development of things here in New York and the people here in New York," remembered Odinga. "He was an inspiration in so many ways."

While learning about Islam and entrepreneurship from Salahdeen and African culture through Sankore, Lumumba and Odinga also hoped to join the Black liberation struggle by enlisting in Malcolm X's OAAU, but their hopes were dashed with Malcolm's assassination. Without its charismatic and driven leader, the organization faltered for a short time before dissolving completely.

"When Malcolm X was assassinated, two so-called brothers of the leadership of OAAU ran like punks," Lumumba recalled later. "A brother who was an OAAU official in Detroit was murdered a few days after Malcolm X. In my opinion, Malcolm X's sister, Ella Collins, assumed the leadership of the OAAU because the so-called men among the leadership ran like punks."

The streets of New York were still smoldering from the 1964 Harlem riots, incited by the fatal shooting of Black fifteen-year-old James Powell by a White off-duty police lieutenant on July 16. The rebellion, which spread throughout central Harlem and Bedford-Stuyvesant in Brooklyn, lasted six days and resulted in one death, 450 arrests, more than one hundred injuries, and $1 million in property damage.

A few days after the shooting, Jesse Gray—a Harlem rent strike organizer who had been beaten by police the night before—addressed the crowd at Mount Morris Presbyterian Church, expressing the prevailing mood in the community: "There is only one thing that can correct the situation, and that's guerilla warfare."

Gray's statements echoed Malcolm X's declaration from only three months earlier, when he predicted that 1964 would be "America's hottest year; her hottest year yet; a year of much racial violence and much racial bloodshed."

As the riots were still underway, the ultra-conservative Senator Barry Goldwater was in San Francisco, where he accepted the Republican nomination for president of the United States on a "law-and-order" platform, denouncing urban unrest while also exploiting the so-called "White backlash" against President Lyndon Baines Johnson's passage of the 1964 Civil Rights Act.

"The growing menace in our country tonight," Goldwater said in his acceptance speech, "to personal safety, to life, to limb and property, in homes, in churches, on the playgrounds and places of business, particularly in our great cities is the mounting concern—or should be—of every thoughtful citizen in the United States."

The rebellion in Harlem, however, was only a precursor to the wave of more deadly race-related riots that soon followed in cities like Newark, Los Angeles, and Detroit. Contending with police brutality, substandard housing, and a lack of education and opportunity, Northern Blacks saw little gain from the civil rights movement, which had largely focused on Southern integration efforts. In the wake of the Harlem riots, the *New York Times* announced the arrival of what it designated "the 'long hot summer' of Negro discontent":

The cycle of discrimination that confronts the Negro in these and other Northern ghettoes is hard to break. There is job discrimination, resulting in low Negro income. The low income plus housing discrimination condemn the Negro to living in the slums. There is apathy toward education, disqualifying many Negroes for many jobs that might otherwise be available. The bleakness of the Negro's future often puts him in conflict with the authority wielded by the dominant white man and breeds hostility toward the enforcer of that authority, the policeman.

The passage of the 1964 Civil Rights Bill, paradoxically, led to a rise in White vigilante violence against Southern Blacks. Launched in June 1964, the Mississippi Summer Project, or "Freedom Summer," organized by the NAACP, Congress of Racial Equality (CORE), Student Nonviolent Coordinating Committee (SNCC), and other civil rights groups, sought to increase the number of registered Black voters in Mississippi. This volunteer-run voter registration drive resulted in the murder of at least six Blacks, including the brutal beating and murder of twenty-one-year-old CORE activist James Chaney; more than a thousand arrests; and numerous bombings and arsons of Black homes, businesses, and churches. Young Black activists surveyed the wreckage and realized that the methods of the older generation—nonviolence, patience, respectability, compromise—weren't working. New methods and different strategies were necessary to survive in America.

"If nonviolence could not win the white racists to biracial democracy and justice," writes historian Manning Marable, "then their brutal terror would be met, blow for blow. If equality was impossible within the political economy of American capitalism, that system which perpetuated black exploitation would have to be overturned. No more compromises; no more betrayals by Negro moderates. Rebellion would supplant reform."

It wasn't enough to trim the branches of institutional racism; the tree itself needed to be chopped down, quartered, and burned.

■

Even before the urban rebellions of 1964 and '65, the seeds had been sown for increased militancy and resistance. Dissatisfied with the incrementalism of the civil rights movement and persecuted by rising Klan and other White supremacist violence against their communities, some Black leaders and activists were, by the start of the decade, already rethinking the movement's commitment to nonviolence, advocating instead for the right to armed self-defense. The most prominent advocate of this ideology at the time, aside from Malcolm X, was Robert F. Williams.

President of the local NAACP chapter in his hometown of Monroe, North Carolina, Williams distinguished himself from the national civil rights organization by openly encouraging "armed self-reliance" and forming rifle clubs to provide community members with guns and weapons training. In May 1959, after a White man was acquitted for the attempted rape of a Black woman in Monroe, Williams stood on the courthouse steps and stated that Blacks "must meet violence with violence" and "must even be willing to kill if necessary" in defense against White aggression. Williams was suspended from his leadership position in the NAACP.

Two years after his suspension, the Freedom Riders stopped in Monroe during their campaign to integrate interstate bus travel. The interracial, nonviolent civil rights activists were brutally assaulted by the Klan and other White residents. Violent confrontations continued over multiple days, with both White and Black vigilantes wreaking havoc across the city. When a White couple drove into Williams's heavily fortified neighborhood, Williams brought the couple into his home, supposedly for their own safety from the Black mob prowling the streets outside. Local law enforcement later accused Williams of kidnapping the couple, and the FBI issued a warrant for his arrest. Williams and his wife, Mabel, fled to Cuba, where they were granted asylum by President Fidel Castro.

By the middle of the 1960s, the civil rights struggle found itself at a crossroads. On one side stood the moderates: the older, largely middle-class leaders who favored integration and nonviolence; on the other side were the younger militants who lionized Robert F. Williams and Malcolm X and argued for Black nationalism and self-defense. These two factions would come together during a pivotal Southern campaign in 1966.

On June 5, a recent college graduate named James Meredith set off on a solo march from Memphis, Tennessee, to Jackson, Mississippi, a distance of 220 miles. The first Black student admitted to the segregated University of Mississippi, Meredith embarked on his "March Against Fear" in order to encourage voter registration efforts and inspire Southern Blacks to stand up to White intimidation. On the second day of his march, a White man ambushed Meredith and shot him with a shotgun. Though he survived his injuries, the shooting galvanized the movement. Mainstream organizations like the NAACP, the Urban League, and the SCLC vowed to continue the march, drawing more than ten thousand supporters to complete the remaining 194 miles along Federal Highway 51. The march—now referred to as the "Meredith March"—would also become notable for exposing the widening rift between the civil rights old guard and the growing militancy of younger activists, as represented by SNCC and its brilliant and captivating chairman, Stokely Carmichael.

What began in 1960 as a student-led nonviolent group, organizing sit-ins and voter registration drives, SNCC (pronounced *snick*) soon attracted Black nationalists and other more radical elements of the movement. In March 1965, SNCC convened in Lowndes County, Alabama, and helped local residents form the Lowndes County Freedom Organization (LCFO), an independent third-party political group, established as an alternative to the Alabama Democratic Party, which was at the time led by rabid segregationist George Wallace. Using a white rooster as its logo, the Democratic Party's campaign slogan was "White supremacy, for the right." The LCFO, in contrast, adopted a different symbol for its campaign: a black panther, teeth bared, claws out, poised to attack. "The black panther is a vicious animal, as you know," said LCFO co-founder John Hulett. "He never bothers anything, but when you start pushing him, he moves backward, backward, and backward, and then he comes out and destroys everything that's in front of him."

Because much of Lowndes County was illiterate and relied on visual images, the illustration of the panther, designed by SNCC members Ruth Howard and Dorothy Zellner, was a powerful voting aid and recruiting tool. The LCFO eventually became known as the Black Panther Party.

Trinidad-born, Bronx-raised, and Howard University–educated, SNCC chairman Stokely Carmichael had been an early adherent of Black nationalist and Pan-Africanist philosophies. Largely as a result of his organizing successes in Lowndes County, Carmichael established himself as leader of the new vanguard of Black militancy. Tall, erudite, and personable yet uncompromising, Carmichael was viewed at the time as the most likely candidate to fill the vacancy left after Malcolm X's death. He was opposed to interracial organizing, going so far as to regard integration "an insidious subterfuge for white supremacy when initiated by blacks." Twelve years younger than Martin Luther King Jr., Carmichael was more attuned to the current mood of the grassroots. He would publicly contradict and challenge the movement's adherence to nonviolence. By the time of the Meredith March, the lines in the sand separating Carmichael's philosophy from King's had been solidly drawn.

Part of the disagreement stemmed from the presence at the march of the Deacons for Defense and Justice—the clandestine, paramilitary, and enigmatic group that organized in 1964 to protect Black Louisianans and Mississippians from the rise in Klan violence. Composed of older, working-class Southern Black men, the Deacons were not a civil rights group or a political organization. Rather, they were, as a correspondent from the *New York Times* described them, "an armed tough-minded league of Negroes, formed to defend members of their race from white terrorism." The participation of these openly armed partisans, as well as Carmichael's insistence that the march remain exclusive to Blacks, caused an irreparable rift between the moderates and the radicals. But it was a single instance, on the evening of June 16, 1966, that would prove to be the march's most memorable and controversial moment.

Just released from a six-hour detention in a jail in Greenwood, Mississippi, where he and two colleagues had been arrested on trespassing charges, Carmichael returned to a gathering of supporters, mounted a nearby tractor trailer, and issued a call to arms that would quickly sweep across the entire nation: "This is the twenty-seventh time I have been arrested," Carmichael told the assembled crowd. "I ain't going to jail no more. The only way we gonna get those white men to stop whuppin' us is to take over. What we gonna start saying now is 'Black Power!'"

The crowd roared with approval. From his makeshift stage, Carmichael led his audience in a chant:

"What do we want?"

"Black Power!"

"What do we want?"

"Black Power!"

This was effectively the final nail in the moderate, interracial movement. "We Shall Overcome" was dead. "Black Power" was born.

Though the phrase itself wasn't conceived by Carmichael—it was used as early as 1954 by author Richard Wright, in his book *Black Power*—it now became inseparable from the young, militant faction of the movement. King tried to suppress it. The NAACP, the Urban League, President Johnson, and Democratic senator Robert Kennedy renounced it. *Time* magazine called Black Power a "racist philosophy that could ultimately perpetuate the very separatism against which Negroes have fought so successfully." The *Saturday Evening Post* feared "a new white backlash." Civil rights leader Bayard Rustin proclaimed that Black Power "[lacked] any clear definition," had no political or social program, and amounted to nothing more than a "slogan directed primarily against liberals by those who once counted liberals among their closest friends."

What "Black Power" actually meant was debated, even among those who professed it. In their 1967 book, *Black Power: The Politics of Liberation*, co-authors Carmichael and Charles V. Hamilton stated that Black Power was "a call for black people in this country to unite, to recognize their heritage, to build a sense of community . . . to begin to define their own goals, to lead their own organizations and to support those organizations. It is a call to reject the racist institutions and values of this society."

Defending Black Power against charges of promoting "reverse racism" or "Black supremacy," Carmichael wrote, in a September 1966 essay: "It is more than a figure of speech to say that the Negro community in America is the victim of white imperialism and colonial exploitation. It is white power that makes the laws, and it is violent white power in the form of armed white cops that enforces those laws with guns and nightsticks."

Some connected Black Power with the anti-capitalist and anti-colonialist struggles happening in the United States and abroad, while others, including middle-class Black business leaders, equated Black Power with Black capitalism—a view that was endorsed by Republican presidential candidate Richard Nixon during his 1968 campaign: "Much of the black militant talk these days is actually in terms far closer to the doctrines of free enterprise than to those of the welfarist thirties," he remarked in a March 28 speech. "What most of the militants are asking is not separation, but to be included in—not as suppliants, but as owners, as entrepreneurs—to have a share of the wealth and a piece of the action."

While the definition of Black Power was being debated and exploited across the nation, the federal government was actively seeking to disrupt the emerging movement. Employing a strategy that would have fatal repercussions for Black radical groups in the years to come, FBI agents spread rumors among SNCC organizers that Carmichael was a CIA agent. The FBI had already begun surveilling SNCC as early as 1960, but in 1967, Director J. Edgar Hoover ordered the surveillance, infiltration, and disruption of other radical Black leftist, nationalist, or separatist groups like the Revolutionary Action Movement (RAM), CORE, and the Deacons for Defense.

But none of these groups would have the impact, or be targeted by the FBI with such single-minded vehemence, as a young, upstart group that borrowed the imagery from the Lowndes County Freedom Organization, the self-defense rhetoric of Robert F. Williams, the youthful charisma of Stokely Carmichael, and the galvanizing fire of Malcolm X. The group that ultimately emerged soon found two enthusiastic converts in New York City.

As Lumumba and Odinga drifted about New York, checking out the various Black nationalist groups, they determined that none of them was adequately representing Malcolm X's vision. They eventually decided to start their own organization, the Grass Root Front, also called Grassroots Advisory Council, and recruited other Black nationalists, including future Panther 21 defendant Larry Mack. They'd sought to implement an anti-poverty program to rival the program managed by the Office of Economic Opportunity, the administrative agency created under President Johnson's "Great Society" legislation. Their intentions were simultaneously vague and ambitious, and the young organizers had difficulty getting their new program off the ground, owing to a lack of experience and consensus: "That was something, after Malcolm passed, that we could figure out a way to carry on what we thought was Malcolm's work and try to put something together," Odinga explained. "But we were so inexperienced. We didn't know what we were doing, and it didn't go nowhere."

"It was a split within the Grass Root Front because Sekou, Larry Mack, and I wanted to inflict a political consequence," Lumumba recalled. "The other brothers did not agree with us. So we quit them and told them that they were jiving."

Meanwhile, on February 3, 1967, at Harlem Hospital, Lumumba and his wife Sayeeda gave birth to their first children, boy-girl twins named Dingiswayo Mbiassi Abdul Shakur and Sekyiwa Jamilla Shakur. "I felt that giving my child a racist, cracker's name would be like cussing the child," Lumumba later explained. "And I felt when my son got about eighteen years old, he would try to kick my ass for giving him a racist, cracker name." Odinga waited with Lumumba at the hospital during Sayeeda's long labor, then the two friends went back to Lumumba's place and celebrated by smoking reefer.

But Lumumba and Odinga were still without an organization to which they could dedicate their restless energy. Each man had come of age in street gangs and then in prison, and each was aware of the need for fraternity and structure. But just as it seemed as though their search would be in vain, a dispatch arrived in the spring of 1967—a light from the distant West Coast that would change the course of their lives, and the lives of everyone associated with them, for decades to come.

On Tuesday, May 2, 1967, thirty members of an unknown group in faraway Oakland marched into the California State Capitol in Sacramento, carrying pistols, rifles, and shotguns. Dressed in black leather jackets, dark sunglasses, and black berets, twenty-four Black men and six Black women overwhelmed the capitol, causing immediate confusion and discord. Demonstrating against a state bill that would outlaw the carrying of loaded firearms in public, the delegation wanted to make a public declaration of the rights and the necessity of Black people to arm themselves to ensure their own survival. Standing before a phalanx of television cameras and newspaper reporters, Chairman Bobby Seale read aloud Executive Mandate Number One:

The Black Panther Party for Self-Defense calls upon the American people in general and the Black people in particular to take careful note of the racist California Legislature, which is now considering legislation aimed at keeping the Black people disarmed and powerless at the very same time that racist police agencies throughout the country are intensifying the terror, brutality, murder and repression of Black people . . . Black people have begged, prayed, petitioned, demonstrated and everything else to get the racist power structure of America to right the wrongs which have historically been perpetrated against Black people. All of these efforts have been answered by more repression, deceit, and hypocrisy . . . A people who have suffered so much for so long at the hands of a racist society, must draw the line somewhere. We believe that the Black communities of America must rise up as one man to halt the progression of a trend that leads inevitably to their total destruction.

It was a perfectly executed publicity stunt. Images of these armed, fearless Black men and women swept not only across California but across the entire nation, receiving extensive coverage on most major media outlets, including the *New York Times*, which reported that Governor Ronald Reagan, accompanied by picnicking schoolchildren, had been caught unawares by the armed Panthers emerging from the capitol. In addition to protesting the pending legislation, the demonstration also served its other goal: increasing Party membership. College students and other young Black men and women flocked to the Party, asking where they could sign up. A rallying cry had gone out across the country, and thousands had answered the call. "That's what really caught my imagination," Odinga later remembered, "and made me think this might be the type of vehicle that we can use here in New York."

4.
BIRTH OF A NATION

WHEN HUEY P. NEWTON and Bobby Seale—college campus organizers in Oakland, California—came together in the fall of 1966, numerous other groups across the nation had already sprung up, each calling itself the Black Panther Party. Inspired by the mobilization efforts in Lowndes County, young activists in such cities as Detroit, Chicago, St. Louis, Los Angeles, and San Francisco had adopted the Black Panther name and symbol, with Stokely Carmichael's approval. "The creation of a national 'black panther party' must come about; it will take time to build, and it is much too early to predict its success," Carmichael wrote, adding that a man "needs a black panther on his side when he and his family must endure—as hundreds of Alabamans have endured—loss of job, eviction, starvation, and sometimes death for political activity."

One of the many activists to take up Carmichael's call was a young organizer from Philadelphia named Maxwell Stanford Jr. Inspired by Carmichael's rhetoric, SNCC's direct-action organizing methods, and the Black nationalist message of the Nation of Islam, Stanford—with fellow college student organizers Donald Freeman and Wanda Marshall—co-founded the Revolutionary Action Movement (RAM), a student-led, nationalist organization with Marxist and anti-imperialist leanings. RAM was also informed by author and scholar Harold Cruse's "Revolutionary Nationalism and the Afro-American," published in the spring of 1962 in *Studies on the Left*, an underground leftist journal. In his article, Cruse contends that Black people are colonial subjects living on American soil, "an oppressed nation within a nation."

"From the beginning, the American Negro has existed as a colonial being," Cruse writes. "His enslavement coincided with the colonial expansion of European powers and was nothing more or less than a condition of domestic colonialism. Instead of the United States establishing a colonial empire in Africa, it brought the colonial system home and installed it in the Southern states."

Beginning in 1963 as a study group at Ohio's Central State University, RAM expanded into Philadelphia and soon grew into a national organization with numerous cells across the country. Malcolm X allegedly advised Stanford during RAM's formation, then became allied with the group after his split from the Nation of Islam and prior to founding the Organization of Afro-American Unity. Audley "Queen Mother" Moore—the esteemed Black nationalist leader, Garveyite, and reparations advocate—also became an advisor, or "second mother," to the young organizers. Robert F. Williams—the NAACP leader and self-defense proponent recently exiled to Cuba—accepted an honorary post as RAM's chair-in-exile. RAM's purpose, declared Stanford, was "to start a mass revolutionary black nationalist movement."

In 1964, RAM created a twelve-point platform, which included calls for the "development of rifle clubs" and the "development of a Liberation Army." RAM argued for the right to self-determination, liberation through armed struggle, and the complete destruction of the "white capitalist structure."

"As revolutionary black nationalists, we do not believe that standing on the street corners alone will liberate our people," Stanford wrote in "We Are at War with White America," published in the fall of 1964 in RAM's bimonthly newspaper, *Black America*. "Revolutionary black nationalists must act as a vanguard to show our people how to seize power so that they may gain some control over their lives."

By 1967, RAM presented enough of a threat to FBI director J. Edgar Hoover, who testified before the House Appropriations Subcommittee that RAM was "a highly secret, all-Negro, Marxist-Leninist, Chinese-Communist-oriented organization which advocates guerrilla warfare to obtain its goals" and suggested that RAM was "dedicated to the overthrow of the capitalist system in the United States, by violence if necessary."

"In an era before the Black Panthers emerged," writes scholar Peniel E. Joseph, "RAM was considered by the FBI to be among the nation's most dangerous black militants."

National news media added to the growing hysteria surrounding Black militancy in general and RAM in particular. In a June 1966 article titled "Plotting a War on 'Whitey,'" *Life* magazine designated RAM as "the most influential and feared of the black revolutionary groups" and described the group as an "umbrella-like fraternity with an estimated 1,000 violence-bent brothers dispersed through the Negro ghettos of the East Coast." *Time* magazine skipped the preamble, defining RAM simply as "a small group of Negro terrorists."

But despite its militant rhetoric, RAM's day-to-day involvement largely consisted of publishing newsletters and arguing amongst themselves over direction, leadership, and ideology. As a revolutionary organization, RAM took part in few revolutionary actions, aside from participating in minor campaigns and demonstrations. Hoping to organize the various militant and clandestine organizations into one aboveground political party, RAM met in Harlem with local activists and plotted how those in the Northern cities could most effectively support the work Carmichael had begun in Lowndes County. Stanford wrote a letter to Carmichael "asking if it was all right to use the name Black Panther," Stanford recalled later. "Through the New York SNCC office the word came back, 'OK, go ahead.'" In August 1966, New York's Black Panther Party was established.

Under Carmichael's tutelage, this Black Panther Party was, in effect, a merger of SNCC and RAM. Not yet associated with later images of gun-wielding, black-bereted Panthers in California, these Panthers resembled something more like community organizers, advocating for the rights of students and workers by coordinating boycotts and strikes. One of the first actions of the Harlem Panthers was organizing the September 1966 picket of a Harlem public school, demanding more community involvement, the hiring of more Blacks in supervisor positions, and the implementation of African and Black history courses. Comprising no more than one hundred members, they were described by the *New York Times* as "an anti-integration group of articulate young militants."

Though Stanford was head of the newly established Harlem Black Panther Party, Carmichael was still seen as the national leader of the Black Power movement. During an August rally at New York's Mount Morris Presbyterian Church, the SNCC chairman was greeted by an enthusiastic crowd of 250 supporters, many of them dressed identically in black pants and shirts emblazoned with the panther logo that was now becoming ubiquitous.

News of this burgeoning organization quickly reached the West Coast, where college students and members of the local RAM chapter began calling themselves the Black Panther Party of Northern California. Established that August, not long after the founding of the Harlem chapter, this Black Panther Party was, like RAM, chiefly concerned with organizing students and workers, writing and distributing periodicals, and arguing for political and economic self-determination. The aim of the Party, wrote Stanford, "was to offer black people a radical political alternative to the political structure of this country." Notwithstanding its advocacy for self-defense, waging armed struggle was not the Black Panther Party's main platform. In a short time, however, changes in the Party's leadership and its objectives would lead to drastic, irrevocable, and fatal outcomes.

In the fall of 1966, determined to move past what he saw as the "intellectualizing and rhetoric characteristics" of local Black nationalist groups, including RAM, Huey P. Newton one day happened upon a pamphlet about the organizing successes of the Lowndes County Freedom Organization in Lowndes County, Alabama. He was especially drawn in by the powerful emblem the LCFO had created as a recruiting tool: "A few days later, while Bobby and I were rapping, I suggested that we use the panther as our symbol and call our political vehicle the Black Panther Party."

A student of law at Merritt College and San Francisco State College, Newton was an academically minded and brilliant thinker, albeit one with a history of legal trouble. Five years older than Newton, Bobby Seale worked for an Oakland youth anti-poverty program and was a natural orator. The two men pored over the writings of Mao Tse-tung, Karl Marx, Vladimir Lenin, Che Guevara's *Guerilla Warfare*, and Frantz Fanon's *The Wretched of the Earth*. Robert F. Williams's 1962 book, *Negroes with Guns*, written while in exile in Cuba, was said by Newton to have "had a great influence on the kind of party we developed." But it was Malcolm X, above all, who served as the Party's lodestar and patron saint: "Malcolm's influence was ever-present," Newton reflected. "We continue to believe that the Black Panther Party exists in the spirit of Malcolm . . . as far as I'm concerned, the Party is a living testament to his life work."

Newton and Seale called their group the Black Panther Party for Self-Defense (they eventually dropped the "for Self-Defense"), founded and distributed their own newspaper, the *Black Panther*, and drafted a Ten-Point Program, which they debuted in the second issue of the *Black Panther*, on May 15, 1967. Headed "What We Want" and "What We Believe," the program defined the group's mission and sought to advance itself as the voice of the Black community and the vanguard of the revolution. Among other demands, the platform called for the rights to self-determination, full employment, decent housing, education, and an "end to the robbery by the capitalists of our black and oppressed communities."

Recruiting members from Oakland's young, working-class or poor population—whom Newton called "the brothers on the block"—the Panthers began its life as a community watchdog group. They were responsible for getting a traffic light installed at a dangerous intersection in North Oakland, taught residents their legal rights, and marched through the streets on armed patrols. Brandishing shotguns and pistols, the Panthers observed or confronted police officers in the middle of interactions, earning the ire of local law enforcement.

As the Party grew, it structured itself as a top-down, "democratic-centralist" organization, establishing the Oakland chapter as the Central Committee, with Newton taking the top rank as Minister of Defense and Chairman Seale as second-in-command. Eldridge Cleaver, a recent recruit to the Party, served as Minister of Information. An acclaimed writer, author of the bestselling *Soul on Ice*, charismatic public speaker, and convicted felon, Cleaver was an especially enigmatic figure.

The Black Panther Party grew slowly in its first months, boasting no more than twenty or thirty members. The Oakland Panthers were still competing with other radical Black groups, including the rival

Black Panther Party of Northern California, based in San Francisco, which was still a RAM-associated group. Just as they were busy establishing themselves as a presence in Oakland, the Black Panther Party was confronted with one of its most decisive moments. In the early morning of October 28, 1967, as Newton and a friend were driving on their way from a party to a soul food restaurant, the two men were pulled over by White Oakland police officer John Frey. After another White officer arrived on the scene as backup, a shootout immediately occurred between the men and, after the smoke cleared, Frey was dead and Newton was wounded with four bullets in his abdomen.

To many in Oakland's Black community, Newton had practiced what he'd been preaching all along: defending himself against racist police aggression. "Newton immediately became a hero in black communities across the country," writes author Curtis J. Austin. "The fact that a police officer had been killed elevated his stature in the minds of millions of blacks and other minorities who knew from experience the brutality of policemen."

The Panthers launched a "Free Huey" campaign, forming an alliance with Carmichael and SNCC, as well as radical White students and organizers, including New Left activists, Vietnam War objectors, and other anti-imperialist groups. The campaign became a national movement, with celebrity endorsements and demonstrations drawing thousands of supporters. Newton himself was fashioned into a cause célèbre—a living revolutionary icon. But Newton's incarceration left a leadership vacuum in the Party during a crucial moment in its development. Though it was now growing exponentially in size and influence, the Party was at the same time in the beginning stages of an eventual split, with early recruit David Hilliard, who had been promoted to Chief of Staff, engaged in a power struggle with Cleaver, whose vision of the Black Panther Party was less a community action and self-defense organization than a heavily armed band of guerilla soldiers engaged in a bloody war against the police.

The abundance of radical Black organizations, as well as the escalation of Black urban rebellions spreading across the country, was perceived by the federal government as a significant threat to the internal security of the United States. In an August 25, 1967, memo, FBI director Hoover instructed agents across the country to implement the agency's Counterintelligence Program (COINTELPRO), intended to "disrupt, misdirect, discredit, or otherwise neutralize the activities of black nationalist, hate-type organizations and groupings, their leadership, spokesmen, membership, and supporters, and to counter their propensity for violence and disorder." Originally enacted in 1956 to surveil suspected communist organizations in the United States, COINTELPRO went beyond the FBI's conventional intelligence-gathering responsibilities to actively destroying, by whatever means available, any organization the FBI deemed subversive. Hoover cautioned that "under no circumstances should the existence of the program be made known outside the Bureau," and agents were encouraged to "take an enthusiastic and imaginative approach" to their endeavors. Using such covert and illegal tactics as fabricating documents and correspondence, planting agents provocateurs, and generating suspicion through spreading rumors or manufacturing evidence—a strategy known as "bad-jacketing"—COINTELPRO targeted RAM, SNCC, the Nation of Islam, and even moderate civil rights organizations and leaders, including the Congress of Racial Equality (CORE), Southern Christian Leadership Conference (SCLC), and Martin Luther King Jr.

In March 1968, Hoover delivered a new memo to FBI field offices, escalating the program's obsessive crusade against Black activism. Going forward, the goal of COINTELPRO was, among other points, to "prevent the coalition of militant black nationalist groups," "prevent black nationalist groups and leaders from gaining respectability," and "prevent the rise of a 'messiah' who could unify, and electrify, the militant black nationalist movement." Hoover acknowledged that Malcolm X might have been that "messiah" if he hadn't been killed and become a "martyr of the movement today." Because King was still committed to "white, liberal doctrines" of nonviolence and the NOI's Honorable Elijah Muhammad was "less of a threat because of his age," Hoover singled out Stokely Carmichael as the most likely candidate for the role of messiah, as he had "the necessary charisma to be a real threat in this way."

On April 3, the FBI issued an ominous memo, stating that "Negro youth and moderates must be made to understand that if they succumb to revolutionary teaching, they will be dead revolutionaries." The following day, Martin Luther King Jr. was assassinated. Two days later, on the night of April 6, seventeen-year-old Bobby Hutton—one of the first recruits to the Black Panther Party—was killed by Oakland police during an ambush following a shoot-out with a dozen Panthers.

The day after King's death, President Lyndon Johnson met with civil rights leaders at the White House. "If I were a kid in Harlem, I know what I'd be thinking right now," Johnson told his guests. "I'd be thinking that the whites have declared open season on my people, and they're going to pick us off one by one unless I get a gun and pick them off first." On that same day, during a press conference at SNCC's Washington headquarters, Carmichael also delivered what would be a particularly prophetic message. "When White America killed Dr. King last night, she declared war on us," Carmichael said. "There will be no crying and there will be no funeral. The rebellions that have been occurring around these cities and this country is just light stuff compared to what is about to happen. We have to retaliate for the deaths of our leaders. The execution for those deaths will not be in the court rooms. They're going to be in the streets of the United States of America."

Riots and rebellions erupted across more than one hundred American cities, in what author Peter B. Levy describes as the nation's "greatest wave of social unrest since the Civil War." Johnson deployed 58,000 military service members and National Guardsmen to twenty-nine states in order to quell the rebellions. When the smoke finally cleared, on May 27, more than forty people were dead, with 3,500 injuries and 27,000 arrests. The moderation and nonviolent protest of the civil rights movement had been losing popularity among younger Black Americans in urban areas, but now it seemed as though all hope for peaceful dissent was permanently dashed.

Hoover had not mentioned the Black Panther Party in his initial memos to FBI agents, as they existed largely under the agency's radar. But six months later, in a September 1968 memo to FBI agents, Hoover now described the Party as "rapidly expanding" and declared that it was "essential that we not only accelerate our investigations of this organization, and increase our informants in the organization but that we take action under the counterintelligence program to disrupt the group."

When emissaries from Oakland journeyed east, in the spring of 1968, the New York Black Panther Party established by Max Stanford had already disbanded. RAM itself had suspended its activities, having been disrupted by a campaign of infiltration and intimidation by the FBI, including the 1967 arrests of Stanford and fifteen other RAM members on dubious charges of conspiring to assassinate civil rights leaders Roy Wilkins and Whitney Young. Stanford was acquitted of the charges, but ongoing FBI surveillance and police harassment, as well as internal organizational challenges, soon proved insurmountable, and by 1968 RAM was effectively finished. Stanford converted to Islam in 1970, changed his name to Muhammad Ahmad, and went on to earn his Ph.D. from Union Institute and University and become a professor of African American Studies at Temple University in Philadelphia.

Though RAM had since dissolved, SNCC still kept a marginal presence in New York City, so when Bobby Seale arrived in the city in April 1968, accompanied by Kathleen Cleaver—Communications Secretary, Eldridge's wife, and the first woman leader in the Black Panther Party—they reported to SNCC's Manhattan headquarters. They conscripted an eighteen-year-old SNCC activist and former Civil Air Patrolman, Joudon Ford, and designated him Acting Captain of Defense for the Black Panther Party of the East. With baby-fat cheeks and a wisp of stubble above his lip, Ford took seriously his new responsibility as commander of a paramilitary unit.

From his command base in Brooklyn, Ford organized and taught political education (PE) classes and weapons training. Yet as seriously as he took his role, he was unable to keep the Party from being infiltrated by undercover NYPD officers. Infiltration had already become such a serious issue in the organization that, at one point, Ford called Chief of Staff David Hilliard in Oakland to inquire how he could keep moles out of the Party. "When I find out," came Hilliard's response, "I'll let you know."

Meanwhile, another Panther had been dispatched to New York from Oakland that April to set up additional chapters and recruit members. Captain Ron Pennywell didn't receive much return for his efforts, apparently only enlisting three men. But the men he found were eager and prepared, as though they had been expectantly waiting, like the Three Kings of the East, for the first appearance of the Good Shepherd.

Lumumba Shakur, Sekou Odinga, and Bilal Sunni-Ali arranged a meeting with Pennywell, whom Lumumba described as "a very grass-root brother." Sunni-Ali was made section leader of a combined Harlem-Bronx chapter, but he was soon arrested and charged with possession of explosives and an excess amount of gunpowder, which he was using to teach Party members how to pack and reload shotgun shells. Rather than face trial, Sunni-Ali went underground and fled to California.

Harlem and the Bronx were then split into two independent chapters, with Lumumba as section leader of Harlem and Odinga in command of the Bronx.

The Harlem office was established at 2026 Seventh Avenue (now Adam Clayton Powell Jr. Boulevard), while section meetings were held at Lumumba's home on West 117th Street. The Bronx section, which didn't yet have an office, held its meetings either at the Harlem office or at the home of an early recruit to the Party, a Harlem Panther named Yedwa Sudan, who hadn't yet been suspected by his colleagues of his true identity.

With Lumumba and Odinga managing Harlem and the Bronx, and Joudon Ford and Chairman David Brothers in command of the Brooklyn chapter, the Black Panther Party in New York expanded its membership quickly in its first few months. One of the first to join, a twenty-seven-year-old married father of three named Bill Hampton, told a *New York Times* reporter that the Panthers were "a service organization for the black community. A service organization and a black liberation army." Depicting what he saw as a war for the survival of Black people, Hampton called the Panthers "young revolutionaries" who "are ready to die for what we believe."

Like their Oakland predecessors, the New York Panthers drew immediate conflict and police provocation. On August 1, 1968, two members of the Brooklyn chapter—twenty-year-old Gordon Cooke

and seventeen-year-old Darrell Baines—were demonstrating outside a Party office in Bedford-Stuyvesant when several police officers
arrived and proceeded to beat Cooke and Baines before arresting
them and charging them with resisting arrest, interfering with an
arrest, felonious assault, and harassment.

The next day, the Crown Heights precinct house received a phone
call reporting a domestic disturbance on Eastern Parkway. When two
patrolmen arrived on the scene, they were ambushed by a shotgun-
wielding assailant and badly wounded from pieces of the shattered
windshield. The assailant or assailants fled and were never identified,
but Assistant District Attorney John J. Meglio declared that the ambush was carried out by the Panthers. At a press conference, Ford responded to these allegations: "The Black Panther Party did not order
those two policemen shot," he said. "It should be clear to all that the
Black Panther Party was not involved, because if we had been . . . the
pigs would be dead."

Weeks after this incident, on August 21, seven Brooklyn Panthers, including the previously arrested Baines, were apprehended
during a skirmish along Nostrand Avenue and charged with resisting
arrest and assaulting a police officer. At a preliminary hearing for
three of the arrested Panthers, around 150 White men packed into
the sixth floor of the Brooklyn Criminal Court building and attacked
a small group of Black Panthers and White supporters from the leftist group Students for a Democratic Society.

The *New York Times* reported that many of the White assailants
were "off-duty and out-of-uniform policemen," some of whom wore
campaign buttons for segregationist presidential candidate George
Wallace and led chants of "Win with Wallace" and "White Power."
Panthers and White supporters were kicked, beaten, and bloodied
with blackjacks and batons. David Brothers, chairman of the Brooklyn Panthers, asserted that he had been kicked more than twenty
times: "I've been all over the South," he told a reporter, "and for
something like this to happen in a court is unbelievable."

While most of the attention was on the Brooklyn Panthers, the
Harlem branch was comparatively quiet. Lumumba and his cadre initially directed their energy to implementing the fourth point of the
Party's Ten-Point Program: "decent housing, fit for shelter of human beings." To help pursue this goal, Lumumba took a supervisor's

position with the Ellsmere Tenants Council, a subsidiary of the Bronx Action Group. He was hired by Harlem Panther Yedwa Sudan, who recalled years later that Lumumba was "always first in the office."

The Harlem cadre boasted that they helped to get a Black principal in a majority-Black school in Harlem and had been appointed to welfare centers in Harlem, the Bronx, Queens, and Brooklyn "to guarantee the welfare recipients their rights, to educate welfare recipients about community control of the welfare centers, also to try to get welfare recipients jobs as case worker aides in the welfare centers."

The Harlem and Bronx chapters were attracting new members from a wide cross section of Black New Yorkers, including high school and college students, veterans, disaffected Black Muslims, nationalists, and former convicts. One member, Sundiata Acoli (born Clark Squire), had been a NASA computer analyst at Edwards Air Force Base in California before becoming finance minister of the Harlem Panthers.

Lumumba's older brother was a latecomer to the Party. Though he'd made the customary name change, from James Coston Jr. to Zayd Malik Shakur, he hadn't previously been especially interested in political work or activism. Like his father, Zayd served in the Navy, ranked Aviation Storekeeper Petty Officer 3rd Class. After the Navy, he worked at the post office, rented an apartment in the Bronx, and ran around with his Navy buddies and old friends from Atlantic City. He was also a jazz enthusiast and knew many of the city's top jazz musicians, and he would deck them out in African-influenced attire, which he would assemble himself. "He was satisfied with what he was doing, which was basically just living the life, enjoying the life," recalled Odinga.

Lumumba and Odinga were persistent in trying to recruit Zayd to the Party, and finally, after six months of their pestering him, in the summer of 1968, Zayd joined the Black Panther Party. Though it took him half a year to agree to join, Zayd was now totally dedicated. "When he came in, he came in body, soul, and mind. He came all the way in," Odinga recalled. "That's the way he did things. He committed. When he decided to do something, he did it."

A young woman who would soon play pivotal roles in the direction of the Party and the future of the Shakur family also joined the Harlem chapter at this time. Alice Faye Williams was a twenty-one-year-old former street gang member who had been drifting aimlessly through New York City, experimenting with drugs and looking for purpose. In the spring of 1968, Williams happened upon a Saturday gathering at Harlem's 125th Street and Seventh Avenue, a famous corner previously occupied by Marcus Garvey, Malcolm X, and several other prominent Black orators. She was halted in her tracks by the assembled crowd—a mix of dashiki-wearers, hustlers with processed hair, domestic workers, mothers, and students, all rapt by the speaker, a mustachioed Black man wearing a black leather jacket and black beret, who was on a recruiting mission from Oakland.

Williams's first impression of Bobby Seale, chairman of the Black Panther Party, was that he was a "cute little nigger," but as she listened to him talk about the Panthers' Ten-Point Program, about taking up arms against police repression, and, most personal to Williams, about channeling private rage into organized, revolutionary action, she realized that this was exactly what she had been looking for.

"All I did then was wait for the Black Panther Party to come to New York," she later recalled. "Somebody told me they were coming; you know, I knew they just had to come, they just couldn't stay on the [West] Coast, I just couldn't relate to that. Nothing that strong could stay in one area. I just knew from the beginning that it would branch out into something beautiful—it had to. I just knew there were niggers all over the place that felt like I did."

The Black Panther Party finally came to New York, Alice Faye Williams changed her name to Afeni Shakur, and neither she nor the Party would ever be the same.

5.
THE DISCIPLE

IN THE SUMMER of 1968, a young, petite, Black woman named Cleo Silvers was called to a meeting of Black Panther section leaders from Harlem and the Bronx. A community mental healthcare worker and former Volunteers in Service to America (VISTA) worker, Silvers had already been acquainted with the Panthers, having worked alongside them at South Bronx's Lincoln Hospital. The assembled Panthers included Lumumba Shakur; his brother, Zayd; and Curtis Powell, a biochemist who had recently received his Ph.D. from the University of Stockholm. Gathered together at Lincoln Hospital, the Panthers sat Silvers down and asked her to join the Party. Silvers was stunned. She began to blush.

"I could not believe that these brilliant, amazing people wanted me to become a member of the Black Panther Party," she later recalled. "I was in awe of this group of people. I was like, 'Yes yes yes.' They said, 'OK, you have to go and sign up.'"

The Panthers told Silvers to go to the Harlem office on Seventh Avenue and meet with some of the Panthers working there, who were expecting her. Silvers set out immediately, running all the way from the Bronx to Manhattan, crossing the Third Avenue Bridge over the Harlem River. When Silvers arrived at the office, she was struck by its splendor, with Black Panther posters decorating the front windows and beautiful Black men and women ornamented in African attire gathered to listen to a recording of Malcolm X's 1964 speech "The Ballot or the Bullet," issuing loudly from a record player outside. Silvers approached a few women sitting in chairs outside the office, each wearing a traditional Nigerian head wrap called a *gele*.

"Good afternoon, sisters, my name is Cleo," she began nervously. "Zayd and them sent me down here to become a member of the Black Panther Party."

Afeni Shakur looked Silvers up and down. It was a hot summer day, and Silvers was dressed lightly, in a short, backless, African-print halter top. After giving Silvers a thorough examination, Afeni declared, "You can't be no Panther woman. Look at you."

Silvers was startled. "What's wrong?"

"You see we all have our *geles* on, and you don't have a *gele*. You can't be a Panther sister without a *gele*," Afeni responded. "I'll tell you what, I'm gonna help you out. Go inside, tell Janet to give you a cloth so you can have a *gele*."

Silvers went inside the office and was met by the Panther officer of the day, Janet Cyril. "Miss Janet," Silvers said, "Miss Afeni sent me in here to get a cloth so I can wrap a *gele*."

Cyril laughed and handed her a cloth. Silvers brought the cloth outside to Afeni, who tied it on Silvers's head, then unwrapped it, gave it back to Silvers, and told her to do it herself. Silvers repeated the motion and successfully wrapped her first *gele*.

Afeni examined Silvers. "OK," she said, nodding approvingly, "go ahead inside and sign your paperwork."

Afeni Shakur was a tough person in every meaning of the word. An intimidating, headstrong, and brilliant woman, she had already lived a difficult life before joining the Black Panther Party in the summer of 1968. Born Alice Faye Williams on January 10, 1947, in Lumberton, North Carolina, but raised in Norfolk, Virginia, Afeni was the youngest of two girls born to Walter and Rosa Belle Williams. Just over a decade after she was born, she would witness her first ethnic uprising against White terrorism, fought between the local Ku Klux Klan and members of the Lumbee Tribe—the largest Indigenous state tribe in North Carolina and the largest state tribe east of the Mississippi.

Descended from the survivors of assorted tribal nations, as well as the intermarriages of Indigenous Americans and freed Blacks, the Lumbee were granted recognition by the U.S. Congress in 1956 but denied the privileges and benefits that come with official recognition. Klan wizard James "Catfish" Cole renounced the recognition, called the Lumbee a "mixed race" people, and led a campaign of intimidation against what he viewed as the "intermingling" between Lumbee with Whites and Blacks. "There's about 30,000 half-breeds up in Robeson County and we are going to have some cross burnings and scare them up," Cole told a reporter from the *Greensboro Daily News*.

The Klan organized a rally for January 18, 1958, at Hayes Pond, near Maxton, North Carolina, but on the evening of the rally only fifty to one hundred people showed up. The small crowd was then surprised by more than five hundred armed members of Lumbee and other supporting tribes, who overtook the crowd and ran them off. The Lumbee later celebrated by burning an effigy of Cole and posing for press photographers while wrapped in a stolen Klan banner.

Commemorated locally as "the Battle of Hayes Pond," this incident took place one week after Afeni's eleventh birthday. Though she hadn't been present at the rally, she would recount this story throughout her life as though it had helped shape her into who she would become: "That was my first taste of *resistance*," she recalled years later. "Resistance is what I felt. *Resist*. A sense of don't let that happen to you."

Afeni's father, Walter Williams, struggled to provide for his family through his work as a truck driver, and his wife, Rosa Belle, would often have to depend on a sympathetic neighbor to put food on the table. Years later, Afeni would remember her father as a "*street nigga . . . loved* by the people in the streets," and as a man of principles and ethics, while also being "stubborn and arrogant"—all traits she believed she'd inherited from him. At the time, however, she'd felt hatred toward her father, because he would often beat her mother.

One day, in the same year when the Lumbee defended themselves from the Klan, Walter made a move to hit Rosa Belle, and the sisters watched as their mother defended herself by throwing hot grease from a skillet on him—offering young Afeni her second example of resistance. Not long after, Rosa Belle left Walter, taking her two daughters briefly back to her hometown of Lumberton before continuing their migration to New York City.

"When I came to New York, I thought I was coming to the land of milk and honey," she recalled later. She was instantly disabused of this heavenly notion. The city "looked sick. It looked nasty and I wanted to go back down South. I couldn't stand the smells, New York smelled terrible. And you couldn't see the stars."

Rosa Belle found work at a low-paying job in a factory that produced lampshades, and she and her daughters shared a single-room apartment on 169th Street and Washington Avenue, in the South Bronx. At Benjamin Franklin Junior High School, Afeni enrolled in a journalism class and wrote for the student newspaper, the *Franklin Flash*; in the ninth grade, she entered a citywide journalism competition, in which she received an award for "outstanding research in a paper on juvenile delinquency," presented by New York City Mayor Robert F. Wagner. When it came time to choose a high school, Afeni's English teacher recommended the Bronx High School of Science or the High School of Performing Arts. Believing Bronx Science would be full of "too many rich white kids," she decided on Performing Arts (PA). But she quickly discovered that she also couldn't relate to the students at PA, who had come from privileged backgrounds, could afford to buy new clothes, and were chauffeured to school in limousines.

While at Performing Arts, Afeni had a brief relationship with Glynn Turman, who'd already had a prominent role at age twelve in the original Broadway production of Lorraine Hansberry's play *A Raisin in the Sun*, as the character Travis Younger, and would go on to find success on the television shows *Peyton Place* and *A Different World*. But Afeni struggled to find her place at school. Besides being new to the city, she couldn't afford the latest clothes, she couldn't afford to buy her own lunch, and other kids teased her for her dark skin, skinny frame, and short-cropped natural hair.

She rebelled the only way she knew how: she fought. She fought boys and girls, White and Black. She fought folks just for looking at her funny. In a strange and imposing city, newly fatherless, and enrolled in a school where she believed she didn't belong, Afeni took refuge behind her fists.

"I thought fighting was the way to compensate for my inadequacies," she later recalled. "I could fight right through my fear. If a pack of motherfuckers attacked me, I'd pick the biggest and the strongest motherfucker and fight for my life."

She would fight for her life for many years to come.

By the time she turned fifteen, Afeni had become president of a street gang called the Disciple Debs—a women's auxiliary to the Disciples gang. She and her Disciples would run wild throughout the Bronx, getting into fistfights, knife fights, and shoot-outs with Puerto Rican gangs, often using the South Bronx's Crotona Park as their battleground. By 1950, at least twenty young gang members had been killed in the area surrounding the public park; seven boys were killed in one year alone, in 1949. Afeni would later remember how every summer "the pool would be red with blood."

During the day, Afeni would come to school drunk on Thunderbird wine; at night she would go out fighting and dodging bullets. She finally walked away from school for good, taking a job with the post office as one of New York's first female mail carriers. She and her best friend, Sandra, hit the Harlem clubs at night, went home with drug dealers, and dabbled in cocaine and weed. She left her post office job after one year because "that kind of work is geared to making you a machine."

Toward the end of 1966, Sandra died from a brain hemorrhage, compounded by an undetected pregnancy and heroin use. Like Afeni, Sandra was only eighteen years old. Sandra's sudden death devastated Afeni. She wandered through the city, unmoored, experimenting with LSD and drifting around to various peace rallies and political demonstrations. At one point, she found her way to a *bembé*—a weekly Afro-Cuban ceremony in which drums and group chanting are used to invoke the orisha deities. The orisha, when summoned, will temporarily possess an individual's soul and provide assistance and guidance on her life path. Attended by scores of Black Harlemites each weekend, *bembés* were held in public parks, at Harlem's Yoruba Temple, or at the adjacent Ujamaa Market, which had been founded in the early 1960s by a Detroit-born Yoruba priest, Adefunmi. Afeni returned regularly to the *bembé*, and her Yoruba teacher soon bestowed upon her the first of her new names, translated from the West African Yoruba language as "dear one" or "lover of the people." Alice Faye was now Afeni.

Baptized with her new name, Afeni recognized that changes in her life were imminent. She had survived deadly gang wars, drug abuse, and the premature death of her best friend. She didn't yet know what path life was going to lead her down, but she knew that her life depended upon a new direction, a renewed purpose. She just had to be patient.

"I knew even then that I was *about* to do something," she recalled, "and I waited for a sign to show me what that something was going to be."

That sign arrived in the spring of 1968.

When she chanced upon Black Panther Party Chairman Bobby Seale, speaking at 125th Street and Seventh Avenue in Harlem, Afeni knew right away that this was the *something* for which she was destined. That summer, she attended political education (PE) class, which was chaired by New York's Deputy Minister of Defense Joudon Ford. During the class, Ford asked the attendees if anyone was interested in joining the Party. Afeni's hand shot up. Since she lived in the Bronx, Ford introduced Afeni to the Bronx section leader, Sekou Odinga.

Odinga helped Afeni to calm her inner rage, to channel her resentment and self-hatred into self-respect, dignity, and love for the community. "He was sincere about what he was saying. He was just such a beautiful person," Afeni recalled. "He was the most pure person I ever met in my life."

Odinga remembered Afeni as being "young, fiery, full of energy, full of curiosity," while also acknowledging that "she was a Bronx girl. She was a hood queen. Didn't take no shit."

Afeni attended a Panther rally at Harlem's Mount Morris Park, organized to garner support for Huey Newton, who was on trial for the murder of Oakland police officer John Frey. Minister of Information Eldridge Cleaver had flown in from California to speak at the rally, but Afeni was most impressed by the care, camaraderie, and confidence of the assembled Panthers.

While at the rally, Afeni noticed a handsome, skinny Black man with a thick mustache and goatee, wearing a black naval coat festooned with insignia in the red, black, and green Pan-African liberation colors. She watched as the man directed others at the rally like a military sergeant. She learned that this man was Harlem section leader Lumumba Shakur.

When Afeni was first becoming acquainted with Odinga and Lumumba, she didn't consider herself political or much of an activist. What she saw in these two close friends was something more visceral, more intimate—something that was directly significant to her. "When I met Sekou and Lumumba it was the first time in my life that I ever met men who didn't abuse women," she recalled. "As simple as that. It had nothing to do with anything about political movements. It was just that never in my life had I met men who didn't abuse women, and who loved women because they were women and because they were people."

Afeni and Lumumba became close, and she was introduced to members of Lumumba's family, including the venerable patriarch, Salahdeen Shakur. Afeni was staggered by the familial love, support, and protection these men offered. As a twenty-one-year-old woman whose personal experiences with men consisted primarily of an abusive father, gangbangers, and drug dealers, when she met the Shakur men—Salahdeen, Lumumba, and Zayd—her "entire view of men and family was shaken up." She found that the "Shakur family was not only strong, but they were independent thinkers."

The feeling was mutual. Lumumba was captivated by Afeni's quick wit and candor. He was impressed by her "political consciousness combined with pure candidness, directness and lots of fire" and with how she "never hesitated to give me constructive criticism on some of my actions."

After receiving Salahdeen's blessing, Lumumba and Afeni married in the fall of 1968. It didn't seem to matter much, at the time, that Lumumba had been married for two years.

He and his first wife, Sayeeda, married in 1966 and were the parents of twin toddlers. Lumumba believed that being a Muslim permitted him to have more than one wife, and even though he had misinterpreted Islamic rules, Afeni and Sayeeda agreed to this arrangement. Lumumba also misappropriated the Islamic wedding ritual, believing that all a Muslim groom needed to do to certify a marriage was to proclaim "This is my wife" three times in front of a witness. With his brother Zayd as witness, Lumumba stood beside Afeni and declared: "This is my wife. This is my wife. This is my wife."

She became Afeni Shakur.

By all appearances, this nonconventional trio coexisted peacefully, if a bit crowded, in their Harlem apartment, with Sayeeda, who was not politically active, keeping home and providing for the twins, while Lumumba and Afeni went out and did Party work. Only later did Afeni discover how much Sayeeda, who would soon fatefully betray her husband, was suffering under this arrangement. But for the first few months, Lumumba and Afeni functioned as a husband-and-wife team. Though Lumumba had since been promoted to lieutenant, the couple were equal partners in the Party, challenging each other as often as they challenged the system.

"I never wanted to get married. I never wanted to be just a housewife. I was too restless," Afeni confessed two years later. "But with my husband it was different. We did things together. I was a revolutionary and he was a revolutionary."

Afeni became a section leader of the Harlem branch and helped launch the Party's Free Breakfast for School Children program, as well as helping organize support during the long and bitter teachers' strike, in the predominantly Black and Puerto Rican neighborhood of Ocean Hill–Brownsville.

Lumumba and Afeni directed most of their work, however, toward helping tenants coordinate rent strikes. Promoted in the early 1960s by Harlem-based tenant organizer and former Malcolm X associate Jesse Gray, by the end of the decade, rent strikes—withholding rent until landlords meet their tenants' demands—had become a popular protest tool to call attention to the squalid and neglected conditions of public housing in Harlem and the Bronx.

Cleo Silvers was awed by Afeni's talent as a tenant advocate, remembering her as "one of the most prolific housing organizers I've ever seen in my entire life. I did it in the South Bronx as a VISTA volunteer, but nothing compared to what Afeni was able to accomplish in Harlem and the South Bronx."

Part of Afeni's success as an organizer, according to Silvers, owed in large part to the kind of values and principles Afeni had cultivated from all the years she'd had to fend for herself. "She was lovely, sweet, kind, sensitive, talented, very smart," Silvers remembers. "But she didn't take no shit off nobody."

Not everything the Panthers in Harlem and the Bronx did was as exciting or provocative as school boycotts and rent strikes. Every rank-and-file Panther was required to stand out on the street and hawk the

Party's newspaper, the *Black Panther—Black Community News Service* (later renamed the *Black Panther—Intercommunal News Service*). At its peak, from 1968 to 1971, several hundred thousand copies of the paper were sold each week; it was the most-read Black newspaper in the country. The paper was one of the Party's main recruiting tools, as well as its primary source of revenue, with proceeds split among the Party members, local chapters, and the Central Committee in Oakland.

The Panthers developed a reputation among older residents in Harlem and the Bronx for always being available to serve the immediate needs of the community, regardless of how small or trivial. And the old folks made sure these young soldiers didn't go hungry. "In the neighborhood around the Black Panther Party office, women would be bringing down pots of food," Silvers recalled. "Old ladies loved us, because Black Panthers were known to carry groceries up to the fifth floor. It's an old lady living on the fifth floor? She's not carrying her groceries upstairs. One of us is gonna carry those groceries upstairs."

While novice Panthers were usually tasked with selling newspapers, attending PE classes, memorizing the Party's Ten-Point Program, and carrying the occasional bag of groceries upstairs for old ladies, they were also instructed in technical education (TE), the Party's term for firearms training. New recruits were taught how to disassemble, clean, and handle different types of firearms, from handguns to automatic rifles. Silvers remembered being driven to a farm in upstate New York, where she and other Panthers were assigned target practice.

Since that spring day in 1967 when a delegation of armed Panthers occupied the state capitol in Sacramento, California, guns had formed the nucleus of the Black Panther Party's popular image. Even more than the Party newspaper, the widely publicized photographs of shotgun-toting Black men and women were perhaps the Party's greatest recruiting tool.

Jamal Joseph, a fifteen-year-old high school honors student, recalled hearing gossip that when you joined the Black Panther Party, "they gave you a gun with a panther on it, a knife with a panther on it, some black sunglasses, and a beret, and you just went out to kill all the devils and savages that there were."

A light-complexioned boy with Afro-Cuban roots, Joseph was raised by doting, churchgoing grandparents in the North Bronx. He attended his first Panther meeting in October 1968, at the Brooklyn office on Nostrand Avenue, alongside a group of fifty men and women, dressed either in the standard black Panther uniform or in African attire. The leader of the meeting, Lieutenant Edmay, began to recite the Ten-Point Program to the assembled group. When he reached point seven—"We want an immediate end to police brutality and murder of Black people, other people of color, all oppressed people inside the United States"—Jamal jumped up. "Choose me, brother," he called out. "Arm me and send me on a mission. I'll kill whitey right now."

The lieutenant called Joseph up to the front of the office, opened a desk drawer, reached inside, and, to Jamal's surprise, pulled out a stack of books, which included *The Autobiography of Malcolm X*; *The Wretched of the Earth*, by the anti-colonialist philosopher Frantz Fanon; and the "Little Red Book" of quotations by Chinese Communist leader Mao Tse-tung.

"Excuse me, brother," Jamal said, confused. "I thought you said you were going to arm me."

"Excuse me, young brother, I just did," replied the lieutenant.

Humbled and embarrassed, Jamal returned to his seat with his new reading material. Jamal's anecdote, however, reflects larger questions about the Party's growth among urban Black youth. Were young Black men and women stirred by the Party's Marxist rhetoric and abstract political theory, or by media accounts and neighborhood gossip of sunglasses-wearing anarchists who were out to "kill all the devils"? Were they motivated by their desire to help organize rent strikes, to wake up at six in the morning to serve breakfast to children, to sell newspapers, and to help old ladies with their groceries? Or did they sign up with the expectation of waging guerrilla warfare against police? Coming from dissimilar backgrounds—the anti-poverty volunteer and mental healthcare worker, the former street gang member, the overzealous high school student—converts to the Party brought their own ideas, visions, expectations, and egos with them into the organization. These internal dissensions would eventually have fatal consequences, for Party members and for the Party itself.

After the Panther meeting had wrapped up, Joseph lingered at the office. As he occupied himself by browsing the Party newspapers for sale, he was approached by "a beautiful woman with dark brown skin and short hair."

"How old are you?" Afeni demanded to know.

Having already been embarrassed once, Joseph added a year to his age, telling Afeni he was "sixteen and a half."

"You look like you're thirteen, maybe fourteen," Afeni replied. "Go home."

Joseph stood his ground, firmly stating his desire to become a Panther.

Afeni studied the brash teenager, just as she had scrutinized the bashful young Cleo Silvers. "Then make sure I see you every time you come in the office," she told him. "I got my eye on you."

Afeni turned and walked away. It was nighttime by the time the meeting had ended, and as Joseph was exiting the office to return home, he was approached by another Panther leader—a tall, physically fit man still wearing his sunglasses. The man informed Joseph that he would be his section leader in the Bronx. He introduced himself as Yedwa Sudan.

Like Judas Iscariot, Yedwa would soon betray his companions, leading to a spectacular trial, during which he finally revealed his true identity, carrying reverberations that lasted for generations to come.

6.
BETRAYAL

WHEN BLACK PANTHER Party Chief of Staff David Hilliard and Chairman Bobby Seale arrived in Brooklyn in the spring of 1968, they were alarmed by what they found. While West Coast Panthers had adopted the uniform of black leather jackets, black berets, and powder blue shirts, these New York Panthers were parading around in dashikis and *geles*. Where Huey Newton and Bobby Seale took inspiration from Mao Tse-tung and North Korea's Kim Il-sung, Lumumba Shakur and Sekou Odinga looked to Pan-African leaders like Kwame Nkrumah. "Some have adopted African names that none of us, even Bobby, who knows a lot about Africa, can pronounce," Hilliard grumbled.

Cleo Silvers remembered the influence of Lumumba and his older brother Zayd on the Panthers' distinctive fashion: "It was Zayd and Lumumba who insisted that the Black Panthers in Harlem wear African clothes."

As leaders in the Party's Central Committee, Hilliard and Seale were tasked with ensuring that these groups were meeting qualifications established by national headquarters. Only groups that followed these conditions—which required the attendance of a six-week training program consisting of political education classes and correct administrative and reporting procedures—were issued a charter, recognizing them as official chapters of the Black Panther Party.

When Hilliard returned to New York, he complained that the Brooklyn chapter had "moved to Harlem, taken over by some veteran movement people and a family named Shakur. With their confusing African names and peculiar New York manner, I can hardly keep track of them."

New Party offices were quickly opening across the country, from such disparate cities as Los Angeles, Bakersfield, Seattle, Denver, Philadelphia, Newark, and Peekskill. Hilliard was overwhelmed by this surge of interest: "We get calls all day long," he said. "Des Moines, Virginia Beach, Atlanta. Since we're three hours behind the East Coast, the requests often start as early as eight A.M. Our replies are always the same: people must come to Oakland, sell the paper, follow Party rules to the letter." With this sudden influx of members and chapters, and with Newton facing trial for the murder of Oakland police officer John Frey, the Central Committee struggled to enforce the organizational structure and to maintain compliance to Party directives.

Of all these new chapters and offices being established from coast to coast, no city had concerned Hilliard as much as New York, which he singled out as the Party's "biggest problem." He placed the blame on Captain Ron Pennywell, an Oakland native who had gone to New York that spring to establish the Brooklyn chapter. Pennywell's "undisciplined, ostentatious style has stamped itself on the group," Hilliard recalled. But though he confessed that Pennywell "shouldn't have started the chapter, called himself or anyone else Panthers, and he certainly has no power to name himself a captain," Hilliard admitted to Pennywell's success in organizing the chapter and "earn[ing] the loyalty of his recruits."

Still, these dashiki-wearing Panthers helped to develop what would become one of the most active cities in the country, with branches not only in Harlem but in Brooklyn, the Bronx, Queens, Corona–East Elmhurst, Staten Island, and Mount Vernon. The Harlem branch, now regarded as the central office for the state, was also one of the busiest. Party members advocated for community schooling initiatives, the hiring of more Black school administrators, and the implementation of African language, science, and arts courses in elementary and junior high schools.

Most of their attention and energy went into supporting tenants' rights. Early Panther recruit Yedwa Sudan was appointed director of the Ellsmere Tenants Council, an Office of Economic Opportunity program, and he hired seven of his fellow Panthers. He made Lumumba deputy supervisor but didn't hire Lumumba's wife Afeni. Yedwa later claimed that it was his refusal to hire Afeni that caused her to go around telling other members he was "a pig," but she had been convinced even before then that Yedwa was "too arrogant for a Panther," waving his guns around too recklessly to be trusted.

Even though membership had seen immense growth since the spring, the Party was facing a national leadership crisis by the year's end. On September 8, Newton was convicted by a jury of manslaughter for the death of Officer Frey and sentenced to two to fifteen years in prison. In November, Eldridge Cleaver—who had assumed a leadership role in the year since Newton's arrest—was ordered to turn himself in to authorities after prison officials determined he'd violated his parole during the April 6 shoot-out between Panthers and Oakland police that left Bobby Hutton dead. Rather than return to San Quentin, Cleaver instead chose exile, fleeing first to Cuba and then to Algeria.

With Newton and Cleaver effectively isolated from day-to-day operations, Seale and Hilliard began to steer the Party away from its militant rhetoric and directed its energy toward newly instituted community programs, particularly the seminal Free Breakfast for School Children program. After launching at St. Augustine's Episcopal Church in West Oakland in January 1969, the breakfast program would become the Party's central agenda. Between 1969 and 1971, Panther chapters across the country, relying on donations from restaurants and supermarkets, served daily breakfast to tens of thousands of schoolchildren in dozens of cities, including Oakland, Los Angeles, Seattle, Portland, Denver, Kansas City, and New York City.

But though such community service programs as free breakfast and tenant organizing did much to improve the Party's public image, some Panthers, particularly those in New York, craved more action. Lumumba threw himself into his work with Ellsmere, but Odinga had little patience for such dreary desk work. As the journalist Murray Kempton observed, these "endeavors at peaceful, if raucous, advocacy for the poor had the meagerest appeal to Sekou's temperament; and restlessly his thoughts turned to scenes more stimulating to the blood."

As a national organization committed to feeding thousands of hungry schoolchildren, offering free community healthcare, and co-ordinating clothing drives—as well as bailing out jailed Party members and procuring enough guns and ammunition for the impending revolution—the Black Panther Party was in constant need of funds. Newspaper sales and donations from sympathetic benefactors only went so far. Additional fundraising methods were needed. The first attempt at such supplementary fundraising, however, was a discouraging one.

On the morning of November 21, 1968, Odinga and another man, William Hampton, were witnessed exiting a State National Bank branch in Stamford, Connecticut. Odinga was outfitted in a green fatigue jacket, and the witness claimed to have seen the barrel of a shotgun peeking out from beneath Hampton's gray tweed coat. After later spotting the same two men driving through town in a Chevrolet, this concerned citizen notified a police cruiser. The police stopped the car, which turned out to have been stolen three days earlier. Upon searching the car, police found two shotguns, three pistols, two wool ski masks, tear gas spray, and fifteen pairs of handcuffs. Whether Odinga and Hampton had been casing the bank or had simply gotten cold feet at the last moment, the police didn't have enough evidence to charge the men with an attempted bank robbery, so Odinga and Hampton were charged only for car theft and held on $25,000 bail.

Four days after their arrest, as the two men awaited arraignment, Lumumba and another man, Ronald Hill, made the forty-mile drive north from New York City to Stamford, and they were promptly stopped by Stamford police for "acting suspiciously." When they searched the car, police discovered a twelve-gauge shotgun. Lumumba and Hill were themselves arrested for possession of the shotgun and held on $5,000 bail. Acting on a tip from a special agent in the New York Panthers—possibly from one Panther who had been particularly singled out by Afeni as being "arrogant"—Stamford police were led to believe that Lumumba had come to free Odinga.

Odinga's bail was soon reduced and he, Lumumba, and the other two men made bond and returned to New York. Whatever their intentions in Stamford had been, Lumumba and Odinga returned home disappointed and dejected, with nothing to show for their efforts.

Resuming his work with Ellsmere, Lumumba, like Odinga, was becoming more and more impatient, with his thoughts also now turned to acts more stimulating to the blood. Though they might've been temporarily set back by the fiasco in Connecticut, it wouldn't be the last time these two Panther leaders would attempt a large, consequential act on behalf of the Party, nor would it be the last time police would interrupt them before they could complete their mission.

On the night of Friday, January 17, 1969, Lumumba and his inner team of trusted Panthers were purported to have placed dynamite in three locations: the Forty-fourth Precinct police station in the Bronx, Manhattan's Twenty-fourth Precinct police station, and the Queens Board of Education office. The alleged plan was for all three bombs to be detonated simultaneously at 9:00 P.M. The first bomb discharged at the Queens Board of Education office, exploding a hole in the side of the building but causing no reported injuries. The second bomb, at the Manhattan police station, failed to ignite at all. But the greatest and most ambitious part of the plan was also the one with the most disastrous results.

Driving a rented red Dodge sedan, nineteen-year-old Harlem Panther Joan Bird steered Odinga and another Harlem Panther, Kuwasi Balagoon, to their assigned position: a grassy slope on the Harlem River Drive in the Bronx, near 170th Street. On the opposite side of the river stood the Forty-fourth Precinct police station. The alleged plan was for the three Panthers to wait for the dynamite to explode, and as police officers ran from the burning building, either Odinga or Balagoon would act as sniper, firing on the fleeing officers from across the Harlem River. The explosion, however, only caused minor damage, shattering two windows. A few minutes later, two patrolmen, Louis Scorzello and Roland McKenzie, who'd happened to be parked nearby, noticed the red sedan. The patrolmen got out of the cruiser and approached the car, where they saw a Black woman sitting behind the wheel and two Black men reaching for something in the trunk.

"What's the trouble?" Scorzello asked.

"Nothing, Officer," Balagoon replied. "Just engine trouble."

Without another word, Odinga allegedly raised his pistol and began firing at the patrolmen. Balagoon then lifted his own pistol and began shooting at the officers, and now all four men were engaged in a close-range shoot-out. Amazingly, none of the men were struck, even though the officers claimed that Odinga and Balagoon had fired a barrage of bullets from a distance of only six feet. The officers ran back to their patrol car and radioed for backup, while Odinga and Balagoon escaped into the nearby woods. After additional patrol cars arrived a few minutes later, Scorzello and McKenzie returned to the sedan, where they found Joan Bird huddled "in a prone position" on the floor underneath the dashboard and a .308 Winchester rifle in the trunk.

The officers dragged Bird from the sedan, and she later claimed she was brutally beaten before being handcuffed and put into the patrol car. The police denied Bird's account, maintaining that she had injured herself as she ducked down in the sedan during the shoot-out, but when she arrived at Harlem's Thirty-fourth Precinct station, she was apparently in such a state that the admitting detective, Frank Ruggeri, asked McKenzie, "Did you work her over?" Photographs would later emerge of Bird with a swollen black eye.

As Bird was being interrogated, police were able to trace the abandoned rental car to Harlem Panther Sundiata Acoli, and they brought him into the Thirty-fourth Precinct soon after midnight. Accompanied by a lawyer, Lumumba arrived at the precinct later that morning to inquire about his captured soldiers, just as he had driven to Stamford, Connecticut, two months earlier. Lumumba was promptly arrested at the precinct as a co-conspirator. Odinga and Balagoon evaded capture and went into hiding.

Lumumba and Bird made bail, and Lumumba went back to work at Ellsmere, but when the time came to submit the routine payroll forms to New York's Human Resources Administration for budget renewal, Yedwa decided it wasn't worth the effort and let the program dissolve. Without the daily burden of a bureaucratic government job, Lumumba and his Harlem Panthers could put their energy toward more immediate and sensational actions. But with Lumumba now facing legal trouble and under scrutiny by authorities, and Odinga underground, command of Lumumba's inner circle fell to Kwando Kinshasa (born William King), a former U.S. Marine. For the next two months, Kinshasa was placed in charge of what Lumumba dubbed the "taking-care-of-business squad" (Kinshasa preferred "Panther Guerrilla Team"). Kinshasa led his team in military drills, obtaining guns and explosives, and scouting downtown department stores and other potential bombing targets throughout the city.

One of the members of this team was a short, soft-spoken man with a mustache and a slight lisp who had known Kinshasa since childhood. He joined the Party in July 1968, and in February he was assigned to Kinshasa's security section, a small and trusted team of six or seven stalwart Panthers who accompanied Kinshasa on reconnaissance missions. He had been so unassuming, so amenable, that no one suspected Eugene Roberts was a detective in the NYPD's Bureau of Special Services and Intelligence.

Roberts furnished the information that led to the April 2 raid, in which hundreds of heavily armed police officers rounded up the Harlem Panthers. But Odinga, once again, managed to avoid being captured that morning.

"I was underground, so I was already thinking about, 'If they ever came, how would I escape?'" Odinga later recalled. "I had my escape route already planned."

When officers arrived at the door of the apartment where Odinga was hiding out, near Prospect Park in Brooklyn, he ran into the bathroom, squeezed through a window, dropped nearly thirty feet onto the roof of a garage, then jumped down to the ground. Finding an unlocked door leading to the basement of a brownstone, he hid for hours as police sealed off the block and searched the area. Finally, when night came and the police abandoned their search, Odinga crawled out from his hiding place and jumped into a jitney cab. He resurfaced one year later in Algeria, joining Eldridge and Kathleen Cleaver, Field Marshal Donald Cox, Larry Mack, and other Panthers in self-exile.

Though their identities hadn't yet been officially revealed, Eugene Roberts and Yedwa Sudan were suspected of being undercover officers following the raid. In the June 14 issue of the *Black Panther* newspaper, Roberts is marked as a "nigger pig," and the author alleges that, by disappearing after the arrests, he had proven himself to "be nothing but another agent for the fascist power structure of America."

Supporting the accused Panthers, as well as performing a bit of public damage control, David Hilliard now spoke out in praise of the same New York Panthers he had dismissed the year before. In an interview published in the *Black Panther* that April, Hilliard called the charges "just another heavy-handed move to wipe out the leadership of the Black Panther Party. In the first place it is very absurd to think of an organization with the magnitude of the Black Panther Party, with some 40 chapters at this point, to risk the distruction [*sic*] of one of our most revolutionary chapters, one of our better organized chapters, by going around talking about blowing up department stores. It is something that our Central Committee does not endorse."

The Panthers' suspicions of members Yedwa and Roberts were finally confirmed when each man took the stand to testify against the defendants and Yedwa was revealed to be undercover detective Ralph White. The defendants also now learned why the dynamite hadn't detonated at Manhattan's Twenty-fourth Precinct, and why the dynamite at the Bronx's Forty-fourth Precinct caused such insignificant damage. Yedwa had discovered the dynamite hidden behind a refrigerator at Ellsmere and secretly replaced it with imitation explosives.

In one of the more dramatic moments of a trial not lacking in melodrama, Lumumba and Afeni would learn that Lumumba's first wife, Sayeeda—quietly seething with resentment and bitterness after he'd taken Afeni as a second wife—had been having an affair with Yedwa and unsuspectingly furnishing him with information on the Panthers' activities.

When Afeni's own infidelities came to light during the trial and Lumumba discovered she'd become pregnant by another man while out on bail, he divorced her in the same informal manner in which he'd married her—by proclaiming "I divorce thee" three times. But Afeni had more pressing concerns to attend to than the end of her marriage.

Representing herself during the trial, Afeni confronted Yedwa on the witness stand, forcing him to confess that, beyond a lot of grandiose talk, he hadn't seen her or any of the other defendants committing any criminal act. Even after her powerful performance in court, however, Afeni didn't have much hope for acquittal. She'd also begun to become estranged from the Black Panther Party itself, after watching the Party's infighting and egotism over the last few years. With most of its leaders incarcerated, the New York chapters were decimated and would never recover.

In the event Afeni was convicted and locked away for the rest of her life, as she believed she would be, she arranged for her sister, Gloria, to raise her child. In March 1971, Afeni wrote a letter from jail, addressed to Lumumba's children as well as "the unborn baby . . . within my womb." Writing from a place of isolation, disillusionment, and sorrow, Afeni's letter is like a prayer, a last will and testament, offering wisdom and guidance to her unborn child and to all children who would one day carry on the struggle:

> I've discovered what I should have known a long time ago—that change has to begin within ourselves—whether there is a revolution today or tomorrow—we still must face the problems of purging ourselves of the larceny that we have all inherited. I hope we do not pass it on to you because you are our only hope . . . I do not regret any of it—for it taught me to be something that some people will never learn—for the first time in my life I feel like a woman— beaten, battered and scarred maybe, but isn't that what wisdom is truly made of. Help me to continue to learn—only this time with a bit more grace for I am a poor example for anyone to follow because I have deviated from the revolutionary principles which I know to be correct. I wish you love.

The child Afeni bore three months later would himself be accused, many years later, of deviating from revolutionary principles. But until then, Afeni would have a second chance at freedom, new friends and lovers, and plenty of new battles ahead.

7.
CIVIL WAR

WHEN POLICE ROUNDED up the New York Panthers, leading to the eventual decimation of the local chapters, it was only one of numerous organized and often fatal actions waged that year by law enforcement across the country against the Black Panther Party. The *Daily World* newspaper called 1969 "the year of the Panthers, or specifically the year of a carefully coordinated conspiracy of federal, state and local agencies to 'get the Panthers.'"

Making good on his promise to bring "law and order" to American streets, Richard Milhous Nixon began his first term as president by encouraging FBI director J. Edgar Hoover to step up the Bureau's campaign against the Black Panther Party.

The FBI wasted no time.

Taking advantage of the existing tensions between the Panthers' Los Angeles chapter and the LA-based, Black cultural nationalist US Organization, FBI agents fabricated and mailed letters to the LA Panthers, claiming that US members "made plans to ambush leaders of the [Party] in Los Angeles" in retaliation for an alleged plan by the Panthers to kill Ron Karenga, the leader of US. The distrust and enmity between the two rival organizations reached a boiling point on January 17, 1969. During a heated disagreement over leadership of UCLA's Black Student Union, US members shot and killed LA Panther leaders John Huggins and Alprentice "Bunchy" Carter.

Emboldened by this outcome, the FBI's field office in Southern California stepped up its covert campaign, illustrating a number of crude, derogatory cartoons lampooning the Panthers and threatening the lives of Panther leaders Bobby Seale and David Hilliard, then publishing these cartoons in San Diego underground newspapers or mailing them directly to Panther members. The hostility between the two rival organizations swelled, with frequent clashes between Panthers and US members. Neither group was yet aware that the FBI's hand was behind these incendiary cartoons.

That spring, the two organizations sought a truce, which was noted by the FBI's San Diego field office. Agents responded by creating additional cartoons and rekindling the conflict. Not long after, US members shot and killed two Panthers, John Savage and Sylvester Bell. Following Bell's death, the FBI field office sent a triumphant message to headquarters, stating: "Shootings, beatings and a high degree of unrest continues to prevail in the ghetto area of southeast San Diego. Although no specific counterintelligence action can be credited with contributing to this over-all situation, it is felt that a substantial amount of the unrest is directly attributable to this program."

Under Hoover's command, the FBI directed its full might against the Party, initiating 233 covert and disruptive actions, forging letters, sowing confusion and distrust among members, and creating factional splits. Hoover even targeted the Panthers' popular Free Breakfast for School Children program, instructing his agents to dissuade churches and grocery stores from donating food, asserting that serving hungry children shows the Panthers "in a favorable light and clouds the violent nature of the group and its ultimate aim of insurrection."

By July 1969, Hoover declared that "the Black Panther Party, without question, represents the greatest threat to the internal security of the country." It was open season on the Panthers throughout the year, with offices raided and mass arrests of Party members. Panthers all across the country had every reason to believe their lives were in imminent danger from law enforcement. These fears were all but confirmed at the end of the year by a fatal encounter in Chicago, Illinois.

In the predawn hours of December 4, fourteen plainclothes Chicago police officers raided a West Chicago apartment shared by multiple Panthers. Armed with pistols, shotguns, a machine gun, and a map of the apartment furnished by undercover informant William

O'Neal, police officers kicked in the front door of the apartment as its occupants slept and immediately began shooting. The police fired more than ninety rounds of ammunition into the home, with only one shot returned by the Panthers. At the end of the police blitz, four Panthers were critically wounded and two were killed: twenty-two-year-old Mark Clark and twenty-one-year-old Fred Hampton, the magnetic chairman of the Illinois Black Panther Party.

By the end of 1969, an estimated forty Panthers were facing life in prison, thirty faced capital punishment, and twenty-eight Panthers had been killed. "The government is absolutely determined to wipe the Black Panthers from the face of the earth," wrote James Baldwin, "which is but another way of saying that it is absolutely determined to keep the nigger in his place."

"In revolution you either win or die," wrote Afeni Shakur from jail in June 1969. "If we cannot win then death will be my tormentor. But the people will win for theirs is a just cause."

After the arrests and incarceration of the Panther 21, the Harlem branch saw an abrupt reduction of leaders and rank-and-file members alike. With the arrest of his younger brother Lumumba, Zayd was tasked with guiding the Party through its sudden deficit, re-assigning members from the more populous Corona–East Elmhurst and Bronx chapters to the newly depleted Harlem branch. He also helped to organize rallies in support of the incarcerated Panthers.

With Zayd's new responsibilities inevitably came increased police harassment. On the morning of Friday, September 18, 1970, a city marshal broke into Zayd's Bronx apartment on Davidson Avenue and found what was described as "a small arsenal" of three sawed-off shotguns, M-16 rifle parts, a revolver, a flak jacket, and more than six hundred rounds of ammunition. Zayd was arraigned in Manhattan Criminal Court the following night, charged with posses-sion of deadly weapons. His $2,500 bail was posted by the actor and leftist activist Jane Fonda. When asked why she'd come to Zayd's assistance, Fonda replied, "He's innocent, isn't he? He's presumed to be innocent, isn't he? And I know Zayd."

Zayd's first turn in the national spotlight, however, came earlier that month, during the Revolutionary People's Constitutional Convention in Philadelphia, held over the first weekend in September.

The purpose of the convention, said Panther Chief of Staff David Hilliard, was "to write a new Constitution that will guarantee and deliver to every American citizen the inviolable human rights to life, liberty and the pursuit of happiness." The convention was to include various factions of the American radical left, including the American Indian Movement, Puerto Rican independence activists, anti-war activists, the Women's Liberation Movement, and the Gay Liberation Movement. The convention would also be notable for the presence of Huey P. Newton, who had been recently released on $50,000 bail.

Before the convention began, it was beset by police provocation. In an echo of the New York raid the previous year, police in Philadelphia conducted an early morning raid of local Party offices on Monday, August 31, arresting fifteen Panthers, stripping them to their underwear, and holding fourteen of the detained Panthers on $100,000 bail each.

The raid came on the orders of Police Commissioner Frank L. Rizzo, who made the tenuous claim that Black Panthers were behind the weekend shootings of police officers, which had left one officer dead. During the raid on the Panther offices, a gun battle ensued between police and Panthers, severely damaging the office on Wallace Street and wounding three officers. The Panthers believed the raid was a coordinated effort, led by the notoriously brutal Rizzo, to disrupt the convention.

During a press conference held on the steps of the Wallace Street office, Zayd—who had arrived in the city to help manage the convention—stated that "the busts were an attempt by the fascist power structure to crush the oppressed people's convention."

"We will have the convention and Huey Newton will address it, no matter what Rizzo or anyone else does to try to stop it," he told a reporter.

On the night of the raids on the Party offices, Zayd happened upon an article in the *Philadelphia Daily News* quoting a recent threat made by Rizzo—who had been photographed the year before with a nightstick tucked into his tuxedo—challenging Black militants to a showdown.

"Tell him to bring his No. 1 man with him," Zayd responded light-heartedly. "Tell him to meet us at 19th and Columbia. Tell him to leave his guns and nightsticks behind. Tell him not to bring his fascist troops and tell him not to wear a tuxedo. We'll take him on, man to pig, and we'll beat him to death with marshmallows."

Asked by a reporter why he and the Panthers refer to police as "pigs," Zayd responded, "We judge people by their practices, by the way they brutalize people in the black community. We judge them by the way they occupy the black community. It's the same way the Nazi pigs occupied the Warsaw ghettos. They value property rights over human rights. They murder black people at whim. We think pigs is a very apt description."

Notwithstanding these interferences, the convention was held as planned the following weekend, at Philadelphia's Temple University and churches and community centers throughout the city. Approximately six thousand people—half of them White—attended workshops and discussion groups and listened to speeches. The conference was promoted as a plenary session to unite the radical left and lay the groundwork for a new U.S. Constitution, acknowledging the plight of all oppressed peoples in the country.

Despite some disagreements between the Panthers and the sundry White radical groups, the Revolutionary People's Constitutional Convention in Philadelphia was a festive and celebratory event. Newton's speeches were excitedly received by thousands of supporters, there was no violence beyond some desultory rock throwing, and no attendees were arrested.

The convention was also notable for the presence of Afeni, who was likewise out on bail. In photographs taken during the weekend, Afeni and her brother-in-law, Zayd, are seen conferring with each other and laughing together, as though neither of them had a care in the world besides looking fly.

Zayd wears a wide-lapel black jacket that hangs off his skinny frame and striped bell-bottom pants. Afeni wears a black leather vest over a black turtleneck, a short black leather skirt, large sunglasses perched atop her head, and a camera slung around her neck. The two Shakurs are the baddest motherfuckers in the room and they know it. The images capture a rare moment of levity in a time of uncertainty, apprehension, and persecution. If one were to look at Afeni and Zayd at this moment, there would be no reason to believe that one person was on trial facing a potential life sentence and that the other would be dead in less than three years.

On May 13, 1971, after an eight-month trial, the jury in the Panther 21 trial acquitted the defendants of all 156 charges against them after deliberating for only forty-five minutes. Family, friends, lawyers, and supporters cheered, cried, hugged each other, and yelled "Right on!" and "Power to the people!" Court officers shouted in vain for the overjoyed crowd to return to their seats. Most of the defendants had been held in jail since the police raids two years earlier, and finally they would get to go home. But the Black Panther Party, as they had once known it, was not the same.

Disaster came in the spring of 1969, with the brutal torture and murder of nineteen-year-old New York Panther Alex Rackley in New Haven, Connecticut. Claiming he'd been dispatched by Oakland's Central Committee to locate and eliminate suspected Party infiltrators following the Panther 21 police raids, a violent and notoriously abusive Panther named George Sams Jr. arrived in Harlem that May and accused Rackley of being a police informant.

Sams brought Rackley to the home of New Haven Panther Warren Kimbro, whose home also served as the New Haven chapter headquarters. Under Sams's orders, Kimbro and a young New Haven Panther named Lonnie McLucas tied Rackley to a chair, beat him, twisted a wire hanger around his neck, and poured boiling water on him. This "interrogation," as Sams called it, was recorded on an audiocassette by Ericka Huggins, a twenty-one-year-old Panther and widow of slain LA Panther leader John Huggins. After torturing Rackley for three consecutive days, Sams, Kimbro, and McLucas drove him out to a wooded swamp on the evening of May 20, and, insisting that the orders came "from national," Sams directed the two New Haven Panthers to shoot Rackley to death.

Police found Rackley's body the next day and arrested Kimbro, McLucas, Huggins, and five other New Haven Panthers. Sams had already left town, but was apprehended that August in Halifax, Nova Scotia, and brought back to Connecticut to stand trial. He testified that he had been acting under orders from Ericka Huggins, as well as national leadership, specifically Bobby Seale, who'd happened to be in New Haven, giving a speech at Yale University, at the time of Rackley's torture and murder. Seale was arrested, and he and Huggins were indicted for conspiracy. Charges against Seale and Huggins were dismissed on May 25, 1971.

The Party's national reputation, however, was badly tarnished. The Black Panther Party was now exposed as an organization whose members were capable of killing their own comrades. Tragically, the murder of Rackley would not be the last time Panthers would shed Panther blood.

The Black Panther Party was at war with itself. The origins of this war began with a feud between the two visionary, influential, and megalomaniacal Panther leaders: Huey Newton and Eldridge Cleaver. From his home-in-exile in Algeria, Eldridge and his wife Kathleen established the Black Panther Party's International Section, forging alliances with the governments of North Korea, North Vietnam, and China, hoping to connect the struggle for Black liberation in the United States to the global anti-imperialist movement. Cleaver was also an open and unwavering advocate for violence and guerrilla warfare, declaring that the "lumpenproletariat" must take up arms and bring about "revolution in our lifetime."

This position put Cleaver at odds with Newton, who, shortly after being released from prison on August 5, 1970, on what was more or less a court technicality, now began to deemphasize armed rhetoric and instead promoted the Party's community social service programs, what he called "survival programs."

Though Panther leaders in Oakland had long disagreed with their New York counterparts, especially regarding the wearing of African clothes and adopting African names, the tipping point came in early 1971, during the final months of the Panther 21 trial. The New York Panthers had already been alleging that thousands of dollars in donated funds had been instead directed to Oakland to pay for Newton's penthouse apartment near Lake Merritt. But when the defendants published their "Open Letter to the Weather Underground" in the January issue of the countercultural newspaper the *East Village Other,* proclaiming the militant, White organization to be "the true vanguard of the revolution," advocating for armed insurrection, and seemingly denouncing the Central Committee as gradualist and reformist, Newton had seen enough insurrection within the Party. He responded at first by expelling only the nine New York Panthers who'd authored the letter, but Newton soon purged nearly all remaining members of the Panther 21.

Newton and Cleaver agreed to hash out their differences with a long-distance phone conversation on February 26 during San Francisco talk show host Jim Dunbar's *A.M. Show.* It was intended to be a display of harmony between the two Panther leaders, but Cleaver instead used this moment, which was broadcast on live television, to demand that Newton reinstate the ousted New York Panthers. Caught off guard, Newton responded by accusing Cleaver of steering the Party toward "counterproductive avenues of violence and adventurism" before ending the phone call. In a follow-up phone call, Newton upbraided Cleaver, accused him of abusing his wife Kathleen, and expelled Cleaver and the International Section. Cleaver responded later that week by himself expelling Newton and threatening to "eliminate" both him and Chief of Staff David Hilliard.

With echoes of Malcolm X and his followers' friction with Elijah Muhammad and the Nation of Islam, the increasingly embattled Newton, Hilliard, and other California Panthers found themselves pitted against the "Cleaverites" in New York City. Though its conduct wouldn't be exposed until years later, the FBI had also been exploiting the hostilities between Newton and Cleaver, by forging and mailing derogatory letters to Panthers and their supporters, locally and abroad. In one such letter, deceptively attributed to Hilliard and written on counterfeit Black Panther Party letterhead, the author declares that Cleaver is "a murderer and a punk without genitals" and cautions that "anyone giving any aid or comfort to Cleaver and his jackanapes will be . . . dealt with no matter where they may be located."

The first casualties in a war are not the generals, the lieutenants, or any other high-ranking official; the first casualties are the rank-and-file, those unfortunate foot soldiers who happen to be caught in the wrong place at the wrong time.

On March 8, 1971, twenty-two-year-old field marshal Robert Webb, a Cleaver loyalist, was shot to death at Harlem's 125th Street and Seventh Avenue. A California native who had relocated to New York and joined the Cleaver faction, Webb had allegedly gotten into an altercation with Party members who had been selling copies of the *Black Panther* newspaper.

At a news conference the day after the killing, Zayd claimed that Webb had been shot while attempting to "confiscate the reactionary rag sheet from two fools." In the inaugural issue of the *Right On!* newspaper—established in April 1971 by the Cleaver faction as a rival to the *Black Panther*—the "Central Headquarters" of the New York Panthers, presumably Zayd, wrote that Webb had been killed by "six or seven mad dog assassins" from the West Coast, that Webb had been targeted because he'd directed a press conference in New York calling for the removal of Hilliard, and that the order had come from Newton himself. Retaliation was inevitable.

On April 17, Samuel Napier—the thirty-two-year-old, San Francisco–based national distribution manager for the *Black Panther*—was gagged and bound to a bed inside the Oakland-aligned Panther headquarters in Corona, Queens, and shot multiple times in the head. The assailants then set the building on fire. When Napier's body was discovered, it was burned so badly that he could only be identified by his fingerprints.

Four Panthers were charged with Napier's murder. All four had been aligned with the Cleaver faction. One of the accused assailants was a leader of the Harlem Panthers, Dhoruba bin Wahad; another was twenty-year-old Jamal Joseph, the former high school honor student and recently acquitted Panther 21 defendant.

The Black Panther Party had reached a point of no return. With the three murders, the FBI encouraging doubt and suspicion among unsuspecting Party members, and the schism between the rival Newton-Cleaver factions, the Black Panther Party had squandered its influence as a national organization. But if the beginning of the 1970s marked the beginning of the decline of the Black Panther Party, it also heralded the arrival of a new group—one composed of disaffected Panthers still loyal to Cleaver, including Zayd and a young former Harlem Panther named JoAnne Chesimard, who later adopted the Shakur name for herself.

Unlike the Black Panther Party, this group went beyond self-defense rhetoric. Believing that revolution was imminent and nothing was off-limits in the struggle for the freedom of oppressed people, this group was decentralized, operated entirely underground, and opted to strike first. Over the next decade, the Black Liberation Army would become the deadliest Black militant organization in United States history.

PART II

8.
AN FBI AGENT BEHIND EVERY MAILBOX

IT WAS CHILLY during the evening of March 8, 1971, in the small, sleepy borough of Media, the county seat of Delaware County, about thirteen miles west of Philadelphia. First settled by Quakers in 1682, Media later became a hub on the Underground Railroad, assisting enslaved Blacks in pursuit of their freedom, as well as offering a safe home for freedmen. By the 1970s, many residents of Delaware County, particularly students and faculty from Swarthmore and Haverford Colleges, were involved in anti–Vietnam War activities, including staging weekly protests at the Media courthouse.

On March 8, much of the county, along with the rest of the world, was momentarily absorbed by the highly anticipated boxing match between Muhammad Ali and Joe Frazier at Madison Square Garden. Billed as the "Fight of the Century," the match was attended by numerous celebrities and viewed on pay-per-view by millions of people across the world as it pitted two undefeated heavyweight champions against each other. Ali, who had been recently stripped of his title for refusing to submit to the draft, had become a symbol of the anti-war movement; while Frazier was seen as an establishment figure, derided by Ali as an "Uncle Tom." The match between these two ideological opposites served as a proxy for what was happening in the streets, colleges, and homes across the nation.

But on that Monday night, while the world was distracted by Ali and Frazier battering each other in the ring of Madison Square Garden, a small group of anti-war activists from Haverford College and Temple University broke into Media's FBI office in search of documents proving the Bureau's surveillance of anti-war demonstrators. What they uncovered would critically damage the reputation of the FBI, prompt an investigation of the federal government's surveillance methods, and uncover shameful secrets about the nation that are still, decades later, being reckoned with.

After the eight-person group made off with their heist, they used a Xerox machine to copy the more than one thousand classified documents and mailed more than a dozen of the documents to members of Congress and the media, identifying themselves as "the Citizens' Commission to Investigate the F.B.I." On March 24, the *Washington Post* was the first to publish the findings; it reported that "one of the documents encourages agents to step up interviews with dissenters 'for plenty of reasons, chief of which are it will enhance the paranoia endemic in these circles and will further serve to get the point across there is an FBI agent behind every mailbox.'"

Reporters would continue to receive documents over the next two months, further revealing the extent to which the FBI, acting under the orders of Director J. Edgar Hoover, surveilled Black Americans, with a particular preoccupation with Black college students. "Increased campus disorders involving black students pose a definite threat to the Nation's stability and security," wrote Hoover in one document, dated November 4, 1970. At Pennsylvania's Swarthmore College, every Black student was under surveillance.

But the most startling and consequential discovery from the trove of stolen documents was the existence of the FBI's secret counterintelligence program, COINTELPRO, which would go on to confirm the movement's most feared suspicions.

While Afeni was incarcerated at the Women's House of Detention in New York's Greenwich Village, still many months away from her eventual acquittal, she'd formed a close bond with other female inmates, some of whom would assist Afeni with such tasks as ironing and starching her clothes before her court appearances. The "House of D," as it was called, was at the time recognized for housing a large population of LGBTQ women and gender nonconforming inmates. The activist organization Gay Liberation Front, which had formed in the aftermath of the 1969 Stonewall uprising, would protest frequently outside the House of D in support of Afeni and fellow Panther 21 defendant Joan Bird.

When Afeni was out on bail in the summer of 1970 and attended the Revolutionary People's Constitutional Convention in Philadelphia, she joined a workshop organized by the GLF and helped develop a list of demands for the Convention Floor, insisting on the inclusion of queer and feminist liberation in the Black Power movement. Afeni told the workshop that after watching GLF protests outside the House of D, she "began relating to the gay sisters in jail" and that she could "understand their oppression, their anger and the strength in them and in all gay people."

Afeni met a young, Black, gay woman named Carol Jean Crooks, a street hustler from Brooklyn. Crooks—or "Crooksie" as she was known—took Afeni as her charge, making sure she was provided with clean, pressed clothes so as to look smart and respectable in the courtroom. "She had a bond with that woman," remembered Afeni's friend Yaasmyn Fula. "Crooksie loved her and respected her, and Afeni had a lot of respect for Crooksie as well."

If the men in the Black Panther Party had been the first to give Afeni a feeling of respect and protection, it was the women—particularly queer women—who now offered her that security. The bond between Afeni and Crooks, however, extended beyond respect and protection. Afeni had just survived a harrowing two years, she had been abandoned by her husband, Lumumba, and she was about to give birth to her first child. She needed someone in her corner, someone to do what needed to be done. To Afeni, Crooks was more than caretaker or protector; she was family. This was especially evident on the day Afeni gave birth to her first child, one month after her acquittal.

When Afeni was admitted at Harlem's Flower-Fifth Avenue Hospital, she was accompanied in the delivery room by two people: her sister, Gloria, and Carol Crooks. At twelve fifteen in the afternoon, Afeni's boy arrived, weighing six pounds, three ounces. The nurse offered the newborn to his mother, but Afeni told the nurse to instead hand him to Crooks, who gave him the name Parish Crooks, with Afeni's brother-in-law's surname, Lesane, as his middle name. The effort of thinking of a name for her newborn only one month after surviving the most traumatizing event in her life was, at that time, too much to handle, so she allowed the two women with her in the hospital room, the two women closest to her at the time, to christen her newborn with their own names.*

With no father to claim paternity, Parish Lesane Crooks was nurtured from the beginning by strong, independent, but turbulent women.

Afeni and Crooks maintained a close relationship over the next year. Crooks gave money to Afeni when she needed it, no questions asked, which Afeni would share with her family or with Black Panthers who needed help with legal fees. In public, the Party looked down on Crooks's line of work, but they took her money all the same. It was a knotty arrangement between Afeni and Crooks, built on a mix of responsibility, need, and unrequited love.

"Crooksie was stone cold in love with her," remembered Fula, but Afeni had more immediate commitments. "Crooksie understood that Afeni was committed and dedicated to the liberation of Black people."

Crooks was arrested in 1972, after shooting to death a former associate of her heroin distribution ring who had allegedly black-mailed her. Crooks pleaded guilty to first degree manslaughter and was sentenced to up to fifteen years at Bedford Hills Correctional Facility, forty-five miles north of New York City. Crooks and Afeni now found each other in reversed roles, with Crooks on the inside and Afeni on the outside. Afeni would soon have an opportunity to return Crooks's earlier kindness.

On Sunday, February 3, 1974, Crooks was placed in solitary confinement following a violent brawl with several prison guards. After twenty-two days in solitary, Crooks was brought before the Adjustment Committee for a hearing. She was convicted of felony assault for the fight, with an additional two to four years added to her sentence and sixty more days in solitary. Citing her "hostile, contemptu-

---

* Many sources list his birth name as "Lesane Parish Crooks," but his original birth certificate confirms the above arrangement.

ous and uncooperative" attitude, the committee extended Crooks's time in solitary again and again. In July, after four months in solitary confinement, with no end in sight, Crooks managed to get word out to Afeni.

By this time, Afeni had been working as a paralegal with Bronx Legal Services, a federal program launched as part of President Lyndon Johnson's War on Poverty. When Afeni learned of Crooks's request for legal assistance, she enlisted the help of a Bronx Legal Services attorney, Stephen Latimer. He and Crooks filed a civil rights lawsuit, arguing that Crooks was not awarded due process before each extension of her time in solitary confinement. The district court agreed and ordered Crooks to be released to general population.

Her victory came with a price, and freedom was short-lived.

On August 29, Crooks got into a fight with another inmate. When Crooks refused to return to solitary confinement without her guaranteed due process, prison authorities brought in male guards from nearby prisons, who entered Crooks's cell, fought with her, restrained her using bedsheets, dragged her across prison grounds, threw her into the back of a station wagon, and transported her back to segregation.

A number of inmates who had witnessed this violent episode demanded to speak with prison authorities, complaining that Crooks's rights had been violated and requesting an update on her condition. Instead, the prison instituted a lockdown. The inmates immediately revolted, overtaking guards and stealing their keys, running throughout the prison and opening cell gates. A rumor spread that Crooks had died and, within hours, two hundred inmates had seized control of Bedford Hills. The women stood in a protective circle in the recreation yard and gave their demands, foremost of which was proof that Crooks was alive. Prison authorities again responded by bringing in armed male guards from nearby prisons, as well as New York state troopers.

Events at this point could have taken a tragic turn. New York had witnessed the disastrous Attica prison uprising three years earlier, in September 1971. What began as a protest against inhumane living conditions ended in a massive assault by police, acting under the orders of Governor Nelson Rockefeller. When the smoke cleared from the uprising, forty-three people were dead, including thirty-three inmates and ten prison guards and civilian employees. Bedford Hills prison authorities and inmates alike would've been mindful to avoid a repeat of Attica.

Bedford Hills guards brought out a water cannon and blasted the women with high-pressure water. They threatened to tear gas the inmates and to bring in the National Guard. Sometime after midnight, the women relented and ended their insurrection. No one was injured, but several alleged leaders of the rebellion were sent to segregation, where they found Crooks—badly injured and in need of medical attention, but alive.

The uprising, which would become known as the August Rebellion, led to sweeping prison reforms across the nation. After spending months in solitary confinement for the fight that led to the uprising, Crooks initiated and won another lawsuit against prison officials, charging denial of due process, followed by a class-action suit brought by other Bedford Hills inmates. In 1981, the court reached an unprecedented settlement with the plaintiffs, establishing an inmate's rights to due process in internal disciplinary procedures, including the right to know the nature of the charges, the right to question witnesses, and the right to be held in solitary confinement no more than seven days without a hearing. The plaintiffs were also awarded $127,000, which they put toward purchasing word processors and computers, copy machines, washers and dryers, and Black and Latino literature for the prison library. In June 1983, using the remainder of the settlement money, Crooks threw an ice cream party for the women at Bedford Hills, which was covered by the *New York Times*, who acknowledged the celebration as being the culmination of "an unusual sequence of events in prison legal history, one that was begun by Miss Crooks nearly 10 years ago and that continues to affect prison conditions in both the state and the country."

Crooks was released from prison later that year and continued to stay in touch with her godson, who was now a teenager and known by a new name: Tupac Amaru Shakur.

Suggested by Afeni's friend Karen Kadison, who had spent time in Peru, Tupac's name was inspired by the eighteenth-century Indigenous insurgent Túpac Amaru II, who led an Andean revolt against Spanish colonial rule in Peru. Born José Gabriel Condorcanqui Noguera, Túpac Amaru II had himself adopted his new name after claiming to be the descendant of the sixteenth-century Incan monarch Túpac Amaru, who'd also led an Indigenous campaign against Spanish occupation. Separated by two centuries, both Túpac Amarus had come to a similar fate: executed and beheaded by the Spanish.

Though no one could have predicted it at the time, the young Tupac Amaru Shakur, conferred now with his new name, was also destined for greatness, notoriety, persecution, and a violent, early death.

The successful outcome of the August Rebellion was in large part due to the tenacious advocacy of Afeni and her partners at Bronx Legal Services. Located on the second floor of an administrative building on the Bronx's Courtland Avenue, Legal Services was a federally funded, nonprofit program designed to assist impoverished and underserved families and individuals with such issues as housing rights, Social Security, welfare rights, and other desperately needed services. The South Bronx in the 1970s was a community in ruins. Ravaged by a heroin epidemic, an increase in crime and street gang activity, extreme poverty and unemployment, and the discriminatory housing practice known as "redlining," the borough faced an exodus of hundreds of thousands of residents over the course of the decade, leaving behind urban decay and abandoned tenements. Unable to rent or sell their properties, landlords often resorted to burning down their buildings to collect the insurance; other buildings were burned by neighborhood arsonists. The South Bronx needed a lifeline.

Before becoming managing attorney at Bronx Legal Services, Richard Fischbein worked as a staff attorney out of the storefront office of Morrisiana Legal Services, an Office of Economic Opportunity federal program. In early 1971, Fischbein was recruited to open a Legal Services office in the South Bronx. One of the first people he hired was Afeni Shakur. After witnessing Afeni successfully defend herself in court during the Panther 21 trial, Fischbein believed she might have a promising career in law. She also had the added credentials of having earned the respect of the people in Harlem and the Bronx.

"She was considered an icon up there. She could do no wrong," Fischbein recalled. "Afeni was wicked smart. Very focused and very tough. You could talk to her and just be amazed that she had no formal education."

Before Afeni could begin her new job, however, she was involved in a serious car accident, which left her bedridden. As she recuperated at her sister Gloria's apartment, Fischbein agreed to let Afeni's friend Yaasmyn Fula work at the office as a temporary replacement. A light-complexioned daughter of a Jamaican immigrant father, Jersey native, and student at the Brooklyn campus of Long Island University, Fula had become acquainted with Afeni during the Panther 21 trial, where she'd joined hundreds of others at the demonstrations held in front of the House of D in support of Afeni and the other defendants.

When Afeni recovered from the accident enough to begin working, Fischbein agreed to let Fula remain on as well, and the two friends worked together at Bronx Legal Services as paralegals. Afeni's responsibilities were similar to the work she'd begun in the Black Panther Party. The housing advocacy and tenant organizing work the Panthers were doing in the Bronx aligned with the mission of Bronx Legal Services, except this was a program instituted by the federal government, which could be viewed as complicit in creating many of the deplorable conditions in these communities. But the needs of the South Bronx were too great for either the Black Panther Party or Bronx Legal Services to handle alone. Fischbein remembered receiving a call at the office one day from members of the Panthers' Bronx chapter: "They called us to say that, if we wanted, they would send people to walk with us in the community and take us to meetings."

A White, Jewish graduate of Brooklyn Law School, Fischbein was an unlikely ally in the overwhelmingly Black and Latino South Bronx, but he had already been known as a community organizer for the troubled borough, which he described as being, in the early 1970s, "a fucking disaster." His unfiltered candor sometimes attracted controversy, like when he was interviewed for a March 19, 1972, *New York Times* article about widespread rent strikes in the South Bronx, and he was quoted as saying his goal was to "break every landlord in this area and for the tenant to take over."

"We identified the worst slumlords in the South Bronx, and we organized each one of their buildings in a rent strike," Fula recalled. "We showed them how to collect rent, how to open escrow accounts.

They were learning independence and the power of unity and organization."

Fischbein had earned the Panthers' trust well enough that they would occasionally hold meetings in his Greenwich Village apartment. He recalled having up to twenty Panthers crammed into his apartment on any given evening, though when Afeni was present, either at the apartment or at the office, it was all business: "You couldn't sit around and bullshit with Afeni, because she didn't have the patience for it."

Afeni often brought her young son to the office, and his joyful energy infected everyone around him. He became a regular presence at Bronx Legal Services, recalled Fischbein: "Afeni would come in to work every day, many days she would bring Tupac."

But sometimes Tupac's unbridled energy would land him in trouble. Fula recalled times when Tupac would act out in front of his mother, prompting the sort of tongue-lashing that could only come from having a mother like Afeni. "You won't disappoint Black people," she would hiss, twisting Tupac's shirt collar. "You won't disappoint the movement."

Though Afeni was a single mother, she wasn't left to raise her young son on her own. Like the old African proverb, the village—in this case, Greenwich Village, as well as East Orange, Harlem, and the Bronx—helped to raise her child. Being who she was and with as much respect as the community conferred upon her, Afeni could count on a strong network of female support.

As Fula recalled, there was a "circle of women who passed Tupac from lap to lap, lavishing him with kisses and adoration." In addition to this circle of women, Fula also remembered that she would sometimes bring Tupac over to his biological father's home for sleepovers, though Billy Garland was still married with three young children. Afeni and Garland made an attempt to negotiate a future together with Tupac, Fula claimed, but the pressures of life as a community worker and activist proved too great for Afeni to commit to conventional family life.

Fula herself had a brief affair with Sekou Odinga, who was living underground after his return from Algerian exile. He, like Garland, had also been married with children when he and Fula got together. Fula soon discovered she was pregnant with Odinga's child. On October 9, 1977, she gave birth to a son, Yafeu Akiyele Fula, who would forge a lifelong friendship with Tupac and later become popularly known as the rapper Yaki Kadafi.

By the end of the 1970s, the damage perpetrated against the Black Panther Party by COINTELPRO was done. The survivors had been harassed, humiliated, and badly scarred. The Party would never fully recover to its influence during its most active period.

Though proud of what the Black Panther Party had accomplished, some members, particularly those in New York, had already begun to align with other, more radical groups. One of these groups was an ultramilitant underground group, composed mostly of former New York Panthers, calling itself the Black Liberation Army.

Another organization, founded in Detroit in 1968, was a Black separatist group that advocated for the creation of an independent Black nation in the American South. Calling itself the Republic of New Afrika, this group would find a loyal and dedicated leader in a young, persuasive activist named Jeral Wayne Williams. A longtime friend of Lumumba Shakur and Sekou Odinga, Williams would later change his name to Mutulu Shakur and help revolutionize American medicine and orchestrate some of the most daring actions ever accomplished during the Black liberation movement.

9.
FREE THE LAND

THE EVENING OF Saturday, March 29, 1969, began pleasantly. Nearly 150 men, women, and children—dressed in conventional attire, African-influenced dress, or army fatigues—had gathered together at the New Bethel Baptist Church at the intersection of Detroit's Linwood and Philadelphia to celebrate the one-year anniversary of the signing of the Declaration of Independence of the Republic of New Afrika.

Pastored by Reverend C. L. Franklin—the renowned minister and father of singer Aretha Franklin—New Bethel was notable as both one of the largest supporters of the civil rights movement and the place where fourteen-year-old Aretha made her first recordings. Reverend Franklin rented his church to Black political groups on occasion, and though he wasn't present on this Saturday evening, he defended the separatist organization by saying its "goals are the same as ours, only they approach them from different directions."

Starting at 8:30 P.M., the anniversary celebration included speeches by RNA founders Queen Mother Moore and Brother Gaidi Obadele, Malcolm X's cousin Hakim Jamal, and civil rights and reparations activist Virginia Collins. Herman Ferguson attended with his second wife, Iyaluua. Eighteen-year-old Mutulu Shakur joined the security detail, composed of around fifteen members of the Black Legion. Also in attendance at New Bethel that evening were several undercover FBI agents, who had been surveilling the RNA since its inception the year before.

The meeting itself was peaceful and largely uneventful, concluding at 11:30 P.M. with a final speech from Brother Gaidi. Ten minutes later, Gaidi and other RNA ministers exited the church, escorted by about a dozen armed legionnaires, and began walking toward their cars. At this moment, two White Detroit police officers, Patrolmen Michael Czapski and Richard Worobec, drove by and noticed "approximately 10 to 12 Negro males with guns entering automobiles."

The patrolmen stopped and got out of their car. Within seconds, the officers were met with a shower of bullets fired from the departing legionnaires. Worobec jumped back into his patrol car and shouted into the radio, "Help! Help . . . Want help!" He attempted to flee in his car but crashed into a nearby dry cleaner's. He had been shot in the back and the leg and he huddled, injured but alive, on the floor of the bullet-riddled car. When reinforcements arrived moments later, they found twenty-two-year-old Czapski lying on the sidewalk in a pool of blood, dead from multiple gunshot wounds. About fifty backup police officers immediately stormed the building, shooting indiscriminately into the church, battering the pews and pulpit with bullets and shattering glass windows as more than one hundred men, women, and children ducked for cover.

RNA legionnaire Mutulu took quick action, ushering Herman and Iyaluua Ferguson to an inner sanctuary and shielding them from the flying bullets and glass. Though he wasn't present that night, Bilal Sunni-Ali remembered hearing afterward about Mutulu's actions: "We were given to understand that he was protecting the lives of senior cadre who were there," Sunni-Ali recalled. "He was giving people orders to lie on the ground—and the old people, he lied on top of them, so if a bullet was to come, he would take the bullet rather than the senior cadre."

Mutulu was born Jeral Wayne Williams, on August 8, 1950, in Baltimore, Maryland. His mother, Delores Williams, suffered from glaucoma, which he inherited. His father, James MacMoore, was a house painter. When Mutulu was seven, Delores left her husband and moved Mutulu and his younger sister to Jamaica, Queens. As the only son and eldest sibling in a new city, Mutulu developed his political ideology from a deeply personal place: helping his sight-impaired mother navigate the labyrinthine and discriminatory social welfare system. Mutulu's experiences with witnessing the lack of medical care and social support provided to his mother and other Black and Brown people would also contribute to his future pursuit of community-focused healthcare.

At thirteen or fourteen years old, Mutulu first met Anthony Coston and Nathaniel Burns, who hadn't yet changed their names, respectively, to Lumumba Shakur and Sekou Odinga. Mutulu lived on the opposite side of Baisley Pond Park in Queens, where Lumumba still lived with his siblings and father, James Coston Sr., who also hadn't yet become Salahdeen Shakur. Mutulu first became friends with Lumumba's younger sister, whom he'd visit often at her home. "I think he was kinda sweet on her," recalled Odinga.

But Mutulu's interests soon gravitated toward something even sweeter. "At a very young age, he had discovered weed," Odinga remembered. "And when he found out that I had some of the best weed around, he started running behind me. Every time I turned around, [he was] trying to get some weed."

A few years away from his religious and political transformation, Odinga was still known as Beany and recognized in the neighborhood for his superior product. Nineteen years old at the time, Odinga regarded Mutulu as a young, overactive boy, always following the older boy around at the heel and smoking too much reefer. "To me, he was a little kid," Odinga recalled. "I wasn't even sure if I should be selling him any weed. 'You're too young to be smoking all that weed, boy.' He would laugh: 'Can I get a joint? Can I get a bag?'"

As a young, fatherless, impressionable boy in a new city, Mutulu looked up to Lumumba and Odinga, who were older, cool, self-possessed, and respected by others. But after both men had been arrested and charged for different offenses—Lumumba for assault; Odinga for robbery—and locked away in Comstock's correctional institution, Mutulu gravitated toward a new mentor—and with his new mentor came new purpose.

A tall, angular, mustachioed Black man, handsome but unassuming, Herman Ferguson was an assistant principal with New York public schools, first at Brooklyn's P.S. 21, then transferring, in 1963, to P.S. 40 in Jamaica, Queens, a school with a nearly one-hundred-percent Black student enrollment. He was described by his colleagues as a "dedicated teacher" and a "sweet guy." The school principal at P.S. 40, Harold Brown, described him as "congenial and friendly. He was absolutely dedicated to seeing that his pupils achieved something." Ferguson's neighbors in Rochdale Village—where he lived in a modest two-story home with his wife, Rose, and their four young children—described him as "mild-mannered" and a "pleasant man who did little mixing with the people on the block and never became involved with local problems."

Ferguson had been quietly active with the civil rights movement, participating in marches and peaceful demonstrations, and later joining Malcolm's fledgling Organization of Afro-American Unity. He had been present at the Audubon Ballroom when Malcolm was assassinated. After Malcolm's death, Ferguson gave up all hope for peaceful reform, writes his second wife and biographer, Iyaluua Ferguson: "Whatever was left of the reformist in Herman was killed in the Audubon Ballroom on that cold February Sunday. Only the revolutionary freedom fighter remained. He now understood clearly that Black folk, if they were to survive, had to separate from this racist system or destroy it."

Ferguson started a South Jamaica–based community organization called the Black Brotherhood Improvement Association (BBIA), styled after Marcus Garvey's Universal Negro Improvement Association, and a Queens-based gun club for Black residents called Jamaica Rifle and Pistol Club Inc. Well into his forties, Ferguson was respected by young Black activists, particularly in South Jamaica, due to his student advocacy and his association with Malcolm X. But after merging BBIA with the militant Revolutionary Action Movement, Ferguson now also attracted the attention of the FBI, who pursued RAM with the same urgency they would later apply to the Black Panther Party.

On June 21, 1967, fifteen members of BBIA and RAM—four women and eleven men, including Ferguson—were arrested by the NYPD in predawn raids. In Philadelphia that same morning, RAM's leader, Max Stanford, was also apprehended. Police seized more than thirty guns, radio receivers and transmitters, walkie-talkies, 275 packets of heroin, "subversive literature," and more than one thousand rounds of ammunition, and discovered ten rifles, a machine gun, three carbines, a shotgun, four knives, and three metal arrows in the basement of Ferguson's home in Jamaica, Queens. The suspects were charged with advocating criminal anarchy, conspiring to commit criminal anarchy, conspiracy to commit arson, and possession of dangerous weapons. The most serious charges, however, were against Ferguson and twenty-two-year-old Arthur Harris, who were accused of conspiring to kill moderate civil rights leaders Roy Wilkins, executive director of the National Association for the Advancement of Colored People (NAACP), and Whitney Young, executive director of the National Urban League.

Ferguson was released on $20,000 bail, raised by supporters. He was suspended from P.S. 40 but was soon hired as an administrative assistant at Harlem's Intermediate School 201, an experimental and controversial school that tested community control of local education. On February 21, 1968, a memorial was held for Malcolm X at I.S. 201 on the third anniversary of his assassination, with speeches by author and activist Amiri Baraka (formerly LeRoi Jones), James Baldwin, and Ferguson. In front of six hundred attendees, Ferguson told the audience to arm themselves in protection against White violence and to practice shooting, so that when "hunting season" comes, the shooter won't develop "buck fever."

"The federal government now has become a police department," Ferguson told the audience. "It has stockpiled armies and new deadly equipment to be dispatched at any time and anywhere to use on us. Let's be ready to die. If they kill us blacks, who are outnumbered, take some of them with you."

The backlash to his speech was swift and severe. The Ford Foundation, who provided financial support to the school, threatened to cut funding unless the school curtailed "racially inflammatory activities." Queens Supreme Court Justice J. Irwin Shapiro, after learning of Ferguson's speech, raised his bail from $20,000 to $100,000, and Ferguson was remanded to the Queens House of Detention. His bail was later reduced to $10,000. At this time, the fight over community control of New York public schools, pitting the majority Black and Puerto Rican school board against White, unionized teachers, was amplifying, with Ocean Hill–Brownsville at its epicenter.

After his wife posted his bail, Ferguson continued to organize support for community control of schools, and he outlined a "Black Survival Curriculum" that would teach a Black nationalist framework to schoolchildren, as well as weapons training, target practice, and martial arts. "It is not enough for us to demand control of our schools," Ferguson wrote in his proposal. "Once we really take this control we must be prepared to teach our black youth how to survive in the hostile society that we do not yet control."

Because of his radical position, Ferguson earned the respect and support of young activists and students throughout Queens. Odinga remembers walking through the neighborhood one day and noticing a large demonstration of mostly young people. He went over to see what it was about and learned the crowd was protesting to get Ferguson reinstated as assistant principal at P.S. 40. "It caught my attention," Odinga recalled. "I seen a few people out there from the projects that I knew from growing up in South Jamaica."

One of the people Odinga recognized was a high school student from Queens—the same kid who was always buying Odinga's weed. Ferguson had been a mentor and father figure to sixteen-year-old Mutulu, raising his political consciousness and introducing him to the writings of Marcus Garvey, Malcolm X, Mao Tse-tung, and Frantz Fanon. "You couldn't hang out with Herman if you didn't read and study," Mutulu recalled years later. After Ferguson's arrest, Mutulu joined the Committee to Defend Herman Ferguson, recruiting young people from Jamaica, Manhattan, and Brooklyn to join rallies to free Ferguson. Though he wasn't a Black Panther, Mutulu worked with local Panthers in what would be his first major political action: organizing more than two hundred people to demonstrate in front of the Queens Supreme Court.

Ferguson's trial began that June. The prosecutor's key witness, a Black police informant named Edward Howlette, had infiltrated RAM two years earlier. On June 15, based largely on Howlette's testimony, Ferguson and Harris were found guilty, by an all-White jury, of conspiracy to commit murder in the first degree. The men were freed, pending appeal, and Ferguson began running a political campaign as a candidate for United States senator on the New York Freedom and Peace Party ticket. Though he ultimately received some ten thousand votes, his campaign was chiefly used to promote a radical platform, in which he called for Puerto Rican independence, the withdrawal of all U.S. troops from Latin America, a denunciation of the war in Vietnam as "racist and imperialist," and an end to the deployment of federal troops, national guardsmen, and police officers to quell urban uprisings.

Ferguson also used his campaign to advocate an even more radical doctrine that had begun to gain support in Black nationalist circles: a separate and independent Black nation within the United States, which Ferguson argued was "the only viable way to bring about freedom, justice and equality for the former slaves." Black people in America, Ferguson argued, were not Americans, as they hadn't been granted the full rights of American citizenship and equal protection under the law. Rather, the descendants of enslaved Blacks in America hold a unique history and heritage that sets them apart from other peoples: "We have a common culture, common perspective and values, a group identity, and a common gene pool, derived from our distinct group history," Ferguson declared. "We are New Afrikans because we, an Afrikan people, evolved from not one but several Afrikan nations and have some Indian (Native/Indigenous) and European genes, melded over the course of two hundred years of slavery."

With his speeches on and off the campaign trail, Ferguson had publicly announced his membership in an emergent Black nationalist and separatist movement, the New Afrikan Independence Movement (NAIM). The beliefs and objectives of NAIM were manifold, but at the heart of the movement was its demand for an independent Black nation within the borders of the United States: the Republic of New Afrika.

The idea of a sovereign Black nation in the United States was not without precedent. Near the close of the nineteenth century, a light-complexioned Black businessman and politician named Edward P. McCabe encouraged Black migrants to settle in what was then the Oklahoma Territory, in hopes of making Oklahoma an "all-Black state," a safe haven where "the Negro can rest from mob law" and could "be secure from every ill of the southern policies." These hopes were dashed when Oklahoma joined the union in 1907 and then passed obstructive segregation laws.

In the 1920s and 1930s, Black communists in the United States and communists abroad proposed an idea called the "Black Belt Republic," an autonomous, Black nation-state in the American South. Endorsed by Soviet leaders Vladimir Lenin and Joseph Stalin, the Black Belt Republic was used as a recruiting tool for the Communist Party and touted as a solution to the "Negro Question." With language that would be echoed decades later by a younger generation of Black activists and nationalists, leading Black communist thinker and member of the Black communist group the African Blood Brotherhood Harry Haywood argued that Black people in the American South constituted an oppressed "nation within a nation."

At the same time as communists were arguing for a Black Belt Republic, a small group of Black separatists, led by Chicago attorney and businessman Oscar Brown, launched the National Movement for the Establishment of the 49th State, a short-lived campaign to pursue an exclusive Black state in the Southern United States. This campaign, too, was futile, as Alaska became the forty-ninth state in 1959.

In the 1950s and early 1960s, as the civil rights movement was sweeping throughout the American South, the Nation of Islam vehemently denigrated civil rights leaders and their calls for integration. Malcolm X echoed Muhammad's assertion that "the only way the black people caught up in this society can be saved is not to *integrate* into this corrupt society, but to *separate* from it, to a land of our *own,* where we can reform ourselves, lift up our moral standards, and try to be godly."

Though the call for a sovereign Black nation was not new or exceptional at the time of Malcolm's speech, it now resonated with Black Americans with a particular urgency. Whites were perpetrating terrorist violence against students, elderly men and women, churchgoers, and others who peacefully demonstrated for civil rights and equal protection under the law. These violent reactions were seen by many as confirmation that Black people in this country would never be treated as anything but second-class citizens. Why go on denying it? Why continue to face arrest, injury, and death, all for the opportunity to sit at a lunch counter next to White people? Many young Black activists came to realize that separation, rather than integration, was the only way to survive in America.

The most durable effort to achieve an independent Black nation-state began on the last weekend in March 1968, when five hundred Black activists, nationalists, and separatists met at the National Black Government Convention to "determine the destiny of the 'captive black nation' in America." Held in Detroit—where Malcolm delivered his influential speech—the convention featured two days of meetings and lectures on issues regarding citizenship, reparations, sovereignty, and self-determination. It was attended by such dignitaries as Malcolm's widow, Betty Shabazz; Amiri Baraka; and the esteemed Garveyite and reparations advocate Audley "Queen Mother" Moore. The convention was organized by two brothers from Philadelphia, Gaidi Obadele and Imari Abubakari Obadele (formerly Milton Henry and Richard Henry), who founded the Malcolm X Society in 1967 with the goal of carrying out what they believed was Malcolm's call for land and independence.

On the second day of the convention, in the auditorium of the Black-owned Twenty-Grand Motel, two hundred attendees gathered to sign their names to a declaration of independence for their new homeland, the Republic of New Afrika.* Asserting that Black people in America were a colonized nation, they renounced American citizenship and instead declared allegiance to the RNA. With the ratification of their Declaration of Independence, the signees founded the Provisional Government of New Afrika (PG-RNA), an independent governing body, complete with executive, judicial, and legislative branches. This government was intended to be temporary, until it could achieve its ultimate goal: the creation of an independent Black nation-state in the area consisting of the five Southern states of Louisiana, Mississippi, Georgia, Alabama, and South Carolina.

With the highest concentration of Blacks in the United States, this region of fertile land, the "Black Belt," had for hundreds of years

---

* The organization originally wrote its name as "Africa," but later changed it to what they believed was the Swahili, pre-colonization spelling.

been cultivated, toiled over, and enriched by enslaved Black people, and the New Afrikans argued that this land was owed to them. "Free the land!" became their battle cry, as well as a form of greeting and show of solidarity. To achieve this rather lofty goal, the RNA called for monetary restitution from the U.S. government in the form of several hundred billion dollars, demanding the "right to damages, reparations, due us for the grievous injustices sustained by our ancestors and ourselves."

The New Afrikans argued that Black people had not consented to becoming assimilated into the United States with the ratification of the Fourteenth Amendment, and they called for a UN-monitored plebiscite where they could hold a vote on whether to remain U.S. citizens or form a nation of their own. Recognizing that the U.S. government has not and would not willfully give up significant territorial land, the RNA formed a military unit, the Black Legion, later renamed the New Afrikan Security Forces, to serve as "a black army to fight for black rights." Robert F. Williams—the exiled former NAACP leader and self-defense advocate—was elected as first president of the PG-RNA, and Gaidi Obadele was designated vice president.

Herman Ferguson was chosen as Minister of Education. When Ferguson joined the PG-RNA, he brought along his young acolyte, Mutulu Shakur, who joined the ranks of the RNA as a political officer and a soldier in the New Afrikan Security Forces. "People who are oppressed must have a specific goal and objective," Mutulu remarked on his motivation for joining the RNA. "The only way Black people in America will be recognized in the world will be if we have a nation which operates in the interests of our people."

Mutulu invited his older friend Beany—now Sekou Odinga—to RNA demonstrations and organizational meetings and convinced him to join the New Afrikan Independence Movement. In the summer of 1968, after filling out some procedural forms, Odinga became a citizen of the Republic of New Afrika. Odinga, who was at the time section leader of the Black Panther Party's Bronx chapter, was soon joined in the RNA by another founding leader of the New York Black Panthers, Bilal Sunni-Ali. Dual membership in the RNA and the Black Panther Party wasn't prohibited, though it was rare and mostly limited to the East Coast.

In defense of their dual allegiance, the New Afrikans highlighted point ten of the Black Panther Party's Ten-Point Program, which, in its original draft, called for "a United Nations–supervised plebiscite to be held throughout the black colony in which only black colonial subjects will be allowed to participate, for the purpose of determining the will of black people as to their national destiny."

For Mutulu, there was never any question about divided allegiance. Though he had many friends in the Black Panther Party, including the two close companions he'd considered older brothers, Lumumba and Odinga, Mutulu never joined the Party. He was a loyal New Afrikan soldier, whose only allegiance was to the RNA. And like any dedicated soldier, his loyalty was tested with his life on March 29, 1969, during the police raid on the RNA's first-anniversary celebration in Detroit.

When the raid on New Bethel Baptist Church ended, only four people inside the church had been injured, but the police arrested all 142 people present and booked them for conspiracy to commit murder. The raid, which would become known as the "New Bethel Incident," was condemned by Gaidi, who charged police of a "bloody, storm trooper-like attack on a black church."

New Bethel's Reverend Franklin also denounced the actions of the police, telling reporters, "They would not have shot up a white church like that." This sentiment was shared by the Black judge George C. Crockett of the Recorder's Court, who asked, "Can any of you imagine the Detroit Police Department invading an all-white church and rounding up everyone in sight . . . Can anyone explain in other than racial terms the shooting by police into a closed and surrounded church?"

Ruling that the police had violated the detainees' constitutional rights, Judge Crockett ordered everyone's release. Three men, Rafael Viera, Chaka Fuller, and Alfred "2X" Hibbit, were later charged in connection with Czapski's murder and the attempted murder of Worobec but were acquitted by a racially mixed jury.

Herman Ferguson, Iyaluua, and Mutulu returned to New York.

Days later, the NYPD would conduct the widespread raids of Panther homes, leading to the Panther 21 trial. The rest of the year would see increased raids, arrests, and assaults on Black militants.

Meanwhile, Ferguson had lost his appeals for his murder conspiracy conviction, and the U.S. Supreme Court refused to hear his case. While he was driving through Queens on the first day of July 1970 with his ten-year-old son Mark beside him, a report from the Queens district attorney came over the radio that Ferguson was to be given a three-to-seven-year prison sentence and would be arrested within twenty-four hours. He pulled the car over near his house. "Well, son, I'll see you later," he told Mark. "Take care of your mother. I will get in touch with y'all as soon as I can." After dropping off his son at home, Ferguson drove to a prearranged safe house. The next day, he was on a plane to Guyana, South America.

For Mutulu, the raid on the church was a formative moment in his evolving radicalism. "I understood that if I was to survive, I would have to defend myself against physical violence," he later recalled. "This particular attack in Detroit explains, in part, my growing militancy."

Years later, Mutulu would find himself at the center of a new battle—not in a gunfight in a Detroit church, but in a fight over a radical new alternative medical treatment program, waged inside a controversial and disreputable hospital in the South Bronx.

10.
ACUPUNCTURE FOR
THE PEOPLE

JUST BEFORE NOON on Tuesday, November 10, 1970, staff members at Lincoln Hospital, in the South Bronx, were beginning to peel off their scrubs, push away from their desks, or return mops and mop buckets to closets, looking forward to eating lunch, getting some fresh air, and taking a much-needed break. At that moment, around thirty-five people—mostly members of radical Puerto Rican liberation group Young Lords but accompanied by a number of Black Panthers, mental healthcare workers, and people with drug addictions—marched into the hospital and took the elevator to the sixth floor. The group erected fortifications and set up a checkpoint, barring police and hospital administrators from entering. Among the group's demands were the implementation of "a drug program that would serve the community effectively and be run by the community" and the promise to "provide an educational program that would teach the true nature of our oppression and the connection between capitalism, dope and genocide."

New York City in the late 1960s and 1970s was in the throes of a devastating heroin epidemic. The New York City Health Department reported more than 650 heroin-related deaths a year by the mid-1970s, with a high percentage of the casualties concentrated in Harlem and the Bronx. The South Bronx in 1970 had the highest rate of heroin addiction in the world, with a mortality rate fifty percent higher than in any other part of the country. An editorial in the *New York Times* complained that the South Bronx was "menaced by 20,000 drug addicts" and quoted one medical doctor saying that the troubled borough was a "necropolis—a city of death." Growing impatient with the lack of drug treatment, local activists took matters into their own hands.

Within five hours of the activists taking over the sixth-floor nurses' residence, police were able to get past the barricade and arrest fifteen of the demonstrators, but hospital administrators soon allowed the activists to set up an inpatient drug detoxification program, housed in the hospital auditorium. The victorious activists took a bedsheet and hand-painted a sign, declaring: "Lincoln Detox is open." On opening day, two hundred people with drug addictions lined up outside the door, seeking treatment.

By the time of the November occupation, Lincoln Hospital had already earned an ignoble and notorious reputation. Founded in 1839 as a nursing home for formerly enslaved and elderly Blacks, the hospital—at the time the only medical facility in the South Bronx—had become, in the words of one *New York Times* reporter, "squalid" and "universally deplored as inadequate and obsolete." Locals were even more unsparing in their judgment, referring to the hospital as a "butcher shop."

The November action was not the first time the Young Lords occupied Lincoln in protest. Earlier that year, on July 14, 150 Young Lords stormed the hospital in an early morning surprise raid and quickly secured the entrance and exit doors and first-floor windows with makeshift barricades. They flew the Puerto Rican flag from the roof and unfurled banners that read, "Seize the Hospital to Serve the People" and "Bienvenidos al Hospital del Pueblo" ("Welcome to the People's Hospital"). Over the twelve-hour occupation, the Young Lords negotiated with hospital officials, listened to the long-standing grievances of community members, and gave a press conference presenting a list of seven demands, which included: "No cutbacks in services or jobs," "Door-to-door health services for preventative care," "A day care center for patients and workers," and "Self-determination of all health services through a community-worker board to operate Lincoln Hospital." The Young Lords and the hospital administrators finally came to a tentative agreement and ended the occupation at five thirty that afternoon.

Whatever success the community may have felt was dashed only days later, however, when a thirty-one-year-old Puerto Rican woman, Carmen Rodriguez, died at the hospital following what should have been a routine abortion procedure. Medical examiners determined that her preexisting rheumatic heart disease had caused her to react negatively to a saline-based solution, but her death only fueled the activists' condemnation of the hospital as a place where Black and Brown people are murdered. "This death was no accident," wrote Gloria Cruz, a leader of the Young Lords, in the Young Lords newspaper *Palante*. "Carmen died because amerikkka is killing our people."

That summer, following Rodriguez's death, the Young Lords and the Health Revolutionary Unity Movement (HRUM)—a Young Lords–affiliated organization of health workers—drafted a list of ten more demands, establishing a protocol of communication between doctors and patients.

This "Patient's Bill of Rights" began with the call for patients to "be treated with dignity and respect," to "have all treatment explained and to refuse any treatment you feel is not in your best interest," to "know what medicine is being prescribed and what it is for and what side effects it will cause," and to "have access to your medical chart." A set of regulated protections and guarantees, modeled on HRUM's original demands, has since been adopted by hospitals across the nation as the Patient's Bill of Rights.

Lincoln Detox received immediate popularity in the community, treating six hundred patients a month, and the program began receiving funding from federal and city governments.* Besides using

---

* The drug detoxification program at Lincoln went by many names, among them Lincoln Recovery, Lincoln Detox Program, Lincoln Detox Center, the People's Program, the People's Drug Program, and the People's Detox Center. In these pages, it will be referred to, in general, as Lincoln Detox.

methadone to help wean users off heroin, staff members also emphasized the politically repressive nature of addiction. Patients were given "The Opium Trail: Heroin and Imperialism," a pamphlet written by "a study group supported by the Committee of Concerned Asian Scholars," which promoted revolutionary ideals, because as "an alternative explanation and another focus for anger, as well as collective support and some sense of direction, the movement can be the best therapy." Patients of the drug detoxification program would go on to participate in local political actions like occupations, rent strikes, and other protests.

"We named it the People's Detox because we wanted the people to feel empowered that this was their program," explained one of the founding members, Walter Bosque del Rio, "so they would come and clean up their act. They'd bring their family and friends and they cleaned up their act. And now we had an extended family and a movement."

Many of the staff and volunteers, especially those who had been members of the Black Panther Party, had also been familiar with Panther 21 defendant Michael "Cetewayo" Tabor's 1969 pamphlet, "Capitalism Plus Dope Equals Genocide," in which he writes that the "government is totally incapable of addressing itself to the true causes of drug addiction, for to do so would necessitate effecting a radical transformation of this society . . . Only a revolution can eliminate the plague."

"What made Lincoln Detox different from any other program is that we were political radicals and we educated them through political education," Bosque recalled. "That's what made Lincoln Detox unique. Because once you liberate minds and hearts and people realize that they're not the problem, that the system is a problem, and that they're just being used and abused, they want to be part of a family."

"We also understood that an individual's addiction wasn't just a physical problem, but a psychological problem," recalled Vicente "Panama" Alba, a member of the Young Lords and a founding member of Lincoln Detox. "It was a widespread problem in our community, not because we as a community were psychologically deficient, but because oppression and brutal living conditions drove us to that."

"These were people that were fiercely in love with making this a better world for the people," remembered Yaasmyn Fula, who volunteered at Lincoln Detox, "and were able to translate ideologies to people and break it down so they could understand: you have a right to live with integrity, your humanity is important. That's the basic premise: self-determination, the right to defend yourself, to live in peace and harmony and protect the community."

The detox program was staffed in the beginning by Young Lords members, people with drug addictions, White and Black doctors, and healthcare workers. One of these workers was twenty-year-old Cleo Silvers, the former VISTA worker who had joined the Black Panther Party in the summer of 1968. After the Panther 21 arrests in April 1969 and the subsequent rift between New York and California Panther leadership, Zayd and another Harlem Panther named Rashid convinced the Young Lords to accept Silvers into their organization so she would not get caught up in the intensifying intraparty feud. Accepting Silvers into the predominantly Puerto Rican group wasn't out of the ordinary; around twenty-five percent of Young Lords members were Black.

Silvers had been employed at Lincoln Hospital since 1969 as a community mental health worker. She helped to implement the Think Lincoln Committee, setting up a twenty-four-hour complaint table in the hospital emergency room, and she was co-chair of HRUM, helping to draft the Patient's Bill of Rights. She soon became one of Lincoln Detox's medical directors. One of her first assignments in her new role was to hire someone from the community who could act as the collective's political education director. One day in 1970, Silvers received word from Zayd and Lumumba Shakur. They said, "We're sending our little brother down to help out with the drug program."

Eight years younger than Lumumba and a decade younger than Zayd, twenty-year-old Mutulu Shakur wasn't a blood relative of the Shakur brothers but was considered a little brother and an adopted son of the patriarch Salahdeen. He'd earned the older men's respect for his involvement in the Ocean Hill–Brownsville school struggle, for organizing community support for Herman Ferguson's defense, and as a legionnaire with the Republic of New Afrika, protecting elder members during the New Bethel Incident. Mutulu was known to be a dedicated young warrior with a seemingly endless supply of energy.

"He had more energy than anybody I know," recalled his child-hood friend Sekou Odinga. "He was really hyper, he really was. To a point where, if he didn't run twice a day—like he would get up in the morning and run five miles, and then before he'd go to bed at night he had to run five miles. He just had too much energy; he didn't know how to control his energy."

Though this overabundance of energy would, a decade later, lead Mutulu and his accomplices to a fateful and spectacular collapse, at the time, his enthusiasm, his élan, as well as his political acumen were believed to make him uniquely qualified at Lincoln Detox, where he began at first with a volunteer position as political educa-tion director but was soon earning a modest $9,000 yearly salary as assistant drug counselor.

"He was very smart and very organized and very confident for a young person," recalled Silvers. "He was the kind of person who was tough enough to organize this wayward group of community activ-ists and drug addicts—because that's what we had there."

His duties were not much different from those of any other admin-istrator: scheduling, attending meetings, representing the program on official business. One of his foremost responsibilities was meeting with policy makers and securing funding. During these negotiations, he was unsparing in his demands and unintimidated by being in the room with these older, straitlaced, White bureaucrats. "White people were scared of him, because he would demand what we needed in order to keep the program going," explained Silvers. "He wasn't play-ing around with them. He was so serious and so committed to the program and making it a good program and making it work."

Not long after beginning work at the collective, Mutulu finally made the decision to cast off his birth name. Legally changing his given name was much more than dropping his "slave name"; it was committing to a particular political agenda, embracing cultural na-tionalist ideologies, and aligning himself with his adopted, revolution-ary family. From now on, Jeral Wayne Williams would be known—to friends, family, colleagues, and the FBI—as Mutulu Shakur.

While many of his colleagues at Lincoln Detox were current or former Black Panthers or Young Lords, Mutulu remained dedicated to the tenets of the Republic of New Afrika, including its call for a sovereign Black nation in the American South. As Minister of Defense of the Provisional Government of the Republic of New Afrika, Mutulu would quarrel with Silvers and others about the revolution's true objectives—enfranchisement or separation—and he refused to yield an inch. Staff members and patients alike would often hear his powerful voice coming from down the hall, shouting "Free the land!" as a way of letting folks know he was in the room.

The Republic of New Afrika, as an organization, had meanwhile undergone its own multiple quarrels and crises. In September, following the police raid on New Bethel in Detroit, Michigan, PG-RNA president Robert F. Williams returned to the United States from his eight-year exile, and New Afrikans were hopeful that the fiery and influential leader would galvanize the embattled organization. Williams, however, distanced himself from the nationalist movement, resigning from his post and focusing instead on fighting his 1961 kidnapping charges. At the same time as Williams's resignation, there were further leadership rifts between RNA's founding sibling members, Imari and Gaidi Obadele. Among other disagreements, Gaidi and his supporters believed RNA headquarters should remain in Detroit and exercise legal and deliberate means to gain support for an independent nation, while his brother, Imari, and his supporters advocated instead for relocating headquarters to Mississippi and immediately beginning to acquire land for their new nation. By July 1970, this fraternal strife had proven insurmountable, leading to Gaidi's resignation.

Now in full control of the PG-RNA, President Imari Obadele moved government headquarters to Jackson, Mississippi, in March 1971, negotiating the purchase of twenty acres of land from a Black farmer, Lofton Mason. During a land dedication ceremony in Hinds County, near the small town of Bolton, the RNA declared El Malik—after Malcolm X's Muslim name—as "the capital of the still unliberated nation." None of this went unnoticed by Jackson police and the FBI, who began a campaign of surveillance and harassment against the organization, culminating in a predawn raid on RNA headquarters on August 18.

Following a twenty-minute shoot-out, pitting fifteen Jackson police officers and fourteen FBI agents against seven heavily armed RNA members, the New Afrikans were finally captured. A Jackson police officer, Lieutenant William Skinner, was killed and one federal agent was wounded. In addition to the seven detained at headquarters, three more New Afrikans were arrested in Jackson that morning in another predawn raid, including President Obadele. The defendants were indicted on charges of "murder and levy of war against the state of Mississippi" and "possession of stolen property." Obadele and several others were convicted on the murder charges and given life sentences in prison.

With the captivity and pending court battles of the "RNA-11," the Republic of New Afrika again faced an existential crisis, but it wasn't the end of the New Afrikan Independence Movement. If anything, these numerous raids and arrests only further convinced New Afrikans of the need for a separate Black nation. Some members, like the Detroit-born Chokwe Lumumba—who would become an influential attorney and future mayor of Jackson, Mississippi—remained in the South to raise money and garner support for "new communities," gradually developing an independent nation, while others would find themselves advancing the struggle by various other means—including inside a small, radical medical clinic in the South Bronx.

Lincoln Detox was the South Bronx's first and only outpatient drug detoxification program. Outpatient methadone maintenance procedures had been available, but Lincoln Detox was the first to use methadone for the purpose of complete detoxification. For the first few years of the program, the only treatment offered to patients wishing to kick heroin was to be administered methadone—a synthetic opioid that is itself an addictive, controlled substance. While it has been shown to help with the effects of heroin withdrawal, staff and patients alike were dissatisfied with and suspicious of methadone, seeing it as another form of addiction, dependency, and control. They sought a natural alternative.

In 1973, three years after the founding of Lincoln Detox, Mutulu happened upon a *New York Times* article that would prove to be a game changer, with outcomes that brought a deep and lasting effect on the practice of naturopathic medicine—not only in the South Bronx, and not only in the United States, but in the wider Western world. The article reported the early successes of a Hong Kong medical team, led by Dr. H. L. Wen, in using acupuncture to help relieve patients of the symptoms of opium and heroin withdrawal. "The treatment yields very quick results, is very gratifying to the patient and seems to replace the urge to take the drug," reported Dr. Wen and senior assistant Mr. Cheung, going on to tout the procedure as simple and economic, with no marked side effects. Mutulu shared the article with some of his colleagues. *Maybe this is what we need here at Lincoln Detox*, they agreed.

The team formed a small collective, composed of Mutulu, Bosque, Hassan Squires and his sister Wafiya, Richard Delaney, Richard Burr, and Michael Smith—a White psychiatrist who worked part-time at Lincoln. Though each person was equally invested in learning acupuncture, according to Bosque, "Mutulu was the leader. If it wasn't for Mutulu's leadership there'd be no collective."

"We read every book available, and there weren't that many back in the seventies," Bosque explained. "But there were enough to teach us what acupuncture was, what the meridians do, and what the acupuncture points in the ear can do."

Before bringing needles to the clinic, the collective first experimented with acupressure, using firm hand pressure to stimulate the meridians. They then began learning the protocol used by Wen's team, using an electrical stimulator in tandem with a needle on the lung meridian.* "We had to convince our community that it was OK to get these funny-looking needles in your ear and in your body," Bosque recalled, "and you weren't going to get high, but you were going to get sober and totally relaxed and eventually help you detox."

---

* In traditional Chinese medicine (TCM), meridians are defined as the channels through which life-energy (chi) flows throughout the body. Acupuncturists or acupressure practitioners stimulate one of the twelve major meridians connecting the body's network of organs. The lung meridian—one of five points located on the outer ear—is believed to support the respiratory system.

The community came around. When they discovered how acupuncture helped them to relax, taking the edge off their withdrawal symptoms, patients began returning to the clinic on a daily basis. The collective soon decided to get rid of the electrical stimulator and focus exclusively on needles. Initially, they'd hired a couple of acupuncturists, including the prominent Dr. Yoshiaki Omura, to teach and administer the procedure, but before long the young radicals and activists grew impatient with being relegated to the sidelines. "After six months of being the assistant to the acupuncturists we realized we could do this ourselves. We don't need them," Bosque recalled. "So we let them go and we took over."

Some of the collective members went to New York's Chinatown to procure acupuncture needles for the clinic, while Mutulu, Hassan, and Smith traveled to the 1974 World Acupuncture Conference in Montreal, where they delivered a presentation on their successes so far in treating addiction with acupuncture. Their presentation impressed Romanian-born physiotherapist and acupuncturist Oscar Wexu. Having learned acupuncture in Paris after fleeing Nazi persecution, Wexu emigrated to Canada with his family, and Wexu and his son, Mario, played an integral role in introducing Chinese acupuncture to North America.

Moved by what this unorthodox crew from New York had largely taught themselves, the Wexus awarded scholarships to Mutulu, Bosque, Delaney, and Burr to study at Oscar Wexu's acupuncture institute in Quebec. In 1976, they each received doctorates in acupuncture from the Acupuncture Association of Quebec.

Upon their return, the collective established the Lincoln Acupuncture School, recruiting students and apprentices from the tristate area. Around thirty students signed up, recalled Bosque, predominantly middle-class Whites. Oscar and Mario Wexu would come down to the South Bronx to give lectures and demonstrations. The school served as kind of a New York auxiliary to Wexu's Montreal institute. None of it—the teaching or the practicing of acupuncture— was approved by the city or the state.

At that time, only medical doctors could practice acupuncture in New York State, and since no one in the collective was yet licensed to practice acupuncture, Mutulu and Bosque traveled to California in 1978, which was then the only state in the United States issuing acupuncture licenses. Their licenses would only permit them to practice acupuncture in the state of California, but, as they justified it, they could at least say they were licensed.

Lincoln Detox suffered its first disaster on October 29, 1974, when Richard Taft—a White, thirty-one-year-old graduate of Baylor University Medical School, one of Lincoln's earliest proponents of acupuncture, and the program's medical director—was found dead in the clinic's storage closet, from an apparent heroin overdose. The unusual circumstances of his death, including the unnatural position of his prone body, recent accusations of threats against his life, and the fact that he was scheduled to meet later that day with an official from Washington about program funding, led some to believe that Taft was murdered by the CIA in an attempt to stop the detox program. These allegations were never confirmed. Michael Smith took over as medical director and the program continued to operate.

During this time, Mutulu had struck up a relationship with another prominent Black activist—someone who, through years of dedication and commitment to the struggle, was likewise highly venerated in the community.

After being acquitted in the Panther 21 trial, Afeni Shakur had gone on to work as a paralegal and housing rights advocate with Bronx Legal Services, and she would sometimes volunteer at Lincoln Detox, bringing along her young son, Tupac. Afeni had since divorced her first husband, Lumumba, but her eventual marriage to Mutulu was much like her first marriage: informal and largely ceremonial, but no less committed, first and foremost, to the movement.

"Mutulu and Afeni's relationship was based on their solid love and commitment to the struggle," explained their mutual friend Yaasmyn Fula. "That was the love that they shared."

On October 3, 1975, Afeni gave birth to her second child, a daughter. To further underscore the bonds among this close-knit family, her parents named her after Lumumba's own daughter: Sekyiwa Shakur.

Sekyiwa, or "Set," also wasn't Mutulu's first child. Eight years earlier, on August 16, 1967, a college student named Sharon Harding gave birth to Mutulu's son, who was given the name Maurice Harding. Born and raised on the south side of Jamaica, Queens, Maurice was given his mother's surname, but he would, years later, follow his father's family tradition and be known to the world as the rapper Mopreme Shakur.

Though Mutulu had his own biological children, he embraced and encouraged Tupac, becoming a father figure to the young, fatherless boy. "Mutulu had integrity," remembered Fula. "He put time and love and energy into Pac. And Pac recognized that."

The marriage of Mutulu and Afeni was a union of equally gifted and equally headstrong organizers, so it was only natural the two would collaborate professionally. In 1975, as the years of illegal surveillance by the FBI were beginning to come to light, Mutulu and Afeni co-founded the National Task Force for Cointelpro Litigation and Research—a coalition of activists and lawyers who would provide legal assistance to Geronimo "Ji-Jaga" Pratt, the former Los Angeles Black Panther leader who had been convicted of first-degree murder in 1972 and given a life sentence. Many in the movement believed Pratt had been targeted by COINTELPRO, and the task force filed multiple Freedom of Information Act (FOIA) requests, combing through thousands of documents pertaining to Pratt's case. Mutulu and Afeni soon discovered just how extensive and pernicious COINTELPRO had been to the New Left movement in general and Black radical groups in particular.

"We felt that the establishment of a National Task Force for Litigation and Research would render an important service to all progressive groups under attack by the state," Mutulu later recalled.

Mutulu and Lincoln Detox were soon faced with a more immediate threat. After accusing them of everything from misappropriating funds to "highly questionable expenditures," being Maoists, and using the medical clinic as a place where doctors offer "a radical political reorientation for patients rather than referrals to more traditional after-care programs," city and state authorities finally decided they'd seen enough.

Health officials had for years accused Lincoln Detox of cheating the city with dubious payroll costs, no-show jobs, and overbilling for patient care. Brooklyn Democratic Assemblyman, Chairman of the Assembly's Subcommittee on City Management and Governance, and future Democratic U.S. Senate majority leader Chuck Schumer accused the Health and Hospitals Corporation of "protecting a ripoff drug-treatment program through years of continuing scandal." New York City mayor Ed Koch was even more severe in his indictment, declaring that "hospitals are for sick people, not for thugs."

"They ran it like Che Guevara was their patron saint, with his picture all over the walls," Koch later recalled. "It wasn't a hospital, it was a radical cell."

On Tuesday, November 28, 1978, Koch ordered two dozen leading members of the detox collective removed from the hospital. Expecting resistance, Koch sent a large squadron of Bronx police to cordon off the hospital, armed with sledgehammers, wire cutters, and crowbars, to assist the city's hospital chief and president of the New York City Health and Hospitals Corporation, Joseph T. Lynaugh, in evicting the workers. Choosing a moment when they knew Mutulu would be away from the hospital, they were able to evict the collective and padlock the doors without much opposition. Lincoln Detox was relocated to a satellite clinic several blocks away and forced to discontinue its radical program. It was rebranded as the Lincoln Substance Abuse Program, with Michael Smith, who had become medical director after Taft's death, effectively in charge. The dozen removed staffers were not fired but reassigned to other hospitals across the city, and they were barred from continuing the political aspect of addiction treatment. Mutulu and Bosque were assigned to a hospital in Brooklyn before Mutulu decided on another course.

In August 1979, Mutulu purchased an apartment in a four-story brownstone at 245 West 139th Street, and established the Black Acupuncture Advisory Association of North America (BAAANA). With space for a consultation room and a therapy room, Mutulu could continue the work he'd begun with Lincoln Detox, practicing and teaching acupuncture under a revolutionary framework.

But while he was no longer restrained by city or state regulations, he likewise didn't receive any city funding, couldn't receive insurance payments, and was almost single-handedly responsible for financing the clinic. Mutulu wasn't an experienced businessman. He was a radical, and he operated the clinic as a radical. Assembling a coalition of militant White and Black activists made up of other

Lincoln Detox exiles, former Black Panthers, Weather Underground veterans, and members of the clandestine Black Liberation Army, this alliance would soon become known by law enforcement and the media as "the Family." Together they would be accused of orchestrating a daring string of robberies, prison breaks, and murders.

11.
REVOLUTIONARY JUSTICE

FLEEING THE UNITED States in 1969 after his Houdini-esque escape during the New York raids, Sekou Odinga and fellow Panther 21 fugitive Larry Mack made their way to Algiers, where they joined Eldridge and Kathleen Cleaver and other self-exiled Panthers at the hilltop villa they had been using as the embassy of the Party's International Section. But in the summer of 1972, the Algerian government had been caught off guard when two American airplanes—in separate incidents and within three months of each other—were hijacked and routed to Algiers. Each plane had been loaded with thousands of dollars in ransom money. The hijackers had not been members of the Black Panther Party but were sympathetic to the cause, and the Algerian government reluctantly agreed to release them into the custody of the Party's International Section. Though the planes and the money were confiscated and returned, the Algerian government was humiliated.

As government officials debated how long to continue to accommodate the Panthers, Eldridge Cleaver published a letter defending the actions of the hijackers and criticizing Algeria's governing officials for giving in to international pressure. Algeria finally decided that the Panthers had overstayed their welcome. The government had also been in the process of restarting diplomatic relations with the United States, as well as negotiating a $1 billion contract with

American oil companies, and the continued accommodation of fugitive Panthers was becoming not only an embarrassment but an obstacle to economic development. The Panthers were placed under a six-day house arrest and their lines of communication were permanently cut off. The message was clear: the Panthers had to go.

When Odinga and Mack returned to the United States in 1973, the Black Panther Party was already well past the point of no return. The rift between the East Coast and Oakland Panthers—or between the Cleaverite Panthers and those loyal to Huey P. Newton—had become terminal, culminating in the 1971 murders of Robert Webb and Sam Napier. Newton himself had become more erratic and unstable since his release from prison in 1970. Holed up in his penthouse apartment in Oakland, in despair over the unraveling of the Black Panther Party, developing an expensive cocaine addiction, and increasingly paranoid and suspicious, Newton established a security force, dubbed "the squad." Its members served as Newton's local mafia goons—harassing, intimidating, and extorting after-hours club owners, drug dealers, and sex workers in an attempt to control Oakland's criminal underworld.

But as Newton spiraled out of control, Elaine Brown had already begun to take over the direction of the Oakland Panthers. In 1972, Brown had been appointed by Newton as Minister of Information, replacing the mutinous Eldridge Cleaver, and she and Chairman Bobby Seale attempted to steer the Party away from radical posturing and toward electoral politics, by running for a seat on the Oakland City Council and mayor of Oakland, respectively. Though both campaigns lost, each candidate had impressive turnouts, with Brown coming in a close second in her campaign, and Seale forcing a runoff in the mayoral election. In 1974, Newton promoted Brown to chairperson—a second-in-command position—after Seale finally left the Party he co-founded. Later that year, Newton fled to Cuba after charges were brought against him of pistol-whipping a tailor and shooting to death a seventeen-year-old sex worker named Kathleen Smith. The Black Panther Party—or what remained of it—was now in Brown's exclusive command.

But not all Panthers, especially those in the more militant faction on the East Coast, were on board with the reformist direction of the Party. They didn't fail to notice that, as the Party attempted to enter the political mainstream, police were continuing to target and kill Black people across the country. In the late 1960s and early 1970s, nearly one hundred Black men under age twenty-five were killed by police every year—a rate ten times higher than Whites and Latinos. The FBI, under the guise of COINTELPRO, had stepped up its campaign of disruption and infiltration, eliminating Black leaders and activists with increased urgency until the program's discovery in 1971. By then, however, many people in the movement had already discovered the need for a more clandestine operation.

Scholar Akinyele Umoja writes how "the increased political repression of the Black liberation movement and particularly the BPP convinced many it was time to develop the underground vanguard." This underground vanguard went beyond the self-defense rhetoric and community outreach programs of the Black Panther Party. It saw itself as waging a "defensive/offensive" operation against police to "defend Black people, to fight for Black people, and to organize Black people militarily, so they can defend themselves through a people's army and people's war."

The opening shots of this war came on what would've been Malcolm X's forty-sixth birthday: May 19, 1971.

During the Panther 21 trial, a police radio car was posted as a precautionary measure outside the home of District Attorney Frank Hogan, on 404 Riverside Drive, beside the Hudson River on the Upper West Side. The police guard had been assigned there after members of the radical White group Weather Underground had firebombed the home of presiding judge John M. Murtaugh one year earlier. Even after the trial was over, police continued to keep watch outside Hogan's home.

On Wednesday, May 19, at 9:00 P.M., the first police car was relieved of its watch by another radio car, occupied by Patrolmen Thomas Curry and Nicholas Binetti, both White and thirty-nine years old. After being on duty for only a few minutes, Curry and Binetti noticed a car turn the wrong way onto a one-way street. The officers made a U-turn and pursued the speeding car. After a six-block pursuit, at the intersection of Riverside and 106th Street, the patrolmen pulled alongside the vehicle's driver's side. The driver of the car ducked down in his seat as the person in the passenger seat reached across the car and pointed a .45-caliber submachine gun out of the window and began firing. The glass of the police cruiser shattered into pieces as a volley of bullets struck the two police officers. The cruiser crashed as the other car sped away.

Curry and Binetti were critically injured during the shooting and taken to St. Luke's Hospital, where they survived. Visiting the recuperating officers at the hospital, Mayor John Lindsay told reporters that he was "very disturbed" that he'd been to St. Luke's for "the third or fourth time in a month and a half to visit with policemen who have been shot while going about their duties." Police Commissioner Patrick Murphy stated that "any policemen [*sic*] at any time has become the target for a killer" and appealed for stricter gun control laws. Detectives in search of the assailants were given a vague description of the getaway car—either a late-model blue or dark-green Pinto or Mustang—and a few possible New York license plate numbers. One of these numbers was a stolen plate reading 8373YA.

Two nights after the ambush on Riverside Drive, on Friday, May 22, at about 7:45 P.M., a young Black woman quietly delivered a package to the studios of the WLIB-FM radio station, at 125th and Lenox Avenue in Harlem. Inside the package was a license plate reading 8373YA. Fifteen minutes later, a Black man delivered a similar package to the lobby of the New York Times Building in Midtown Manhattan. This package contained the companion license plate, as well as a .45-caliber cartridge and a typewritten letter. The letter, typed in black capital letters, read:

May 19, 1971

All power to the people.

*Here are the license plates sort [*sic*] after by the fascist state pig police. We send them in order to exhibit the potential power of oppressed peoples to acquire revolutionary justice.*

The armed goons of this racist government will again meet the guns of oppressed Third World people as long as they occupy our community and murder our brothers and sisters in the name of American law and order; just as the fascist Marines and Army occupy Vietnam in the name of democracy and murder Vietnamese people in the name of American imperialism are confronted with the guns of the Vietnamese Liberation Army, the domestic armed forces of racism and oppression will be confronted with the guns of the Black Liberation Army, who will mete out in the tradition of Malcolm and all true revolutionaries real justice. We are revolutionary justice.

All power to the people.

Justice.

"Revolutionary justice" and the closing "Justice" were typed or underlined in red ink.

Shortly after the two packages had been delivered, at about 10:00 P.M., two patrolmen—twenty-eight-year-old Joseph A. Piagentini, who was White, and thirty-three-year-old Black officer Waverly M. Jones—responded to a call in the Colonial Park housing development about a woman who had been injured. After the woman—who may have only been a snare for the patrolmen—had refused their aid, Piagentini and Jones began walking back to their squad car, passing two young Black men leaning against the fender of a car. As the patrolmen passed, the two men raised .45-caliber automatic pistols and began shooting. Jones was shot once in the back of the head and three times in the spine. He died instantly. Piagentini fell but didn't die right away. The two assailants took the service revolvers from the fallen patrolmen's holsters and continued shooting their victims. The assailants then ran and escaped. Piagentini died on the way to Harlem Hospital.

Immediately after the ambush of Piagentini and Jones, another typewritten letter was delivered to WLIB. This letter began:

*All power to the people. Revolutionary justice has been meted out
again by righteous brothers of the Black Liberation Army with the
death of two Gestapo pigs gunned down as so many of our brothers
have been gunned down in the past. Revolutionary justice is ours.*

By May, seven New York police officers had been killed and thirty
were wounded. As many officers had been killed in the first five
months of 1971 as had been in the entire year before, which led the
police to wonder if they were in the midst of a war against cops. But
the war between the police and the Black Liberation Army was just
beginning. The moderate factions of the Black Panthers, together
with liberal White benefactors and supporters, could only watch in
horror.

Though its existence hadn't been announced until that fateful
spring of 1971, the Black Liberation Army was years in the making. As early as 1964, the Revolutionary Action Movement (RAM)
included in its twelve-point program the development of a "Liberation Army." RAM later published a document, "On Organization of
Ghetto Youth," that recommended developing a youth-led parami-li-
tary organization referred to as the Black Liberation Army.

In 1968, the Black Panther Party stated in its official rules that "no
party member can join any other army force other than the BLACK
LIBERATION ARMY." But no such liberation army had yet existed,
other than in the imagination of the more militant Panthers. Clandestine paramilitary units had flared up now and again throughout
the first half of the century, such as the Communist Party–affiliated
African Blood Brotherhood and the civil rights–era Deacons for Defense and Justice. A very small group calling itself the Black Liberation Front, organized by future Panther 21 defendant Robert Steele
Collier, was accused of a plot to dynamite the Statue of Liberty in
1965. Not until 1971, with the violent rupture of the Black Panther
Party, had the Black Liberation Army begun to take shape.

From its beginning, the Black Liberation Army (BLA) was intended
as a decentralized movement, with small, clandestine cells working
independently in different cities throughout the country. Realizing
that working aboveground, as the Black Panther Party had, only in-

vited police and federal infiltration, the BLA—whose membership numbers will never be accurately known—resolved to remain underground, operating under various aliases and never disseminating any information about itself, aside from the occasional anonymous communiqué. Just as the Black Power movement in general, and the Black Panther Party in particular, had grown out of mounting frustration with the reformism and incrementalism of the civil rights movement, the BLA emerged from disillusionment with the reformist policies and factionalism of the Black Panther Party. BLA membership consisted largely, though not exclusively, of Black Panther Party veterans and defectors, especially the Cleaverite faction, who were concentrated predominantly in New York City. But while the Black Panther Party—effectively a top-down, hierarchical organization—may have held them back from the increased militancy they viewed as necessary to bring revolution, these former Panthers were now free to throw themselves fully into armed insurrection.

After being ousted from Algeria with the other exiled Panthers, Odinga and Mack wandered for a bit before returning to the United States. "We decided to come back because Amerikkka is where our struggle was, where we felt we could be most effective," Odinga later wrote. Though the Panther 21 defendants had been acquitted in 1971, Odinga and Mack, because they had evaded arrest and trial, were still considered fugitives of the law. Odinga returned to New York City the same way he'd left four years earlier: clandestinely and without fanfare. He stayed underground while reconnecting with comrades who hadn't yet been captured or killed. Returning to the Black Panther Party wasn't an option, but Odinga had never been much of a Party man anyway. He'd been more interested in armed revolution than in selling newspapers. Odinga sought out a new formation, someplace he could be most effective in the struggle.

Since being acquitted in the Panther 21 trial, Odinga's oldest friend, Lumumba Shakur, had begun working with another veteran New York Panther, Bilal Sunni-Ali, in the National Committee for the Defense of Political Prisoners, seeking to bring attention to the plight of incarcerated Black activists and leaders. But Lumumba and his twin children, Dingiswayo and Sekyiwa, soon joined Sunni-Ali in New Orleans, selling cultural crafts and clothes brought in from West Africa. Lumumba appeared to be leaving behind militarism and was now following in the entrepreneurial footsteps of his father, Salahdeen Shakur.

Lumumba's older brother, however, had remained in New York to carry on what was left of the movement. Zayd Malik Shakur had gone in the other direction. He had become a founding member of the Black Liberation Army.

But membership in an underground paramilitary unit didn't pay the bills. While the Black Panther Party had depended on newspaper sales and monetary donations, the Black Liberation Army was not afforded the same luxury. There could be no fundraisers, no appeals to well-to-do White supporters. And though the costs of running a clandestine guerrilla war were not as high as running a national organization, there were still weapons and ammunition to purchase, safe houses to rent, getaway cars to procure.

The BLA initiated a campaign of sticking up drug dealers, robbing Black social clubs, and committing armed bank heists, which members called "expropriations." The BLA was quick to justify the difference between everyday thievery and revolutionary expropriation. "Bandits indulge in rip-offs for individualistic reasons, for personal gains," Zayd declared. "The guerrillas deal with expropriation of funds for the purpose of financing the revolution." Still, few of these guerrillas were experienced outlaws. They were also desperate for cash, and desperation and inexperience often lead to mistakes. One of the first slipups would come in the early morning hours of June 5, 1971.

A maroon Buick Rivera drove up and parked in front of the Triple-O Social Club, an after-hours club in the Bronx. In the back seat of the car were Augustus "Gus" Qualls and a Panther named Irving Mason, who would be connected to the murder of the *Black Panther* newspaper distribution manager Samuel Napier two months earlier. In the passenger seat was eighteen-year-old Jamal Joseph— the once-wide-eyed teenager who'd eagerly joined the Harlem Panthers at age fifteen. Behind the wheel was twenty-five-year-old Panther Dhoruba bin Wahad, who had been a mentor to the young Joseph. Bin Wahad and Joseph had both been defendants in the

Panther 21 trial, and after bin Wahad jumped bail that February, they had gone together into hiding. They, too, would later be indicted for Napier's murder. But now, four months after disappearing, bin Wahad and Joseph turned up outside this Bronx social club just after 4:00 A.M., with the two other men as backup.

Bin Wahad, Joseph, and Qualls walked into the club carrying a large duffel bag, having told Mason to stand watch on the corner. Moments later, Mason heard the sounds of gunfire coming from inside the club. He ran inside and up the stairs and saw fourteen men and twelve women lined up against a wall, stripped naked, with the gunmen rummaging through the clothes for money and jewelry. Joseph and Qualls were each holding a shotgun in one hand and a pistol in the other. Joseph ordered Mason to return to his post, but when Mason peered out the door, he saw police officers surrounding the building. Mason ran back upstairs and reported this to bin Wahad, who ordered everyone to get dressed and calmly exit the club.

When the would-be robbers attempted to blend in with the others, one of the club patrons identified them to the police, who immediately apprehended the four men. The police found two shotguns, a .45-caliber Colt, a .357 Smith & Wesson Magnum, a 9mm Browning automatic, a .45-caliber submachine gun, and an Army hand grenade. When ballistics tests were run on the submachine gun, it was discovered to be the same gun that was used on Patrolmen Curry and Binetti eighteen days earlier. Furthermore, bin Wahad's and Joseph's fingerprints were shown to match prints on the packages that had been delivered earlier to the *New York Times*.

In court, all men pleaded guilty to the attempted robbery but denied the other accusations. Bin Wahad defended the holdup as a "political act," and Joseph said he targeted the social club because it was a place frequented by "pimps, cocaine sellers, drug pushers and other undesirable people."

The men also pleaded guilty to manslaughter in connection to Sam Napier's murder. Joseph was given a four-year sentence, to be served concurrent to the attempted robbery charges. Bin Wahad was found guilty of the attempted murder of Curry and Binetti and was sentenced to life in prison. Upon being advised by State Supreme Court Justice Joseph A. Martinis of his right to appeal, bin Wahad replied: "My appeal will be over the barrel of a gun."

The incarceration of the men didn't bring an end, or even an interruption, to BLA activity. On August 4, 1971, two months after the failed holdup of the Triple-O, a small group of purported BLA members entered a Harlem bar called Thelma's Lounge, at Seventh Avenue and 148th Street, and robbed the thirty people inside of $6,000. Having been alerted to the holdup, police quickly arrived on the scene, where they were met with gunfire from the robbers. The group escaped by jumping into a taxicab and ordering the driver, James Pratt, to flee. The cab was caught in traffic three blocks away, and one of the members—a hotheaded twenty-year-old named Twymon Ford Myers—jumped out of the cab with an automatic rifle and began shooting. Police returned fire and Pratt was struck and killed by police bullets. Myers fled on foot and escaped, but the three others, who had remained inside the cab, were arrested.

Though they had locked up dozens of low-level criminals and had ostensibly solved the shooting of Patrolmen Curry and Binetti, New York detectives hadn't yet had any solid leads in the May assassination of Patrolmen Waverly Jones and Joseph Piagentini. But on the night of August 28, police would finally find a break in the case—clear across the country in San Francisco.

Sergeant George Kowalski, of the San Francisco Police Department, was stopped at a red light near Folsom and 16th Streets when a two-door, black Oldsmobile occupied by two Black men pulled up alongside his radio car. One of the men stuck a submachine gun out of the window and pulled the trigger, but nothing happened; the gun had apparently jammed. The car peeled off, and Kowalski gave chase, calling for backup. The passenger in the speeding Oldsmobile leaned out of the side window with a handgun, firing off shots at Kowalski.

When police reinforcements joined in the chase and impeded the car, the driver crashed into another car. The two men traded gunshots with the approaching officers, but Kowalski and two patrolmen shot and wounded the gunmen and were able to apprehend them. Inside the Oldsmobile, the officers discovered a .45-caliber submachine gun, a Colt .45 automatic, and a .38-caliber Smith & Wesson revolver. The revolver was soon discovered to have belonged to the slain Piagentini.

The two apprehended men—thirty-year-old Albert "Nuh" Washington and nineteen-year-old Anthony Bottom (later Jalil Abdul Muntaqim)—were affiliated with the BLA, and Bottom allegedly confessed, to a jailhouse informant, to a number of earlier, as-yet-unsolved police shootings and station house bombings throughout San Francisco. Bottom, Washington, and another purported BLA member named Herman Bell were alleged to have traveled to New York that spring to kill police officers. Bell was later apprehended in New Orleans after police matched his fingerprints to those left on the scene of Jones and Piagentini's murder. The three men were convicted and sentenced to twenty-five years to life. But again, BLA activity continued unabated.

The day after the attempted murder of Sergeant Kowalski, on the evening of August 29, three Black men strode into the Ingleside District police station in San Francisco and began shooting. A clerk was injured during the shooting, while one gunman shot forty-five-year-old Sergeant John Young at close range with a shotgun, killing him instantly.

On the following Tuesday, the *Sun-Reporter* received a letter from the "George L. Jackson Squad of the Black Liberation Army."* Claiming credit for Young's murder, the letter declared that this act of "revolutionary violence" was retaliation for "the recent intolerable political assassination of Comrade George L. Jackson in particular and the inhumane torture of inmates in POW (Prisoner of War) Camps in general."

By this time, COINTELPRO had already been exposed, and FBI director J. Edgar Hoover subsequently declared that the illegal surveillance program had been discontinued. But after these recent assassinations of police officers by the BLA, President Nixon told Hoover to carry out a "no punches pulled" investigation. "By God, let's get these bastards," Nixon told Hoover in a conversation after the May killings of Jones and Piagentini.

---

* George Lester Jackson was an influential and militant author and prison inmate, who was killed by a prison guard on August 21, during an alleged escape attempt at San Quentin State Prison.

"I'll go all out on the intelligence on this thing," Hoover replied.

"Go in with everything you've got," ordered Nixon. "Surveillance, electronic and everything."

Hoover initiated a new operation dubbed NEWKILL (New York police killings) and set about rounding up New York Panthers, particularly the "Cleaverites" and other members of radical Black groups, directing his field officers to list "supporters and affiliates of these groups with your file numbers on each, if you have a file. If you have no file, open files."

Many BLA members, however, had already fled New York City and traveled south to Georgia, where they rented a frame house in Fayetteville, about twenty miles south of Atlanta, to be used as a guerrilla training camp. Led by thirty-eight-year-old Army veteran John Leo Thomas, the group conducted target practice and learned firearm maintenance, wilderness skills, first aid techniques, and bank robbery procedures.

After one month of training, on October 7, they robbed their first bank, a branch of the Fulton National Bank. One month later, on November 3, Twymon Myers—who had eluded arrest in New York—and a young BLA newcomer named Fred Hilton (later Kamau Sadiki) allegedly shot to death twenty-seven-year-old Atlanta police officer James Richard Greene as he sat in his police van on a coffee break. After shooting Greene, Hilton and Myers tore off his badge and took his service weapon.

Soon after the shooting, the Fayetteville group abandoned Georgia and drove north, stopping briefly in Chattanooga, Tennessee, and then continued east through North Carolina, where they got into a gunfight with Lieutenant Ted Elmore during a traffic stop. Elmore was shot and paralyzed, and two members of the group were arrested. The few remaining members of the group continued driving until they reached Florida.

Meanwhile, the BLA cell in New York City had its own near misses. On the morning of December 20, two police officers in a cruiser noticed a man acting suspiciously in a Pontiac parked outside a Bankers Trust bank branch in Queens, New York. Moments later, two additional men and one woman entered the car. The officers called in the license plate number and learned the car was stolen. When the Pontiac began to drive off, the cruiser fell in behind them, hitting the lights. After a chase, a window in the Pontiac rolled down, and one of the vehicle's occupants pitched a hand grenade at the police car. The grenade exploded near the cruiser, damaging the car and leaving the officers with slight injuries. The four people jumped out of the Pontiac, hijacked a car, and escaped.

After such a turbulent year and violent end to 1971, the beginning of 1972 could have been an opportune time for the BLA to regroup, strategize, and enjoy a moment of convalescence while hiding out. Instead, the BLA would claim credit for the most ruthless police assassination yet.

On the night of Thursday, January 27, two rookie New York police officers—a White patrolman named Rocco Laurie and Black patrolman Gregory Foster, both in their early twenties—were walking their beat on the Lower East Side when they passed three young Black men at East 11th Street and Avenue B. As soon as they passed, the men turned, raised their guns, and began shooting into the officers' backs. After they fell to the ground, the shooters walked over and emptied their guns into the prone bodies, aiming deliberately for their heads, eyes, and groins, then leaned down to steal their service weapons. According to a witness, one of the three men danced over the bodies and fired a pistol triumphantly into the night sky before escaping.

Like the earlier shootings of police officers, this, too, was followed by a communiqué, sent to the United Press International. The letter began

This is from the George Jackson Squad of the BLACK LIBERATION ARMY about the pigs wiped out in lower Manhattan last night. For too long black people have been callously murdered for the sake of property. Never again! For everyone [sic] of us that are murdered two of you will die. Thinka' bout it! No longer will we tolerate Attica and oppression and exploitation and rape of our Black community. This is the start of our spring offensive.

The communiqué went on to take credit for other bank robberies and police ambushes and signed off as being from the "Olugbala tribe of the Black Liberation Army."

Believed by followers to be an African word meaning "love for the people," Olugbala was adopted by several BLA members, including Twymon Myers, whose tribal name was Kakuyan Olugbala, and Zayd Malik Shakur, who took the tribal name Dedane Olugbala.

Though the BLA had no chain of command or central authority, Zayd was considered, at least by authorities, as an apparent leader of the BLA. He also served as its chief propagandist. In a statement published after the double killings of Patrolmen Piagentini and Jones and Laurie and Foster, Zayd again defended the murders as "revolutionary executions" and "revolutionary justice" and pushed back against critics in the community who objected to the fact that two of the officers—Jones and Foster—were Black. "Many Black people say, 'Right On!' when white policemen have been snuffed out, but have hang ups when it comes to moving on Black policemen," Zayd wrote. He continued:

The Black policeman, Waverly Jones, met with Revolutionary Justice along with his white counterpart Joseph Piagentini in May of last year (1971); and Gregory Foster caught up with the same fate along with his crime partner, Rocco Laurie, in January of this year (1972). The pigs tried to play on the sympathy of the people. Every reactionary and his cousin went into a Machiavellian divide and conquer bag . . . But revolutionary executions are not a question of Black and white. It's a question of who wears the midnight blue.

In the two years after the schism of the Black Panther Party, the deaths of twenty police officers across the country were attributed to the Black Liberation Army. The NYPD pursued suspected BLA members aggressively, making arrests and rounding up suspects, though they hadn't yet gone public with any information about the underground group, whose existence had so far only been conjecture. But finally, on February 17—the day after another shoot-out between the BLA and police in St. Louis, Missouri, which left one BLA member dead and two arrested—a front-page story in the *New York Times* declared that this recent exchange was "regarded by detectives here as the hardest evidence to date of the existence and operations of the Black Liberation Army, a group described by the police as a network of black terrorists gunning for policemen."

The NYPD issued a nationwide alarm for four suspected BLA members and five others who were wanted for questioning in connection with the police murders and bank robberies. Among the five people wanted for questioning, only one was a woman. She was a diminutive, young, intelligent former Black Panther from Queens, and police would soon consider her "the soul of the gang, the mother hen who kept them together, kept them moving, kept them shooting." Her name had come up frequently in connection with BLA activity, as early as the May 1971 ambush outside Hogan's house on Riverside Drive. She was known at first, by her associates and the NYPD, as JoAnne Deborah Chesimard, but she would soon change her name and become infamous, far beyond the boundaries of New York City, as Assata Olugbala Shakur.

12.
THE STUDENT

THE FIRST PHOTOGRAPHS appeared on February 9, 1972, on page three of New York's *Daily News*. Two grainy photographs, printed side by side, near the bottom of the page. The photograph on the right shows a young woman with a stunning Afro, a wide smile across her face, proudly raising her hand high, as though waving to a crowd—or hoping the teacher will call on her for the correct answer. The photograph on the left shows a woman wearing eyeglasses and a wig, frowning and looking over her shoulder, as though anticipating trouble. In her right fist she is gripping a pistol, pointing it at something or someone in front of her. The caption explains that the photo on the right is from JoAnne Chesimard's 1971 Manhattan Community College yearbook. The other photo, from August of the same year, was taken by a hidden surveillance camera and alleges to show the same woman holding up a Queens bank.

The article reports that a national police alarm has been announced, naming Chesimard as one of five Black Liberation Army members "wanted in connection" with the January 27 ambush murder of Patrolmen Gregory Foster and Rocco Laurie in the East Village. Police also suspect Chesimard of being connected to the May 19 machine-gun assault of Patrolmen Nicholas Binetti and Thomas Curry on Riverside Drive, the May 21 ambush murder of Patrolmen Waverly Jones and Joseph Piagentini in Harlem, and the December 20 grenade attack of a police car during a high-speed chase through Queens. In addition to these allegations, Chesimard was also a suspect in the August 23 theft of $7,697 from a Bankers Trust Company bank in Queens, as well as a series of bank robberies in Georgia and Florida.

But how did this bright twenty-four-year-old college student, with no previous criminal record and raised by a supportive family, develop into an alleged serial bank robber, convicted police killer, and fugitive of the law, eventually becoming the first woman to be placed on the FBI's "Top Ten Most Wanted Terrorists" list? How did JoAnne Chesimard become Assata Shakur?

On July 16, 1947, at 4:00 A.M., JoAnne Deborah Byron was born in Brooklyn Women's Hospital, a four-story maternity hospital on Eastern Parkway. Her mother, Doris Johnson, was a schoolteacher who had recently separated from her husband, a World War II veteran. The labor had been long and difficult, and Doris was bedridden at home for a month after her delivery. As she recuperated, baby JoAnne was cared for by Doris's younger sister, Evelyn, who took charge of changing her, feeding her formula, and rocking her to sleep. For the first three years of her life, JoAnne, Doris, Evelyn, and JoAnne's grandparents Frank and Lulu Hill all lived together in a row house in South Jamaica, Queens, in a neighborhood known as Bricktown. When JoAnne was three, her grandparents sold the house and brought Doris and young JoAnne south to Wilmington, North Carolina. JoAnne's grandparents were native North Carolinians, and the family moved into Frank Hill's large and pleasant childhood home on Seventh Avenue, near Cape Fear River. JoAnne would later reminisce about swinging on a green swing on the house's wraparound porch, with "rosebushes in the front yard and a pecan tree in the back."

Her grandparents were proud, Southern-raised Blacks who promoted self-sufficiency, economic security, and personal dignity as the best means of uplifting the race, and they groomed their granddaughter to become a part of Wilmington's "Talented Tenth" of college-educated, prosperous Black Americans. Frank and Lulu Hill taught their granddaughter to be respectful to adults, speak confidently, and never allow herself to be disrespected by anyone, especially White folks. Frank and Lulu Hill could be stern, uncompromising, and frustratingly redundant, but their message nonetheless stuck with JoAnne: "The tactics that my grandparents used were crude, and i hated it when they would repeat everything so often," she later remembered. "But the lessons that they taught me, more than anything else i learned in life, helped me to deal with the things i would face growing up in amerika."*

JoAnne's maternal forebears, the Freemans, carried a certain level of prestige in North Carolina. After gaining emancipation in the years following the Civil War, Alexander and Charity Freeman—whose surname derived from the common practice of formerly enslaved Blacks taking the name Freeman to replace the enslaver's name—acquired ninety-nine acres of underdeveloped beachfront property near Myrtle Grove Sound. By the time of Alexander's death in 1872, he and Charity had added 180 acres to their property. In 1876, the couple's eldest son, Robert Bruce Freeman Sr., purchased an additional 2,500 acres of land in the area between the Atlantic Ocean and Cape Fear River, making him one of the largest landholders in New Hanover County. Upon his death in 1905, his family inherited 5,000 acres, which his son Robert Bruce Freeman Jr. parceled into separate tracts to be occupied by the Freemans and other local Black families.

The Freeman heirs soon helped develop the small hamlet of Seabreeze into a popular destination for Black vacationers, and established, at the northern end of Carolina Beach, the small recreational area known as Freeman Beach. Because Black people in the South were barred from enjoying most beaches, Freeman Beach—one of only two beaches in North Carolina open to Blacks—became a popular destination for Black Carolinians, and the beachfront area euphemistically came to be referred to as Bop City, due to its abundance of lively juke joints. Frank and Lulu Hill moved the family from Queens

---

* In her published writings, Assata uses a lowercase "i" when speaking about herself (except when beginning a sentence), as well as using lowercase for certain proper nouns. When quoting from her work in these pages, her capitalization preferences will be followed.

to Wilmington in hopes of using Lulu's family connections to capitalize on the popularity of Seabreeze and Freeman Beach. In 1951, one year after arriving in Wilmington, they opened Monte Carlo on the Sea—a café, dance hall, and hotel, only a short stroll from the Atlantic Ocean. In its first few years, Freeman Beach brought thousands of visitors during the summer, and Monte Carlo on the Sea developed a reputation as "Seabreeze's finest lodge." JoAnne spent most of her days playing on the beach with her cousins, collecting shells, reading books in the sun, or doing various chores for her grandparents. Years later she would fondly remember those young and carefree days on Freeman Beach: "For me, the beach was a wonderful place, and to this day there is no place on this earth that i love more."

This tranquil beach life was interrupted on October 15, 1954, when Hurricane Hazel made landfall and destroyed most of the buildings in Seabreeze and on Freeman Beach, including Monte Carlo on the Sea. The loss was devastating to Frank and Lulu Hill, who had watched helplessly as their life savings were reduced to rubble. Though some businesses were eventually able to rebuild, it was the beginning of the end for Bop City.

JoAnne was sent back north to New York City to live with her mother and stepfather. She began third grade at P.S. 154 in Queens, a majority-White school. Though she continued to spend summer vacations with her grandparents in Wilmington, she learned about New York life from her aunt Evelyn, who would take her to museums, parks, restaurants, and her first concert: Frankie Lymon and the Teenagers at the Apollo Theater. She would later call Evelyn the "heroine of my childhood," and Evelyn would remember JoAnne— "Joey," as she called her—as "eagerly curious and precocious," attracted at an early age to fine art and poetry. When she learned her best friend, Barbara, was Catholic, JoAnne decided to convert to Catholicism. Before sixth grade was out, she had taken her first communion and would later be confirmed.

As she grew older JoAnne would spend more and more time away from home, wandering the city alone. She would soon begin to leave home for days at a time, staying overnight with new friends she'd meet in the city. When her mother and stepfather separated, Doris took JoAnne and JoAnne's younger sister, Beverly, and moved into an apartment in Parsons-Gardens, a cooperative housing complex in Flushing, Queens. But JoAnne and Doris were now fighting often, and one day JoAnne packed her clothes and left her mother's home for the last time. A young, free-spirited, and rebellious thirteen-year-old, JoAnne was attracted to the bohemian nightlife of Greenwich Village. She stayed in a seedy hotel room, was harassed by men, narrowly avoided being sexually assaulted, and met older people who taught her various street hustles.

JoAnne's life, like all lives, could have gone in many different directions. If she had remained with her grandparents in Wilmington, North Carolina—if Hurricane Hazel hadn't laid waste to the entire property—she may have gone on to inherit the family business and become a respected owner of valuable beachfront property. If she hadn't run away from home at age thirteen, she might not have learned about street life and how to fend for herself. If she hadn't been discovered by a family friend wandering down St. Mark's Place and promptly returned to her aunt, she might've one day ended up strung out or dead in some anonymous Village tenement. And if she hadn't been rescued by Evelyn, encouraged to continue her education, and enrolled in the Borough of Manhattan City College, she might not have joined the Black Panther Party or become the voice of the Black Liberation Army.

JoAnne moved into Evelyn's brownstone apartment on the Upper West Side, and she settled back into her earlier routine of visiting museums and art galleries and strolling through city parks. Though she still liked to wander, her aunt was a hard taskmaster and didn't tolerate JoAnne staying out too long or straying too far.

JoAnne pored over Evelyn's extensive home library and engaged her aunt in wide-ranging discussions. "Evelyn was a store of knowledge and she knew about a whole range of subjects," she recalled. "We were always discussing or debating something. Hanging out with Evelyn, i started to think that i was cool and sophisticated and grown up and that i knew it all. You couldn't tell me nothing. I was just too cool."

Evelyn Williams worked as a social investigator for the Department of Welfare and as a juvenile probation officer in New York City

Children's Court. She went on to study law at St. John's University School of Law in Brooklyn and was one of only two Black students to graduate in an entering class of five hundred.

In 1954, when she was thirty-two years old, Williams was appointed to investigate the welfare of the two children of Ethel and Julius Rosenberg, the married couple and accused communist spies who had recently been executed for conspiracy to commit espionage during World War II. The young boys, Michael and Robert, had been shuffled around from home to home before being placed in the temporary care of the songwriter and noted communist Abel Meeropol and his wife, Anne. Williams's assignment was to determine whether the children should remain with the Meeropols, be placed in custody of their grandmother Sophie Rosenberg, or be institutionalized in the Jewish Child Care Association in upstate New York. Though she admired the Meeropols' care and genuine love for the children, she recommended the boys live with their grandmother to avoid the possibility of later institutionalization. The boys were placed with Sophie Rosenberg, but several months later the Meeropols completed the adoption process to become Michael and Robert's legal guardians, and the boys were returned to their home on Riverside Drive.

Reflecting years later on what had been a complicated, high-profile, and heated case, Williams stated that this experience had been the first time in her professional career that she was "exposed to the way in which lives, especially those that have been the focus of national attention and fall within judicial jurisdiction, can be permanently altered by prejudice and arbitrary decisions." By the time JoAnne moved in with her, Williams had passed the New York State bar exam and had become a criminal defense lawyer, but this earlier career experience with the Rosenberg children would prepare her for another prominent and notorious case some two decades later—with a defendant with whom she was much more familiarly invested.

On Williams's urging, JoAnne attended Cathedral High School—a private, all-girls, Catholic school in Manhattan—but after six months

Afeni Shakur and her husband, Lumumba Shakur, are escorted from an NYPD station, following their arrest during a predawn raid on their Harlem apartment on April 2, 1969. More than a dozen members of the Black Panther Party's Harlem branch were rounded up in police raids that morning and arraigned on charges of conspiracy to kill cops and bomb multiple sites throughout New York City. The defendants soon became known as the Panther 21 or the NY 21, and the ensuing trial would become the longest and most expensive trial in New York City history to date. | **Jacob Harris/AP Photo**

Members of the Black Panther Party's New York chapters march on July 22, 1968, in support of Black Panther Party co-founder and Minister of Defense Huey P. Newton, on trial for the murder of an Oakland, California, police officer. One year later, many of these demonstrators would face their own high-profile trial as Panther 21 defendants. *Left to right:* Lumumba Shakur, unidentified, Zayd Malik Shakur, unidentified, Michael "Cetewayo" Tabor, "Debbie," Sekou Odinga, Ralph "Yedwa Sudan" White, Kuwasi Balagoon, and unidentified others. | **MPI/Stringer**

After his assassination in 1965, Malcolm X (El-Hajj Malik El-Shabazz) became a martyr and patron saint to younger generations of Black militants, who had grown weary of the incrementalism and failed promises of the civil rights movement. Malcolm's message of self-determination, self-defense, and Black nationhood inspired the students and activists who would go on to form the Black Panther Party, the Revolutionary Action Movement, and the Republic of New Afrika. | **Herman Hiller/***World Telegram & Sun*

The storefront office of the Black Panther Party's Harlem chapter, 2026 Seventh Avenue, Harlem, New York City. | Fred W. McDarrah/MUUS Collection via Getty Images

Afeni was bailed out from the Women's House of Detention in 1970 through donations from supporters. She was tasked with hosting fundraisers and delivering public speeches, such as this one on April 4, to draw attention to the ongoing case and to raise bail funds for her fellow defendants. | David Fenton

Rally in support of the Panther 21 defendants, New York City, November 17, 1969. | **David Fenton**

Zayd Malik Shakur, Minister of Information for the Black Panther Party in New York and older brother of Lumumba. | **Stephen Shames/Polaris**

"Free the Panther 21" buttons. | **Schomburg Center for Research in Black Culture, Art and Artifacts Division, The New York Public Library**

While out on bail, Afeni attended the Revolutionary People's Constitutional Convention (RPCC) in Philadelphia, along with her brother-in-law, Zayd (*in striped pants*). Organized by the Black Panther Party and held over four days in September 1970, the convention brought together multiple radical left organizations and attracted thousands of attendees from across the country. | **David Fenton**

Afeni and Zayd sharing a light moment at the RPCC. Though Afeni faced a potential life sentence and Zayd was tasked with keeping the Harlem Panther chapter afloat while its leaders and members were in jail, Afeni and Zayd still held fast to moments of warmth and levity. | **David Fenton**

Afeni at the RPCC.
| **David Fenton**

Top right: In the summer of 1970, while out on bail, Afeni had an affair with a New Jersey Black Panther named Billy Garland and soon discovered she was pregnant. The child grew inside of her as she defended herself in court against charges that threatened to put her in prison for the rest of her life. Her son, Tupac Amaru Shakur, was born one month after she and her co-defendants were acquitted on all charges. | **Stephen Shames/Polaris**; *Bottom right:* During a break in the Panther 21 trial, Afeni speaks with her father-in-law and Shakur family patriarch, Salahdeen Shakur, outside the Manhattan Criminal Courthouse. | **Stephen Shames/Polaris**

A young, intelligent, and eager recruit to the Harlem chapter of the Black Panther Party, JoAnne Chesimard quickly grew disillusioned with the Party and joined other defectors in the clandestine offshoot group the Black Liberation Army (BLA). She changed her name and within a few years had become infamous as Assata Olugbala Shakur, accused by authorities of being the "high priestess" and "mother hen" of the deadly BLA, who "kept them together, kept them moving, kept them shooting."
| **Stephen Shames/Polaris**

As a legionnaire of the Republic of New Afrika, community organizer, and clinic administrator, Mutulu Shakur had an unbridled energy and enthusiasm for Black liberation that inspired friends and colleagues, while also eliciting the occasional complaint of arrogance and hubris.

Mutulu and Afeni began an intimate relationship in the mid-seventies and had a daughter together, Sekyiwa Shakur, born on October 3, 1975. Mutulu holds Sekyiwa at a birthday party at a family friend's home in the Bronx. | **Yaasmyn D. Fula**

Mutulu was recruited into the South Bronx's radical Lincoln Detox collective in 1970 as a political education instructor. But after discovering acupuncture as an effective tool for combating heroin withdrawal symptoms, he became a certified and licensed acupuncturist, going on to revolutionize grassroots community healthcare.

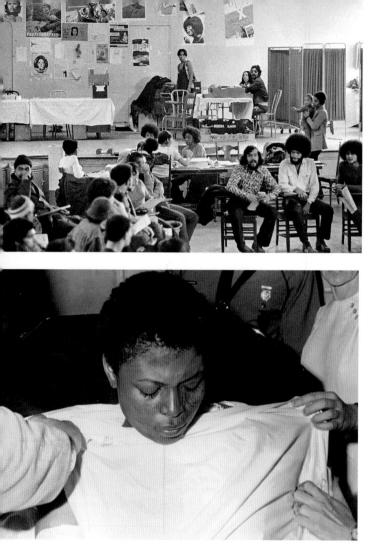

In 1970, members of the Young Lords and the Black Panthers established Lincoln Detox, a drug detoxification center inside an auditorium in the South Bronx's Lincoln Hospital. People with heroin addictions were given a radical political education along with holistic treatments to help them kick their addictions. (Notice Che Guevara, Mao Tse-tung, Angela Davis, and Malcolm X posters on the wall, November 16, 1973.) | **Neal Boenzi/***The New York Times***/Redux**

Assata in Middlesex County Hospital, after her capture on the New Jersey Turnpike in May 1973. She accused New Jersey state troopers of beating her, resulting in multiple injuries and wounds. | **Middlesex County, New Jersey, Prosecutor's Office**

On October 20, 1981, two police officers and a guard were killed during the robbery of a Brink's armored truck in Nanuet, New York. The robbery led to multiple raids and arrests of suspected radicals in the movement throughout New York and New Jersey and initiated a nationwide manhunt for the group's purported ringleader, Mutulu. | **AP Photo/File**

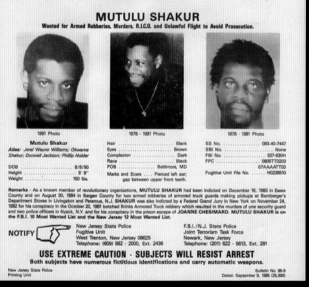

Wanted poster for Assata and Mutulu, distributed by New Jersey State Police. Mutulu was accused, among other charges, of aiding in Assata's 1979 escape from prison. Assata fled to Cuba, while Mutulu remained a fugitive until his capture in Los Angeles in 1986. | **New Jersey State Police Printing Unit**

Top right: Fourteen-year-old Tupac in Baltimore, Maryland, 1985. | **Yaasmyn D. Fula**

Bottom right: Sekou Odinga is led by police officers to his arraignment on February 11, 1982. Charged with racketeering, conspiracy, and aiding in Assata's 1979 prison escape, Sekou argued he was a political prisoner and a prisoner of war. "I am a New Afrikan soldier," he told the court, "and we have an absolute right to fight for our freedom." | **Bettmann via Getty Images**

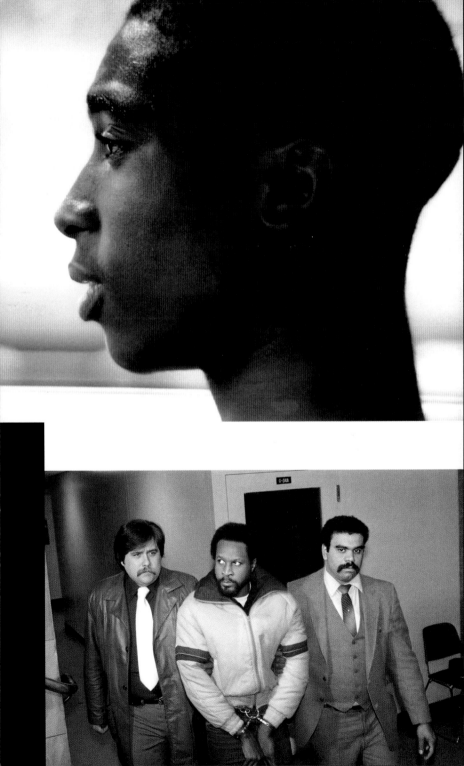

Top left: Tupac with family and friends, visiting the Shakur family patriarch, Salahdeen. *Back row, left to right:* Tupac, unidentified, Afeni, Salahdeen, Sekyiwa, and Shadia Odinga (Sekou's daughter). *Front row, left to right:* unidentified, Ali Bey Hassan, and Anochi Odinga (Sekou's son).
| Yaasmyn D. Fula

Top right: Tupac and his mother, Afeni, share a personal moment. Tupac maintained a deep respect and admiration for Afeni throughout his life, continuing to learn from her and seek her guidance. (Notice the Digital Underground's "The Humpty Dance" poster on the wall.)
| Yaasmyn D. Fula

Tupac at his aunt Gloria's home in New York City in 1992, with (*left to right*) his cousin Jamala Lesane; Panther 21 defendant Ali Bey Hassan; his sister Sekyiwa; and his mother, Afeni. Tupac is holding a copy of *Sunviews*, written by Panther 21 defendant Sundiata Acoli, who was serving a life sentence at the time for his role in the 1973 fatal shoot-out on the New Jersey Turnpike. After five decades in prison, Sundiata was granted parole in May 2022.
| Yaasmyn D. Fula

Assata in Cuba, holding the manuscript pages of her autobiography, October 7, 1987. | **Ozier Muhammad/***Newsday* **RM via Getty Images**

In May 2005, the rappers Yasiin Bey (formerly Mos Def), pictured here, and Talib Kweli, together with New York City Council member Charles Barron, hosted an "Assata Shakur Is Welcome Here" demonstration, in protest of the recent million-dollar bounty placed on Assata (the bounty has since increased to two million dollars). | **Johnny Nunez/WireImage via Getty**

An interactive museum exhibit exploring Tupac's life and career, called *Wake Me When I'm Free*, opened in Los Angeles in January 2022. The exhibit also features a tribute to Afeni and her work in the Black Panther Party. This sculpture, *Hang In There*, created for the exhibit by Manza Studios, shows a dripping Black Power fist raised above an American flag surrounded by three hundred handcuffs, representing the three-hundred-plus-year sentence Afeni and other Panther 21 defendants faced if convicted. The exhibit includes a reproduction of the Harlem Panther office, with Panther flags and red, black, and green liberation flags hanging from the ceiling. More than fifty years after the Panther 21 raid and historic trial, the legacy of the Shakur family is still inspiring new generations of students, artists, and activists. | **Valerie Macon/AFP via Getty Images**

she transferred to a public high school before dropping out altogether at age seventeen. She worked a series of menial jobs, drifted in and out of friendships and relationships, idled her days away, and grew listless and dissatisfied with the monotonousness of her routine. She was searching for purpose and growing restless: "My patience was zero," she recalled. "I didn't want to wait for something to happen. I was into living and living for now. I was hungry, starving for life, but at the same time i was growing more and more cynical every day. I wanted to go everywhere, do everything, and be everything, all at the same time. I wanted to experience everything, know how everything felt."

JoAnne realized she would eventually need a more lucrative occupation than these tedious, low-paying jobs, so she decided to go back to school. After her aunt helped her obtain her GED, JoAnne enrolled in Borough of Manhattan Community College (BMCC). Unlike the other schools she'd attended, BMCC had a high percentage of Black and Brown students, and she entered school when Black nationalism and Afrocentrism were at the height of popularity in college campuses across the country, especially in New York. From attending poetry readings and African cultural events to learning about the history of slave rebellions to befriending students who identified as Black Muslims, Garveyites, and New Afrikans, JoAnne was, for the first time in her life, exposed to a new way of thinking, a new consciousness. She went to demonstrations and protests. She had impassioned late-night arguments with friends about revolution, socialism, nationalism, and anti-imperialism. She and one hundred other students were arrested on trespassing charges after chaining and locking the entrance to a building on campus to demand more Black studies programs and the hiring of more Black faculty members. She took an African name, Ybumi Oladele—which she promptly discarded. She cut her conk and grew a natural. By and large, it was a typical college experience for a young Black woman in the 1960s.

After graduating from BMCC, JoAnne enrolled in the City College of New York (CCNY), where she met student, activist, and U.S. Air Force veteran Louis E. Chesimard. The couple quickly married, but they just as quickly discovered they'd had different notions of domestic life, and they separated after one year. They made their divorce official three years later, but JoAnne kept her husband's last name. When she and Louis separated, JoAnne dropped out of CCNY and moved across the country to Berkeley, California.

The Bay Area at the start of the 1970s was the epicenter of countercultural movements and youthful idealism. Anti-war demonstrators, Chicano activist groups, Asian American activist groups, Black liberation groups, women's liberation groups, "Third World" liberation groups, students' rights groups, and free speech activists fanned out across college campuses, city parks, and street corners, giving speeches, distributing leaflets, and organizing rallies and sit-ins. For a young, newly conscious woman who had never ventured outside of New York City or Wilmington, the Bay Area was cloud nine, and JoAnne went bounding through San Francisco and the East Bay, exploring one group after the other. She eventually found her way to Oakland to visit the national headquarters of what she remembered as being the "most important organization on my list to check out." As JoAnne approached the front gate of the Black Panther Party headquarters, she had little reason to believe this would be the moment that would determine the rest of her life.

"A brother opened the door and i nervously blurted out that i was from New York and had come to check out the Party," she recalled. "He acted like he was glad to see me and brought me into a room to meet some of the other Panthers."

JoAnne had already been familiar with the Black Panther Party, having seen the images and read the stories of the armed takeover of the California State Capitol in 1967. She had also witnessed with anger and frustration the roundup of the New York Panthers, whom she considered "some of the baddest, most politically educated sisters and brothers in the Party." But though she had respected the Party and had gotten to know some of the Panthers back home, she had been hesitant to join, due to what she perceived as the arrogance and chauvinism of some members. Nevertheless, she was impressed by the Oakland Panthers and found herself often returning to headquarters, visiting other Bay Area offices, working for newspaper distribution, and becoming friends with Party members. By the end of her California visit, she had converted. "Of all the things i had wanted to be when i was a little girl, a revolutionary certainly wasn't one of them," she later reflected. "And now it was the only thing i wanted to do."

JoAnne returned to New York in the summer of 1970 and went directly to the Harlem Panther office on Seventh Avenue to sign up. She joined, however, during an inauspicious time for the Party. The Panther 21 conspiracy trial was underway, with much of the local leadership in jail, and the enmity between the New York and Oakland Panthers was escalating day by day, with each side accusing the other of either mismanaging funds or steering the Party in misguided directions. But operations meanwhile continued to function, and JoAnne was kept busy selling newspapers, attending political education classes, and waking up early to serve free breakfast to children. She was also assigned to the Party's medical cadre, where she was responsible for scheduling health appointments for Party members and administering free tuberculosis and sickle-cell anemia tests to the community. Though Lumumba Shakur was incarcerated and Sekou Odinga was in Algerian exile, a number of Panther leaders were out on bail, including Afeni Shakur, Joan Bird, Jamal Joseph, Cetewayo, and Dhoruba bin Wahad, all of whom helped train the new recruit. But JoAnne would find her closest friend and ally in Lumumba's older brother and Deputy Minister of Information for New York, Zayd Malik Shakur.

Thirty years old and now tasked with leading the New York Panthers through the organization's most consequential moment—with Panther fighting against Panther and most of the New York leadership facing potential life sentences in prison—Zayd remained a figure of patience and calm, even while unsuccessfully attempting to make peace between Huey P. Newton and the expelled New York Panthers. He and JoAnne would share deep conversations about politics, organize fundraisers and raise support for the Panther 21, or just sit around JoAnne's Hamilton Heights apartment talking about music and literature.

To JoAnne, Zayd was a rare exception in the Black Panther Party: sophisticated, polite, and respectful to women. JoAnne experienced what Afeni had herself experienced when she first met Zayd's brother, Lumumba, and his father, Salahdeen, two years earlier. "Zayd always treated me and all the other sisters with respect," she remembered, adding that he "refused to become part of the macho cult that was an official body in the BPP."

As much as she respected Zayd, JoAnne soon began to lose patience with much of the other Party leadership, including Newton himself, whom she viewed as uninspiring, erratic, and pompous. Newton, now calling himself the Supreme Commander and the Supreme Servant, had built up a cult of personality about himself, expelling renegade Party members while holed up in his penthouse apartment, surrounded by bodyguards. Not only that, but she noticed that even New York Party members were becoming more doctrinaire, suspicious, and convinced that moles had infiltrated the Party and that their offices would be raided by the police at any moment.

Despite Zayd's efforts, the schism between New York and the Central Committee in Oakland had become insurmountable, and JoAnne's frustration grew as she watched the community programs like healthcare and free breakfast for children get shelved or abandoned. The Party's earlier sense of unity and purpose, too, had become replaced by factionalism and contempt. "This Party was a lot different from the Black Panther Party i had fallen in love with," she recalled. "Everything felt different. The easy, friendly openness had been replaced by fear and paranoia. The beautiful revolutionary creativity i had loved so much was gone. And replaced by dogmatic stagnation."

One day, JoAnne asked Zayd to come over to her apartment, where she spoke for hours, confessing her concerns over the direction of the Party. Zayd was the Party leader she trusted most, and he was one of her closest friends, so she believed he would agree with her or at least hear her out, but when he abruptly left her apartment without offering either consolation or support, she was crushed. She and Zayd wouldn't speak again for a long time. Shortly after, in 1971, JoAnne decided to leave the Black Panther Party, less than one year after joining.

But even after quitting the Party, JoAnne continued to be affected by fear and paranoia. She believed her home was tapped, that the FBI was recording her phone conversations, that detectives were following her everywhere she went, even though she hadn't been part of Party leadership and had only been a rank-and-file member, low in the organization's hierarchy. She hadn't had any prior trouble with the law, aside from her arrest for trespassing during a college campus protest four years earlier, as a student at BMCC. She was, at the time of her departure from the Party, not a significant priority to the New York Police Department or the federal government.

She could have quietly returned to City College, where she was still enrolled as a student, and finished her studies without incident. She would later claim that police were rumored to be monitoring her because they believed she might lead them to bin Wahad and Cetewayo, the Panther 21 defendants who had recently jumped bail and went underground, possibly even hiding out in JoAnne's Hamilton Heights apartment. Whatever the reason behind her suspicions, JoAnne decided to disappear, too, to abandon her apartment and join the other renegade Panthers and go underground. Her relative anonymity wouldn't last long.

On the evening of Monday, April 5, 1971, a twenty-three-year-old woman arrived at the Statler Hilton Hotel in Midtown Manhattan and knocked on the door to one of the rooms. The occupant of the room, C. Richard "Rick" Gibbons, claimed to be a proprietor of a ski shop in Taylor, Michigan. When Gibbons answered the door, the woman asked, "Is there a party going on here?" When Gibbons replied that there was no party, the woman took out a revolver and demanded money. Gibbons and the woman began to fight over the gun, and it discharged into the woman's stomach. Severely wounded, she fled the hotel but was apprehended two blocks away by an off-duty police officer. The woman was brought by police to French Hospital on West 30th Street, where she was booked on charges of attempted robbery, felonious assault, reckless endangerment, and possession of a deadly weapon. The woman was described by police simply as being a "student at City College" and identified as JoAnne Chesimard.

From the hospital, JoAnne called her aunt and asked her to represent her on the felony charges. But after posting bail, JoAnne disappeared again. Williams wouldn't hear from her niece until two years later, when she heard a startling news flash at 1:30 A.M. on May 2, 1973. By that point, the "eagerly curious and precocious" young woman she'd called Joey—who had once loved nothing more than to play on her family's beachfront property, accompany her aunt to museums and art galleries, and write poetry—had become Assata Olugbala Shakur: the subject of a nationwide manhunt, wanted for a series of bank robberies and police shootings in New York, Georgia, and Florida, and described by police as the "soul" of the Black Liberation Army.

13.
JOANNE OF ARC

WHEN ASSATA SHAKUR was apprehended on the New Jersey Turnpike on the night of May 2, 1973, she wasn't widely known beyond New York law enforcement and a small inner circle of underground Black militants. She hadn't even yet been known as Assata Shakur; she was still JoAnne Chesimard, one of a handful of suspects wanted in connection with a series of bank holdups and other robberies. She hadn't been a popular orator, political organizer, or revolutionary theoretician. Her time in the Black Panther Party had been so brief and inconspicuous, moreover, that she was not acknowledged, in newspapers or police statements, as a former Panther. What fame or notoriety she'd had at the time of her capture two years later had, ironically, been largely manufactured by the police, specifically NYPD Deputy Commissioner Robert Daley, who was responsible for Assata's later portrayal as "the soul of the movement" and the "mother hen who kept them together, kept them moving, kept them shooting." Local newspapers ran with this story line, printing that the captured suspect had been the "Black lib chief," a "fanatical black 'Joan of Arc,'" and the "high priestess of the Black Liberation Army."

But these sensationalist, hyperbolic, and racist and sexist characterizations were, by and large, media inventions. These portrayals of Assata not only inaccurately represented her role in the Black Liberation Army; they misrepresented the BLA itself as a tightly structured, disciplined, guerrilla army. What newspaper reporters and the general public didn't understand is that, when she was captured on that fateful May night, Assata Shakur was more of an enigma than a leader.*

Between the time of the hotel robbery attempt and her capture two years later on the turnpike, little is known for certain about Assata's activities. All that can be confirmed about this brief time with any level of certainty are the numerous charges brought against her. But during those two years she spent on the run, the allegations against Assata continued to grow in size and scope until it became impossible for the public to separate the real Assata Shakur from the police fabrication. Nevertheless, while she may not have been the most active or integral member of the BLA, she would go on to become its most prominent member.

The path that led her to this prominence was winding, unplanned, and frequently violent, beginning at around the same time as the origin of the BLA itself. After leaving the Black Panther Party in early 1971, Assata connected with a small group of other breakaway Panthers, who had gone underground with the intention of waging guerrilla warfare against the police. Using a town house at 757 Beck Street in the Bronx as their meeting place and safe house, they amassed weapons and medical supplies. This group, which hadn't yet adopted the name Black Liberation Army, consisted primarily of young Cleaverite Panthers, including the fugitive Panther 21 defendant Dhoruba bin Wahad, a Queens Panther named Andrew Jackson, Frank Fields, Mark Holder, and Assata. All were in their early twenties, with the exception of Holder, who was still a teenager, and bin Wahad, who, at twenty-six, had seniority. This small, loosely organized clique began by robbing drug dealers and so-

---

* Though she hadn't yet changed her name from JoAnne Chesimard and wouldn't become famous as Assata Shakur until after her 1973 arrest, for the sake of consistency she will be referred to as Assata Shakur for the remainder of these pages.

cial clubs for money. "We bashed down a lot of doors, man," recalled bin Wahad years later. "We were like black cops."

On April 19, the group suffered its first casualty, setting off an irreversible chain of events. Two police officers—Sergeant Howard Steward, a Black officer, and White patrolman Anthony Plate—were alerted by a passerby to three Black men on Harlem's West 121st Street, allegedly discussing a robbery. When the officers ordered the men—Harold Russell, Robert Vickers, and Anthony "Kimu Olugbala" White, all members of the Beck Street clique—into a tenement hallway to frisk them, one man, believed to be Anthony White, pulled out a pistol and began shooting.

Officer Plate was hit three times in the face; he was critically wounded but survived. Officer Steward was shot in the upper thigh as he returned fire, emptying his service revolver. Reinforcements soon arrived and found White critically wounded and hiding in a basement with four bullet wounds in his chest. Police arrested him and brought him to Harlem Hospital to recover, charged him with the attempted murder of the two police officers, and held him in the Manhattan House of Detention. Twenty-year-old Harold Russell died from Steward's bullet. Vickers had been shot in the upper body but managed to escape. He returned to the Beck Street safe house, where Assata—applying the training she'd received as part of the Black Panther Party's medical cadre—was able to remove the bullet.

The group demanded retribution for Russell's death. As Malcolm X's birthday fell exactly one month later, on May 19, this date was chosen as the first official action of the Black Liberation Army: the machine-gun assault of Officers Thomas Curry and Nicholas Binetti on Riverside Drive. But this fledgling and leaderless group soon lost whatever counted as its main organizer. Bin Wahad was arrested on June 5 after the attempted holdup of the Triple-O Social Club, and he was later charged with the attempted murder of Curry and Binetti. He and six other New York Panthers, including Holder, Jackson, Fields, and Jamal Joseph, were later indicted for the April murder of *Black Panther* newspaper distributor Samuel Napier.

Regardless of these setbacks, the BLA didn't retreat or dissolve; in fact, the group stepped up its campaign, graduating from robbing drug dealers and social clubs to robbing banks.

The first successful bank job was on August 23 at the Bankers

Trust bank branch in Queens. A half dozen armed BLA members—four men and two women—participated in the robbery, making off with almost $7,700. Soon after, surveillance photos of the disguised but unmasked suspects were printed in newspapers and plastered across subway stations and bank teller windows throughout the city. Police believed one of the two women—wearing a towering wig and thick-rimmed eyeglasses—to be Assata, who was still a fugitive after the failed hotel stickup. She was also wanted for questioning in the murder of Napier, as well as the May shooting of Patrolmen Curry and Binetti.

Deciding that they needed to skip town until the heat died down, Assata and several other fugitive BLA members left New York in the late summer of 1971, drove south to Georgia, and marshaled at a house on Fayetteville Road, outside of Atlanta. In the nearby woods, they were alleged to have engaged in guerrilla warfare training exercises—wilderness survival, weapons cleaning, and target practice—with Assata providing first aid lessons. The seventeen-person group was largely made up of the Beck Street clique, including Fields, Holder, Jackson, Twymon Myers, and Kamau Sadiki. The group soon scattered into smaller units, taking up residence at temporary safe houses and motels throughout the South. For three months, from October to December, police would attribute numerous bank and store robberies in Georgia and Florida to the BLA, as well as the November 3 murder of Atlanta police officer James Greene and the November 11 shooting of sheriff's deputy Ted Elmore in Catawba County, North Carolina. The BLA, however, did not get away entirely unscathed.

On November 7, Andrew Jackson, Ronald Anderson, and Samuel Cooper were arrested in Atlanta under suspicion of robbing a supermarket. Four others were arrested on November 11 for the shooting of Deputy Elmore. Weakened and diminished, what remained of the original team were now scattered and left to their own devices. Most headed back north. Jackson, Anderson, and Cooper escaped from DeKalb County jail on December 12 and eventually joined the others in New York. The final three holdouts reconvened in Florida and checked into a hotel in Odessa, a small suburb of Tampa, on December 30. When a suspicious hotel employee called the police, FBI agents arrived the next day and quietly arrested thirty-nine-year-old John Leo Thomas and a twenty-three-year-old woman named Ignae

Ruth Gittens, who were both wanted for the Queens bank robbery. Rather than surrendering, twenty-three-year-old Frank Fields engaged the agents in a brief gun battle before being shot and killed.

After the fugitive guerrillas regrouped in New York at the start of 1972, the NYPD and the FBI would begin to connect the BLA to the growing epidemic of robberies, stickups, and police assassinations throughout the city. And though the BLA professed to be a leaderless and autonomous militia group, law enforcement set their sights on one member in particular as its implicit commander, as the "'matriarch' of the Black Liberation Army." Meanwhile, as allegations against Assata continued to mount, so did her growing notoriety.

On March 16, 1972, a Brooklyn bank was robbed of $90,000, with one police officer shot in the hand and neck. The getaway driver was reported to be a woman. "Was That JoAnne?" asked the *Daily News*. But by the end of the year, some members of the BLA apparently decided robbing banks carried too much risk, now that many of their photos were plastered across the city and posted in multiple banks in connection with earlier robberies. Still in need of money, they returned to stickups and petty larceny.

On December 28, Assata and four others were alleged to have entered Iesha's Dugout Bar and Grill in Brooklyn armed with shotguns and pistols. Assata emptied the cash register of $50, and the bartender, James Freeman, was abducted and driven to the former Brooklyn Navy Yard. The kidnappers left behind a ransom note demanding $20,000 from the bar owner, but Freeman managed to escape and called the police. Five days later, on January 2, 1973, Assata and three others, including Andrew Jackson and Twymon Myers, were alleged to have robbed a social club in Brooklyn. During the robbery, thirty-one-year-old Richard Nelson was shot and killed.

Later that month, on January 23, the BLA suffered its next casualties when Anthony "Kimu Olugbala" White, who had recently escaped from the Manhattan House of Detention, and Woody "Changa Olugbala" Green—wanted in connection to the 1972 murder of police officers Foster and Laurie—were killed during a late-night shoot-out with police at the Big T Corner Lounge in Brooklyn. Just like when Harold Russell was killed during the shoot-out in Harlem two years earlier, the BLA demanded retaliation.

On the evening of Thursday, January 25, Patrolman Vincent Imperato and his partner and younger brother, Carlo, were sitting in their squad car in the Brownsville section of Brooklyn when a Black man wearing a tan raincoat stepped out of a nearby car and began firing on them from an automatic rifle. The officers managed to drive away and escaped with minor wounds. Two days later, Officers Roy Pollina and Michael O'Reilly were similarly ambushed by three people, who fired a barrage of bullets from a shotgun and two automatic rifles, including a submachine gun, as the officers idled at a stoplight on Baisley Boulevard in St. Albans, Queens. These two officers also escaped with nonfatal wounds. Police named six familiar suspects, including Myers, Jackson, Sadiki, and Assata.

After this second ambush, Police Commissioner Patrick V. Murphy authorized one thousand extra tours of duty for officers in the Brooklyn North Command, then received approval from Mayor John Lindsay to add seven thousand additional tours of duty across the entire city, supported by plainclothes officers and unmarked squad cars, along with the hiring of six thousand more police officers. Robert McKiernan, president of the Patrolmen's Benevolent Association, announced his plans to equip every patrol car with a shotgun. "We have a guerrilla war in New York City today," he said, "and the Police Department should be taking the necessary steps to meet this challenge before any more policemen are attacked."

"Every cop on the streets of New York yesterday was on the lookout for six Black Liberation Army members," declared the *Daily News* on Tuesday, January 30. "Former residences and known hangouts of Black Liberation Army members were under surveillance by heavily armed detectives. Friends and relatives of the militants also were being sought for questioning."

By this point, Assata's reputation was cemented, owing in large part to Daley, whose article "Target Blue: The Story Behind the Police Assassinations" was published in the February 12, 1973, issue of *New York* magazine, weeks before Assata's capture. Daley connected multiple BLA actions to Assata and declared without proof that she "may in fact be their leader—a City College girl who was once shot in the stomach during a stickup and who later said she was glad she had been shot because now she no longer feared police bullets." Regardless of the veracity of these claims, local media ran with this romantic idea of Assata as the quintessential leader of a roving band of American bandits and outlaws. As the *Daily News* hyperbolically reported in May: "In a 15-month period her criminal reputation exceeded such heralded female felons as Bonnie Parker and Ma Barker."

While the NYPD combed the streets of New York and the FBI conducted a multistate manhunt for Assata, her aunt, Evelyn Williams, anxiously kept herself updated with news and rumors of her fugitive niece: "For two years I had spent my nights monitoring the radio news stations," she later recalled. "In the early hours, before eventful news breaks were reported, dead spots were filled in with rumors of what militants called 'Assata sightings.' She was reported to have been seen in different states. On the West Coast. Conducting a training camp in the use of weapons and guerrilla warfare on a farm in Georgia. Hiding out in a Brooklyn armory. Leisurely walking along East 23rd Street in New York City, flanked by serious-looking Black men who inspired such fear in the observing policemen that they refused to apprehend her without a platoon backup."

Williams would finally hear from her niece in early May 1973, when she received a phone call from Middlesex General Hospital in New Brunswick, New Jersey, where Assata lay in critical condition, with multiple gunshot wounds, shackled to a hospital bed and guarded around the clock by shotgun-wielding state troopers.

The New Jersey Turnpike is one of the country's busiest thoroughfares, extending from the southernmost part of the state to the northernmost, a distance of more than one hundred miles. It had a reputation for being a road where Black drivers were more likely than Whites to be stopped and harassed by state troopers. If you were a Black driver with Black passengers in the early 1970s, explained attorney Richard Fischbein, "you could guarantee that, if you drove from New York down to Atlantic City, at least once but probably two or three times you'd be pulled over."

The three occupants of the 1965 white Pontiac LeMans were aware that driving on the turnpike late at night was hazardous. They knew they would be noticed by New Jersey state troopers, and yet they decided it was worth the risk, or else they had been on the lam for so long—living underground, running from place to place—that their judgment was clouded. Behind the driver's wheel was Sundiata Acoli (formerly Clark Squire), the NASA computer programmer, finance minister for the Harlem Panthers, and acquitted Panther 21 defendant. In the passenger seat was Assata. Sitting in the back seat was Zayd Malik Shakur, who had been Assata's closest friend and confidant during her short tenure in the Black Panther Party. Though she and Zayd's three-year friendship had been especially formative to Assata's political development, she revered the thirty-six-year-old Acoli as an elder Panther as well as a kind and devoted warrior. "There is something about Sundiata that exudes calm," she would later reflect. "From every part of his being you can sense the presence of revolutionary spirit and fervor. And his love for Black people is so intense that you can almost touch it and hold it in your hand."

Assata, Zayd, and Acoli were heading south on the turnpike just after midnight on May 2. Police would later assert that Zayd and Acoli were taking Assata to a hideout in Philadelphia, then planning to continue to Washington, D.C. Assata would testify that she was on her way to Baltimore to begin a bar waitressing job arranged for her by Zayd, as though the most wanted woman in the country could simply tie on an apron and begin a new life serving cocktails. Regardless of the purpose of their trip, they were not halfway through New Jersey before they were noticed.

After stopping for snacks at a Howard Johnson's restaurant at the Alexander Hamilton rest stop near Newark, the trio continued south, passing the East Brunswick section of the turnpike when, between 12:30 and 12:45 A.M., twenty-nine-year-old New Jersey State Trooper James M. Harper spotted the Pontiac bearing Vermont plates, with three Black occupants. He hit the lights. Harper would later claim that he pulled the car over either because it was "slightly" exceeding the speed limit or "because it had a faulty tail light." Because of the notoriety of the turnpike, however, the most likely traffic violation the occupants committed was driving while Black.

Acoli pulled over near exit 9, about two hundred yards south of the Turnpike Authority's administration building. Harper stopped his vehicle behind the Pontiac and radioed for backup. Thirty-four-year-old Trooper Werner Foerster arrived soon after. Harper approached the driver's side, asked Acoli for his license, and, allegedly noticing a discrepancy on the license, told Acoli to step out and stand with Foerster at the rear of the car for questioning. In another testimony, Harper claimed that Foerster had reached into the Pontiac and held up an automatic pistol and ammunition clip and said, "Jim, look what I found."

Harper testified that he ordered Assata and Zayd to place their hands in their laps and not move, but Assata's "hand kept moving down to the right side of her right leg." All at once, Harper claimed, "her eyes went wide open, her teeth were showing," and she fired a single shot, striking Harper in the shoulder. Harper—who continued to be inconsistent with his later recollection of events—either ducked for cover behind his cruiser and fired his gun wildly into the Pontiac, or staggered, confused and bleeding, into the Turnpike Authority building and said modestly, "I've been shot. My car's outside."

As Harper sheltered inside the administration building, Acoli jumped back into the Pontiac and sped off as three patrol cars in the area followed in pursuit. Five miles south on the turnpike, Trooper Robert Palentchar spotted the Pontiac on the side of the road and saw Acoli escaping into a nearby wooded area. Palentchar shouted for him to stop. When Acoli continued running, Palentchar began shooting, firing all the rounds in his gun, but he didn't strike Acoli. Moments later, he saw Assata walking toward him from fifty feet away, her arms covered in blood and raised to the sky in surrender. In a nearby ditch on the shoulder of the road lay the mortally wounded body of thirty-three-year-old Zayd Malik Shakur.

Trooper Foerster's body was found up the road, dead from multiple gunshot wounds. An ambulance brought Assata to Middlesex General Hospital, with gunshot wounds in her left shoulder and both of her arms. A massive manhunt was conducted for Acoli, with helicopters, bloodhounds, and a house-to-house search in East Brunswick and Milltown. He was discovered nearly forty hours later, hiding in a thick underbrush, two miles away from the abandoned Pontiac. He was unarmed, covered in dirt, and exhausted. "I give up, man," he said as he surrendered.

Zayd Malik Shakur's funeral service was held on Monday, May 7. He was wrapped in a white shroud, according to Islamic rites. Since he was a Navy veteran, he was interred at the Long Island National Cemetery. Services were held at the Marcus Jackson Funeral Home in Harlem, attended by hundreds of mourners, while supporters outside distributed leaflets that said, "Support the Black Liberation Army." Zayd's coffin was decorated by two floral sprays, as well as a red, black, and green liberation flag, a Black Panther flag, and a Puerto Rican independence flag. Six bullets of various calibers were placed on his chest.

Among the mourners were Zayd's younger brother, Lumumba; his father, Salahdeen Shakur; and Salahdeen's wife, Mariyama. Zayd was the first casualty for the Shakurs, and the family wept and consoled one another. With a gray cloak across his shoulders and a white skullcap on his head, Salahdeen said his eldest son "was a struggler, he was a revolutionary—he died for a good cause." Pointing out that his son had never been convicted of a crime, Salahdeen added, "The only crime he was convicted of was being black in America."

The violent confrontation at the side of the New Jersey Turnpike marked the end of Zayd's years of leadership, companionship, and radical insurrection. But it was only the beginning of Assata's long and agonizing ordeal—and the beginning of her transformation from a largely unknown soldier in the Black liberation struggle into an international icon.

14.
NOTHING TO LOSE
BUT OUR CHAINS

HER FACE IS bruised and swollen. Her hair, which had once been styled into a large and proud Afro, is now only a few inches long. She is grievously thin. Her right arm is wrapped in a sling, paralyzed from when the trooper's bullet severed her median nerve. Her clavicle has also been shattered, by a bullet passing through her shoulder. A bloodied bandage covers a bullet wound in her chest; the bullet hasn't been removed, nor will it ever be. As Assata Shakur recovers at New Brunswick's Middlesex General Hospital, a phalanx of state troopers stands nearby, hurling racist epithets and threats against her.

While still in her hospital bed, she is arraigned on numerous charges, including first- and second-degree murder, assault and battery against a police officer, assault with intent to kill, and illegal possession of a weapon. She calls her aunt, Evelyn Williams, who arrives at the hospital that Friday, May 4. After a procedural and hurried legal consultation, Assata's mother and sister enter her hospital room. It's been more than two years since her family has seen her in person, aside from the "wanted" photos displayed all over town and in the papers. Assata is overjoyed to see them but worried about what they might think, what they might say. Her mother, Doris, approaches her bedridden daughter, kisses her, and says, "I'm proud of you."

"The words spin around me, weaving a warm blanket of love," Assata thinks. "I am so happy. I can hardly contain myself. My mother is proud of me. She loves me and she is proud of me."

The family reunion is over in minutes, and hard reality sets in. The indictments against Assata come quickly, stacked one on top of the other like firewood, waiting to be burned. In addition to charges of shooting the state troopers, Assata is indicted for the April 1971 robbery at the Statler Hilton Hotel; the August 23 bank robbery in Queens; the September 1972 bank robbery in the Bronx; the December kidnapping of the bartender James Freeman in Brooklyn; the January 1973 murder of Richard Nelson at a Brooklyn social club; and the attempted murder, also that January, of police officers Roy Pollina and Michael O'Reilly in Queens. The FBI opens a new file, called CHESROB (Chesimard robbery), attempting to connect Assata to nearly every bank robbery or violent crime allegedly committed by a Black woman on the East Coast.

Because she was still a relative unknown in the liberation struggle at the time of her capture, she was portrayed by media as a common criminal, bank robber, and bloodthirsty murderer. Assata realized she'd need to shape her own narrative, to "talk to my people and let them know what i was about, where i was really coming from." Written in early July and preserved with a tape recorder—reluctantly provided by Williams—Assata's first public remarks served as an introduction to herself and her ideology and provided a sort of Black Liberation Army mission statement. Like the Apostle Paul's prison epistles or King's "Letter from Birmingham Jail," Assata's communiqué, "To My People," would be shared, heralded, reprinted, and recited for many years to come. Broadcast on local radio stations on July 4, the nation's Independence Day, and reprinted in the October issue of the *Black Scholar* journal, her statement begins with a greeting and introduction:

> *Black brothers, black sisters, I want you to know that I love you and I hope that somewhere in your hearts you have love for me. My name is Assata Shakur (slave name JoAnne Chesimard), and I am a field nigga who is determined to be free by any means necessary.*

By that I mean that I can never be free unless all my people are free along with me. By that I mean that I have declared war on all forces that have raped our women, castrated our men and kept our babies empty bellied.

I have declared war on the rich who prosper on our poverty, the politicians who lie to us with smiling faces, and all the mindless, heartless robots who protected them and their property.

I am a black revolutionary, and as such I am the victim of all the wrath, hatred and slander that amerikkka is capable of. Like all other black revolutionaries I have been hunted like a dog, and like all other black revolutionaries, amerikkka is trying to lynch me.

She continues by defending the Black Liberation Army from its negative portrayal in the media, reproaching the U.S. government for its military involvement in Southeast Asia and Africa, and criticizing Nixon and his accomplices for the still-unfolding Watergate scandal. "They call us murderers," she states before citing the many ways the country has targeted and killed Black leaders, activists, prisoners, and children, whether through assassination, discrimination, poverty, unjust imprisonment, or inadequate access to healthcare. "They call us thieves and bandits," she continues. "They say we steal. But it was not us who stole millions of black people from the continent of Africa. We were robbed of our language, of our gods, of our culture, of our human dignity, of our labor and of our lives."

Assata's only remorse or regret is when she admits to the ill-advised decision to travel on the turnpike at night. With the turnpike's reputation for being a road where Black drivers are routinely stopped, Assata believes that she let down not only her guard that night but the Black community as well: "I want to apologize to you, my black brothers and sisters, for being on the New Jersey Turnpike. I should have known better. The Turnpike is a check point where black people are stopped, searched, harrassed [*sic*], and assaulted. Revolutionaries must never be in too much of a hurry or make careless decisions. He who runs when the sun is sleeping will stumble many times."

She closes her statement with a flourish of elegiac prose, paraphrasing from a Malcolm X speech and setting in motion the transformation of the Black Liberation Army from a small, loosely connected group of bank robbers, stickup artists, and cop killers into a perennial and everlasting ideology, a creed, and a revolutionary spirit that guides the liberation movement like a beacon:

> *There is and always will be, until every black man, woman and child is free, a Black Liberation Army. The main function of the Black Liberation Army at this time is to create good examples to struggle for black freedom and to prepare for the future. We must defend ourselves and let no one disrespect us. We must gain our liberation by any means necessary.*
> *It is our duty to fight for our freedom.*
> *It is our duty to win.*
> *We must love each other and support each other.*
> *We have nothing to lose but our chains!*

After Assata's arrest, what remained of the BLA was a small group of fugitives, now doggedly pursued by a joint task force of the FBI and NYPD. Some members carried out a few desultory bank robberies and stickups, but mostly they stayed in hiding, without direction or purpose. Their time was running short, and it wasn't long after Assata's capture that police would round up most of the last remaining fugitives.

On Thursday, June 7, twenty-year-old Kamau Sadiki was apprehended in Brooklyn after a police and federal stakeout. Early the next morning, a dozen agents and detectives broke down the door of an apartment on West 80th Street, belonging to twenty-six-year-old Denise Oliver, and surprised her and Andrew Jackson, also twenty-six, who were sleeping in bed together. Described by police as Assata's former boyfriend and one of the leading members of the BLA, Jackson surrendered without struggle. A former member of the Black Panther Party and the Young Lords, Oliver was also arrested and charged with harboring a fugitive. During a news conference, Police Commissioner Donald F. Cawley said the arrests had a "substantial impact" on destroying the BLA and that its strength had "diminished considerably," but he added that the group still remained a threat.

In a journal belonging to Oliver, discovered by police during the raid and later reprinted in the *Daily News*, Oliver describes the desperation faced by the remaining BLA fugitives. "In the end, jail or death is the resolution. So why postpone it? Maybe there is a chance for us to have a future, children, a farm to organize. But now each day is precious, paranoid, no time to think of tomorrow, except in basic survival terms and the tension is a slow death." In an entry dated on the day of the fatal shooting on the New Jersey Turnpike, Oliver muses on the despair and confusion she felt upon hearing the news about Assata's capture and Zayd's death:

Today it was Joanne—who I have never met . . . but I feel as if I know her . . . even though it has been knowledge gained through the half-baked lies and propaganda of the news media. And today it was Zayd . . . poor Zayd . . . the field mouse . . . always scurrying from one side to the other . . . never trusted, ever the romantic. This is one time he erred in judgment and failed to pick a winner. He is dead. I never thought he would wind up a corpse on the New Jersey turnpike . . . He died and Joanne lived—ironic when you consider that Zayd, the opportunist, had a great will to live and Joanne, the anarchist, seemed to constantly tempt death.

The capture of the remaining BLA fugitives meanwhile continued apace. On Sunday, September 2, twenty-five-year-old Herman Bell—wanted for the 1971 murder of police officers Waverly Jones and Joseph Piagentini in Harlem and the fatal shooting of Sergeant John Young in San Francisco—was arrested in New Orleans. Two weeks later, on September 17, BLA members Robert Hayes, Avon White, and Melvin Kearney were apprehended following a gun battle with police detectives at an apartment in the South Bronx. The

BLA was now "substantially crippled," said Commissioner Cawley, but still not yet broken.

At last, on Wednesday, November 14, the NYPD and the FBI located the BLA's most hot-tempered member and one of the FBI's most wanted fugitives: twenty-three-year-old Twymon Myers, wanted in connection with the 1971 murder of police officer James Greene in Atlanta, the 1972 murder of officers Rocco Laurie and Gregory Foster in New York's East Village, and a string of bank robberies and other stickups. After a seven-month pursuit in which Myers evaded detectives at every step, he was spotted strolling outside his safe house apartment near Tinton Avenue and 152nd Street in the Bronx, which detectives had been staking out for days. When a police detective approached and made a move to grab him, Myers spun around and began firing from an automatic pistol before switching to a 9mm submachine gun. More than one hundred nearby undercover officers opened fire, riddling Myers's body with bullets, killing him instantly.

The *New York Times* reported that Myers was "the seventh alleged major member of the Black Liberation Army to die in a shootout with police officers" and that "at least 18 others identified as key figures in the movement have been arrested." With Myers's death, Commissioner Cawley could triumphantly tell reporters that they "have now broken the back of the B.L.A."

Myers's funeral service was held on Tuesday, November 20, at the Marcus Jackson Funeral Chapel in Harlem. It was attended by hundreds of activists and radicals, as well as busloads of schoolchildren visiting from a Brooklyn community center sponsored by the Black United Front. During the service, police sharpshooters in flak jackets perched on rooftops, peering at the large group through rifle scopes as police helicopters hovered above. The funeral was notable also for the appearance of not only Black mourners, but Whites, too, particularly young White women. Though they may have attended out of curiosity or sympathy for the movement, this funeral would mark a turning point in at least two of their lives, setting them on a course that would have lasting consequences.

Susan Rosenberg was a young Jewish woman raised in a middle-class home in Manhattan. "That funeral was just one of the heaviest things that I'd ever been to in my life up to that point," Rosenberg recalled. "There are always these moments where you are posed with these choices, and I think that that funeral was one of those times for me, where I thought, 'Oh, I'm in big trouble now. This is so heavy. This is such serious stuff.'"

The young Italian-born Silvia Baraldini also attended and remembered that "seeing all these sharpshooters, on practically every rooftop in Harlem, you realized there really was a war going on. I think that was the day I decided to join them."

One of the more notable attendees at the funeral was a young Black member of the Republic of New Afrika. He had been an employee at Lincoln Hospital for two years but had only recently begun practicing acupuncture in the hospital's drug detoxification program. An intense and commanding presence, he walked around the funeral now, introducing himself to the other mourners, conveying his hope that Myers's death—his supposed martyrdom—would galvanize the movement.

"Mutulu came up to me at that funeral," Rosenberg remembered. "I was with a couple of other people, and he said, 'We've gotta remember this brother, we've gotta remember this brother.'"

The destinies of Mutulu Shakur, Susan Rosenberg, and Silvia Baraldini would, years later, become critically intertwined with that of Assata Shakur, but in the meantime, Assata was sitting alone in Middlesex County Workhouse—where she had been relocated after her harsh treatment and insufficient medical care at Middlesex General Hospital—awaiting the first of what would be many arduous and contentious criminal trials.

It took a while for the movement to take up Assata's fight. In the October following Assata's capture, Angela Davis—who had herself been a target of the FBI and jailed for sixteen months on spurious charges—spoke at a "Women in Prison" conference at Princeton University, where she called Assata a "freedom fighter" and a "political prisoner" and called for the five hundred attendees to demonstrate in front of the Middlesex Superior Court in New Brunswick and "pack the courtrooms" every day until all charges against her were dropped. On the first day of Assata's murder trial, however, only twenty-five people showed up and stood quietly outside the courthouse.

From the beginning of her incarceration, much of Assata's support came from sympathetic White women activists, who viewed her as a symbol of Black female resistance against the racist and patriarchal

American justice system. Jennifer Dohrn, sister of Weather Underground fugitive Bernardine Dohrn, told a reporter from the *New York Times,* "I don't think Joanne's going to get a fair trial. Under the present court system, blacks just don't get fair justice." Another Weather Underground fugitive, Kathy Boudin, composed a poem, "For Assata Shakur," in which she gushes, "You moved among your people a gentle wind, invisibly winding into their lives," and closes by reflecting that "When you were captured, sister, I wept, for all of us."

Updates on her trials were provided in bulletins written by various support groups. She would be lauded by supporters for her frequent acts of defiance and courtroom outbursts. She also grew her Afro back out and arrived at court wearing long, beautiful African dresses, with her hair wrapped in a *gele.*

Similar to when Huey P. Newton's incarceration propelled him from the leader of a small, local Black Power organization to a world-famous political prisoner, Assata's own incarceration would soon turn her into a cause célèbre.

But the most inexplicable and astonishing moment came in January 1974, when it was first reported that Assata had somehow become pregnant six to eight weeks earlier, during her trial for the Bronx bank robbery. Authorities couldn't offer an explanation. Blame and responsibility was passed around. Questions remained unanswered. "How can a woman who has been in jail for the last nine months suddenly turn out to be six weeks' pregnant?" asked the *New York Amsterdam News.* Assata herself wouldn't answer any questions as to what, by all appearances, seemed to be an immaculate conception. But soon doctors, the press, and authorities were able to pinpoint the likely moment of conception: a very brief occasion in early December when she and Kamau Sadiki had been detained in a holding room in Manhattan Federal Court. The circumstance that led to Assata and Kamau being held together in this room was itself a display of remarkable theater.

As the jury was still being decided for the 1972 Bronx bank robbery trial, Assata frequently disrupted proceedings, shouting at the judge and pounding her fists on the counsel table, accusing Judge Lee P. Gagliardi of not allowing the defense time to prepare for the trial. When Assata refused to be quiet, Gagliardi threatened her, in an echo of Bobby Seale's now-infamous mistreatment in court nearly five years earlier. "We may bind, gag and shackle you to your chair if you don't behave," the judge declared. Assata in turn accused the judge of "violating the rules of humanity" and taunted that he was "bought and paid for." Her codefendant, Sadiki, backed up Assata and joined the disruption, finally prompting Gagliardi to eject both defendants from the courtroom, holding them in an adjacent room for the duration of the trial, with a loudspeaker placed inside broadcasting the proceedings.

What happened inside that small room would prompt interrogations, accusations, and even an FBI investigation. Both defendants were presumed to be kept in separate cells, under constant guard by federal marshals. Assata and Sadiki would not have had even one private moment together. Writing for the *Amsterdam News* one month following the revelation of Assata's pregnancy, journalist James L. Hicks accused the U.S. marshal guarding the defendants of watching Assata and Sadiki have sex on a table inside the holding room and later laughing about it with a supervisor. To Hicks, there were sickening reverberations of the days when enslavers allowed Black men and women to fight and screw to their hearts' content, so long as they didn't bother White folks.

But Assata would later write in her *Autobiography* that her and Sadiki's relationship had grown more intimate over the course of the trial, that they had "begun to touch and to hold each other and each of us was like an oasis to the other." She writes that they had discussed sex and the possibility of becoming pregnant. "If you become pregnant and you have a child, the child will be taken care of," Sadiki assured her, adding that she "may never have another chance to have a child." Assata relented, telling herself, "I'm gonna live as hard as i can and as full as i can until i die. And i'm not letting these parasites, these oppressors, these greedy racist swine make me kill my children in my mind, before they are even born."

It was itself a brazen and rebellious act. By asserting her freedom to love, to feel tenderness, and to bring a new life into the world, while facing the possibility of life in prison, Assata was defying the system that sought to destroy her and strip her of her bodily autonomy. She also must have been thinking of her friend Afeni Shakur, who had herself become pregnant during the Panther 21 trial and had gone on to give birth to a healthy and well-loved son.

A mistrial was declared for the state trooper murder charges, out of fear of Assata suffering a miscarriage, and her trial was separated from that of her codefendant Sundiata Acoli, whose trial continued without her. Though Acoli could've viewed this separation as an abandonment of her codefendant and accomplice, Assata writes that Acoli was instead "elated" upon hearing the news of her pregnancy and called it "absolutely beautiful." When Assata later learned that the FBI was conducting an investigation into the details surrounding her pregnancy, Assata responded that if they came around asking questions, she'd "tell them that this baby was sent by the Black creator to liberate Black people. I'll tell 'em that this baby is the new Black messiah, conceived in a holy way, come to lead our people to freedom and justice and to create a new Black nation."

On September 11, 1974, at 4:00 A.M., at Elmhurst Hospital in Queens, Assata gave birth to a daughter, Kakuya Amala Olugbala Shakur—the newest addition to the Shakur and Olugbala tribes. Assata was allowed to remain at the hospital to nurse Kakuya, but after two weeks her daughter was released to the custody of Assata's mother, Doris, and Assata was brought back to the Women's House of Detention at Rikers Island. She accused prison authorities at Rikers of abusing her and putting her in shackles for refusing an invasive medical examination. She was placed in solitary confinement for two weeks and eventually stopped eating. Though she wouldn't admit as much to her jailers, the depression she felt at having to give up her new baby was evidently tremendous.

Assata still had many more trials ahead of her, necessitating frequent changes of venues and detention in deplorable conditions at numerous correctional facilities. But as the months and then the years ticked by, Assata's eminence steadily grew, with supporters now flocking to courthouses, filling spectator benches or demonstrating outside. Her friend Afeni, who at the time was a highly revered movement veteran and currently working as a legal assistant, visited Assata in January 1976 to offer support and encouragement. White and Black demonstrators handed out leaflets on streets and plastered posters on walls, leading to the arrest of a handful of supporters, including Susan Rosenberg, who'd paid a $30 fine after pleading guilty to putting up "Free Assata Shakur" posters on New Brunswick public property.

Yaasmyn Fula, who worked with Afeni and Mutulu in the National Task Force for Cointelpro Litigation and Research, recalled driving around the city, often with young Tupac in tow, in search of Black women who resembled Assata to be used in a police lineup. "He was in my car, in the back seat," Fula said. "And he knew what we was doing . . . He would look and he would see someone that looked like Assata, and he would smile and point at them and say 'There's Assata!'"

Witnesses would predictably fail to identify the real Assata from the stand-ins.

A new, clandestine group calling itself the May 19 Communist Organization—named for the shared birthday of Malcolm X and Ho Chi Minh, comprising a handful of radical White activists—proclaimed that Assata "stands in a long line of Black women—from Harriet Tubman and Sojourner Truth to Rosa Parks . . . who, from the first days of kidnap and slavery, have fought for the survival and liberation of their people." Where only two dozen people had shown up to her first murder trial in 1973, her retrial in 1977 brought 150 protestors to the New Brunswick courtroom, with an additional two hundred students and supporters attending solidarity events and benefits on college campuses, with poems and speeches by such notables as the activist and writer Amiri Baraka, poet Jayne Cortez, and venerated political activist Yuri Kochiyama. Fundraisers were held featuring such entertainers as Harry Belafonte, Ossie Davis, and Ruby Dee. Within four years of the shooting on the New Jersey Turnpike, Assata Shakur had become a freedom fighter, political prisoner, and undaunted symbol of Black resistance.

"People are always looking for heroes in the movement, especially in women," Fula reflected years later. "They're always looking for women to be superwomen, for Black women to be super warriors, and they were none of that. Afeni wasn't a superwoman. She just did superhuman things. It's the same with Assata. She wasn't a superwoman, but she did some superwoman damn things. That's what happens in the movement when it becomes hero worship and people are assigned these legendary characteristics. They're just regular people that are fighting because they believe so hard and so strongly in what they're fighting for."

In those four years, between her capture in 1973 and her final trial in 1977, Assata managed to score successive victories. She was acquitted for the Bronx bank robbery; she was acquitted of the kidnapping of the bartender James Freeman; attempted murder charges for the ambush shooting of policemen Michael O'Reilly and Roy Pollina were dismissed for insufficient evidence; and she was acquitted for the Queens bank robbery charges after the jury decided that the widely circulated surveillance photo of a Black woman in a wig and eyeglasses, gripping a handgun, was not Assata. When this acquittal was announced, spectators who had been packed inside Brooklyn's Federal Court cheered and burst into applause. Assata turned and waved to the adoring crowd. "I love you all," she called out.

Her luck would run out in 1977, during Assata's retrial for the deadly shoot-out on the New Jersey Turnpike. Acoli had already been found guilty, in March 1974, for the murder of Trooper Werner Foerster and sentenced to life in prison. Before sentencing, Acoli addressed the court with a prepared twenty-minute statement: "The Black Liberation Army has been accused of killing policemen. All we do is stop the police from killing us," he declared. "If the police don't want to get killed, they should stop murdering blacks and Third World people. The poor people of the nation are being victimized by the system. The Black Liberation Army has been fractured, but it will continue until the oppression is stopped."

It had been four years since the shoot-out. Though she had defeated all her other charges, the murder of a state trooper was a much more forbidding accusation, not quite so easily dismissed. Police and the FBI had pursued Assata zealously for years, chasing her from New York to Atlanta, and they'd had to watch with embarrassment as she won back-to-back acquittals or dismissals, all the while becoming a hero and role model to both Black and White progressives. They were not going to let her get away so easily this time.

At the start of jury selection, Superior Court Judge Theodore Appleby refused the defense's request for a change of venue from Middlesex County after the results of a poll showed that ninety percent of county residents were already familiar with the woman known as JoAnne Chesimard and seventy percent believed she was guilty. Of the 408 potential jurors questioned, seven women and five men were ultimately selected—all of them White.

The trial lasted for nine weeks, attracting hundreds of daily demonstrators to the courthouse and receiving regular press coverage. During the trial, the prosecution claimed that the gunfight had started "on command" of Assata, who had pulled out an automatic handgun and shot Harper in the shoulder as he approached the Pontiac. Harper testified that he returned fire, wounding Assata and fatally shooting Zayd, then escaped to report the shooting, in which time Assata allegedly left the car to assist Acoli, who was struggling with Foerster. On the witness stand, Assata denied shooting either Harper or Foerster, testifying that Harper shot her after she'd raised her arms in compliance with his demand. Assata's defense team brought in a neurosurgeon and a pathologist, who'd each examined Assata's X-rays, to demonstrate how she had been shot in her arm and chest by Harper while her arms were raised, severing her median nerve and paralyzing her arm, rendering her unable to fire a weapon or pull a trigger. It wasn't enough to convince the jury.

On Friday, March 25, after a twenty-two-hour deliberation, the jury found Assata guilty on eight counts, including first-degree murder. Judge Appleby sentenced her to mandatory life imprisonment, plus twenty-six to thirty-three years on assault and weapons charges, the maximum possible sentence. Wearing a floor-length bright yellow dress and matching head scarf, Assata addressed the judge: "I have no intention of applying to you for justice; no intention of applying to you for mercy," she said. "The final result was not a trial, not even a mock trial. It was a sham, a charade, a lynching." She called the jurors "racist and misled," denounced them as having "convicted a woman who had her hands in the air, who is innocent," and confessed that she was "ashamed that I have even taken part in this trial."

Judge Appleby told the court attendants to "remove the prisoner."

"The prisoner," Assata declared, "will walk away on her own feet."

No one at that time could have realized just how serious she was.

15.
LIBERATION

IN THE FOUR years between Assata Shakur's 1973 arrest on the New Jersey Turnpike and her conviction in 1977 for the murder of Trooper Werner Foerster, the nation itself had undergone momentous and extraordinary events. Richard Milhous Nixon became the first and only American president to resign from office, after he was indicted for impeachment over the Watergate scandal. America's military involvement in Vietnam came to an end. After a series of investigations, the United States Select Committee to Study Governmental Operations with Respect to Intelligence Activities, the "Church Committee," uncovered years of domestic spying, infiltration, disruption, and other intelligence abuses by the FBI, CIA, and National Security Agency (NSA), directed against American leftists in general but especially targeting Black activists and leaders through COINTELPRO.

This four-year period also corresponded to the time from when Mutulu Shakur first happened upon a little-known holistic treatment called acupuncture to earning his doctorate in acupuncture from the Acupuncture Association of Quebec and helping to revolutionize drug addiction treatment. Only two years after earning his doctorate, however, New York City mayor Ed Koch ordered Mutulu and two dozen others to be removed from the Lincoln Hospital's drug detoxification program. But Mutulu wasn't sidelined for long, going on to open the Black Acupuncture Advisory Association of North America (BAAANA) in a four-story brownstone in Harlem's

St. Nicholas Historic District, known as Strivers' Row. A two-block-long enclave of brownstone and terra-cotta row houses, Strivers' Row is as distinguished for its stately architecture as it is for its prominent former residents, from the "Father of the Blues" W. C. Handy to Congressman Adam Clayton Powell Jr. to entertainer Bill "Bojangles" Robinson. The neighborhood lies on the opposite side of St. Nicholas Park from City College of New York (CCNY), where Assata was briefly a student, and is a five-minute stroll from the historic Abyssinian Baptist Church, where Powell first made a name for himself as a pastor before going on to become the first Black congressman from New York, a position he kept for twelve terms.

Mutulu and his financial partners established a holding company called the Straight Ahead Realty Corporation on August 16, 1979, and purchased the ninety-year-old brownstone from Harlem physician Dr. Edward Dukes and his wife, Mae. The inside was in poor condition, and Mutulu spent months repairing, renovating, and equipping it as a place to practice and teach acupuncture. There was a waiting room downstairs with a front desk, sofa, and chairs, and there was an upstairs classroom with a large conference table. Because educational material on acupuncture was scarce, books and papers were shared or photocopied on a Xerox machine. Revolutionary posters decorated the walls. Many of Mutulu's first recruits had been his former colleagues and students at Lincoln Detox, including Richard Delaney, Kamau Bayette (born Pete Middleton), Mtayari Shabaka Sundiata (born Samuel Smith), Nehanda Abiodun (born Cheri Laverne Dalton), and Susan Rosenberg.

They had all studied at the Lincoln Acupuncture School and now loyally followed Mutulu, whom they called "Doc," into his new enterprise. BAAANA was established to continue the work begun at Lincoln Detox: treating poor Black and Brown members of the community with a combination of acupuncture and political education. For legitimacy, they brought in doctor and progressive activist Barbara Zeller and her physician-activist husband, Alan Berkman, as medical advisors. The clinic treated ten to fifteen patients a day, charging $50 for the first visit and $25 for follow-up visits, but the clinic would often waive the fee altogether, avowing that "we'd much rather see our people get well."

Rosenberg was in her early twenties when she graduated from

the Lincoln Acupuncture School. She'd first met Mutulu at Twymon Myers's funeral in November 1973, and she followed Mutulu to BAAANA, where she was one of a handful of White acupuncturists at the clinic. She recalled Mutulu as holding a "very strong political position and a very strong ideological position," adding that he was a "very charismatic kind of guy." Rosenberg also recalled meeting Afeni Shakur a few years earlier, when Afeni had been organizing White support for political prisoners and providing legal support for victims of COINTELPRO harassment. Rosenberg understood then that the Shakur surname was more than a name: "It was a collective. It was a community. It was a family. The Shakurs were like this incredible clan. They were a New Afrikan tribe."

One of the newest members of the Shakur tribe was a young, attractive American Airlines flight attendant from Texas, born Anita Hearns. She had been living in New York for about a year, and one day in 1978, as she was walking home along West 96th Street between Amsterdam and Columbus Avenues, a man leaned out of the window of his apartment and hollered at her. She and Mutulu would strike up a relationship and eventually marry, and Anita Hearns would change her name to Makini Shakur. She remembered Mutulu as "a person that garners respect" and "a badass. I'm talking about, you know, a 'man's man,' but a good man. When I say good, I mean principled. He's a man of honor and integrity and respect."

Of course, Mutulu was at the time married to Afeni, but their marriage had been ceremonial and not legally binding. Mutulu and Makini's marriage, however, was officially certified by the State of New York. Though the couple did have genuine affection for each other and Makini considered Mutulu her best friend, their marriage was one of convenience: as the husband of a flight attendant, Mutulu could travel the world. When Mutulu wasn't working at the clinic, the couple flew together to such idyllic destinations as Jamaica, Barbados, Venezuela, and Antigua.

But though Makini had only agreed to the marriage as a favor to Mutulu, Afeni disliked and distrusted her—not because Afeni viewed the new woman as a threat, but because Makini was "not part of the movement." Makini didn't have the same background as the others. She hadn't sacrificed for the struggle, hadn't been targeted by the police or the federal government for her beliefs, hadn't watched as her comrades were murdered by the police or unjustly imprisoned. Makini liked to wear makeup and nice clothes and travel the world. Nevertheless, Makini soon learned how to practice acupuncture and became BAAANA's administrative director.

She recalled her husband as "one of the most brilliant people I'd ever met. Huge heart. Very compassionate. Mutulu took care of a lot of people." But with that brilliance and compassion, he was also known to overextend himself at work, taking on too many responsibilities and not leaving much room for others. Makini remembered Mutulu as "the kind of guy that was always on the job. Always working . . . I used to tell Mutulu this all the time, because he was one of those people who could be up all night long, get a couple of hours of sleep, and then be up on the case, doing whatever he had to do, make an appointment, doing this, doing that. And I used to tell him, 'You do everything.' People wouldn't show up, wouldn't do what they're supposed to do. 'You keep doing that, but if something happens to you, shit's gonna fall apart' . . . He was the glue."

Mutulu's longtime friend Sekou Odinga also recalled him being "a high energy dude. Part of his problem was he wanted to be involved in everything. I always told him that was more of a hindrance than a help . . . I always told him, 'You want to do everything. Your problem is you want to compete with everybody.' He thought he could do whatever anybody was doing, as good as they could do it."

BAAANA officially opened for business in August 1980, after a year of renovations. The Harlem brownstone that housed the clinic served not only as an acupuncture clinic and school but also as living quarters for Mutulu; his wife and clinic administrator, Makini; former American Airlines flight attendant Asha Sundiata (born Rene Thornton); the acupuncture doctor Richard Delaney; Mutulu's former student at Lincoln and loyal protégé, Kamau Bayette; and James E. Wilson, who served as an accountant for the clinic in exchange for room and board and acupuncture training. Mutulu had envisioned BAAANA as a space where he could continue the work he'd begun nearly a decade earlier: treating drug addiction and other ailments with a combination of acupuncture and political enlightenment. Patients would often leave the clinic with their ears still pricked by acupuncture needles that were inscribed with the motto

"Choice of Health Care Is Your Human Right" above BAAANA's address and phone number.

But Mutulu's strengths, which at times could be his flaws, were his unique intelligence, his enthusiasm, and his obdurate commitment to the movement—not his administrative acumen. During his tenure at Lincoln Detox, Shakur wouldn't hesitate to go downtown, storm into the offices of the Health and Hospitals Corporation, pound on tables, and demand funding for the program. As the owner of a private clinic, however, without the promise of city or state funds, he had to rely on other means of raising capital. The negligible treatment fees BAAANA charged patients, when they charged at all, didn't bring in enough to sustain the clinic, with its monthly mortgage payments and ongoing repairs. Mutulu and his colleagues were compelled to find more creative means of keeping BAAANA operational. Fortunately for them, they already had plenty of experience in how to obtain some quick cash.

After Odinga ended his Algerian exile in 1973, he reconnected with his former mentor, the patriarch Salahdeen Shakur, and traveled with him from New York, New Jersey, and Philadelphia to New Orleans, selling African clothing, jewelry, and incense to shopkeepers or peddling their wares to tourists from folding card tables. But Odinga also was upset to find the liberation movement in disarray, crestfallen to see his fellow soldiers lacking direction or organization. "The one main thing that has been missing from the Black Liberation struggle is continuity," he wrote in a notebook that April, one month before the fatal shoot-out on the New Jersey Turnpike. "What we have today is a few loosely organized aboveground organizations and a bunch of loosely organized underground units or cells." The following January, Odinga rented an apartment at 350 Omega Street in the Pittsburgh, Pennsylvania, suburb of East Liberty, under the alias "Ralph Smith," to be used as a safe house for a new organization. This group would soon come to be known by its members as the Revolutionary Armed Task Force and by law enforcement and the press as "the Family."

Veteran Black Panther, Republic of New Afrika member, and musician Bilal Sunni-Ali challenged the media portrayal of this coalition of Black and White anti-imperialists as a posse of criminals and outlaws: "They hear the word 'family' constantly being projected," he explained, "and don't understand the dynamics and the nuances of the Afrikan community at that time, and why people refer to themselves as family. The whole community refers to themselves as family."

One of this nascent group's first expropriations was carried out in Pittsburgh, early on Monday morning, December 6, 1976. For the job, Mutulu enlisted a twenty-five-year-old Delaware man named Raymond Q. Oliver and thirty-year-old Cecilio "Chui" Ferguson—a U.S. Army veteran, member of the Republic of New Afrika, assistant director of a Brooklyn drug rehabilitation program, and former Lincoln Detox volunteer. Though he had by then taken part in at least ten bank robberies throughout New York, New Jersey, and Connecticut, Odinga abstained from taking part in this job, recognizing Mutulu's relative inexperience with expropriations. He was concerned that things wouldn't go smoothly. His premonitions turned out to come true.

"He had a very good grasp of national and international politics," Odinga recalled. "He was a pretty good spokesperson. I always thought that if he had just did the organizing that we'd needed aboveground it definitely would've been a lot more helpful."

The plan itself wasn't particularly bad. Mutulu, Oliver, and Ferguson stayed at Odinga's Omega Street apartment that Sunday night, got up early the next morning, and stationed themselves outside the Mellon Bank in downtown Pittsburgh. Mutulu and Ferguson hid behind a large pillar near a side stairwell, and Oliver was posted at the bottom of the stairs. An armored truck containing almost $1.5 million pulled up, and two guards exited the truck and began loading the money sacks onto a dolly to deliver it to the bank. Mutulu and Ferguson emerged and displayed their revolvers.

One of the guards promptly fainted. The other guard complied with the men's orders and stood against the wall with his legs spread. Mutulu and Ferguson were getting ready to handcuff the guards and make off with the loot when Ferguson, who'd been prone to muscle spasms, was now stricken by one, causing him to accidentally fire his gun.

The gunshot alerted two nearby county detectives and two city policemen, who gave chase to the three fleeing men. Ferguson and Oliver were both apprehended only a few blocks from the bank. Mutulu got away and returned defeated to Odinga's Omega Street apartment, shaken and humbled. If Mutulu was going to make another attempt at this, he needed help from the veteran Black Panther leader, the closest the movement had to an elder. Odinga agreed to help Mutulu. This was the beginning of a partnership that would itself end in disaster for both men.

Mutulu wasn't dormant for very long after the botched robbery attempt in Pittsburgh. He and Odinga recruited new soldiers to replace Oliver and Ferguson, who were both in a county jail facing armed robbery charges. One of his first recruits was thirty-year-old RNA Minister of Defense and Vietnam War veteran Tyrone Quincy Rison. Odinga brought in Larry Mack, a trustworthy soldier and fellow Panther 21 fugitive who had known Odinga since the founding of the Harlem and Bronx Black Panther chapters. The four men spoke at length about the drug scourge ravaging Black communities and the U.S. government's likely complicity, the police occupation of Black communities, and the need for Black people to have self-determination in this country.

With Odinga now assuming control over the small team, the next robberies went much more smoothly. Their first hit was May 26, 1977, at the House O' Weenies meatpacking plant in the Bronx, a few blocks south of Lincoln Hospital. The next job was October 19, at a Citibank branch in Mount Vernon. The four men divided the $13,800 amongst themselves, putting aside a few thousand dollars for future actions.

One year would pass until their next robbery, at a Chase Manhattan bank, on the Lower West Side, on October 12, 1978. For this job, Mutulu was replaced by Kuwasi Balagoon—a former Panther 21 defendant who had recently escaped from Rahway State Prison in New Jersey, where he'd been held on charges of shooting at police officers during an attempted bank robbery. The Chase Manhattan robbery garnered $8,380. Mutulu rejoined the group on December 19 for its next action: the holdup of two Coin Depot Corporation armored truck guards in Livingston, New Jersey. This job netted an impressive haul of $200,000.

No one was harmed during any of these robberies. The jobs were quick, clean, and efficient. Because the authorities believed they had neutralized the BLA with the killing of Twymon Myers in 1973, they had no reason to believe these holdups were anything more than the work of a few crooks. In many respects, they were correct. Mutulu, Odinga, and the others had each joined the Black liberation struggle at a time when revolutionary fervor was sweeping the nation, when activists were organized, united, disciplined, and had the support of celebrities and the New Left movement at large. But nearly a decade had since passed. The Black Panther Party was by now all but obsolete. So many comrades were either dead or in prison. And what did the survivors have to show for all their work, all their sacrifices? A life spent underground, perpetually on the run, sustaining themselves on armed robberies. Meanwhile, the systemic repression of Black Americans had only intensified. The movement, as they'd once known it, had become reduced to a fight for survival. They needed to do something big, something to galvanize the movement. Ironically, this moment would come soon after the addition of White people to the group.

Silvia Baraldini, Susan Rosenberg, and Judy Clark had all been active as former members of White militant group Weather Underground and the anti-imperialist Prairie Fire Organizing Committee before going on to establish the May 19 Communist Organization (M19CO). Consisting exclusively of White women, M19CO's objective was to form alliances with the Black Liberation Army and the militant Puerto Rican liberation group Fuerzas Armadas de Liberación Nacional (FALN), in hopes of joining the "people's war."

"In order to be part of the alliance, white people have to be willing to engage in armed struggle," said one M19CO document later found by the FBI, "to break with the white leftist history of mouthing revolution—always years in the future—and abandoning Third World comrades on the front lines."

Baraldini, Rosenberg, and Clark were joined by Kathy Boudin, another former Weather Underground member who had become a fugitive since the accidental and fatal detonation of a homemade bomb in a Greenwich Village town house in 1970. Besides coming from relatively privileged, prominent, and left-leaning families, what all four women had in common was their unswerving and uncompromising commitment to assisting Black activists in the struggle.

But the most notable White woman to align with the Black liberation movement was the Texas-born, attractive, intelligent thirty-one-year-old Marilyn Jean Buck. A former honor student and a longtime supporter of leftist and anti-imperialist causes, Buck had been arrested in San Francisco in 1973 after being caught using a fake name to purchase guns and ammunition from a gun shop. An investigation by the Bureau of Alcohol, Tobacco, and Firearms soon found that Buck had also purchased guns and 1,450 rounds of ammunition in Oregon, Arizona, and New Mexico, and they traced some of those guns to BLA actions in San Francisco, Georgia, and New Orleans. Twenty-six years old at the time, Buck earned the distinction of being the only White member of the Black Liberation Army. Buck was convicted of gunrunning for the BLA, sentenced to the maximum ten years, and sent to the Federal Correctional Institution at Alderson, West Virginia. Four years into her sentence, in the spring of 1977, Buck was granted a one-week furlough and was released into the custody of the lawyer Susan Tipograph, in New York, to work on her appeal. Though Buck only had eighteen months left in her reduced sentence, she made up her mind not to return to Alderson.

That December, Buck met with Baraldini and others in a Brooklyn apartment. She told them she wasn't returning to prison, that she wanted to reconnect with the struggle, and she needed their help. She was first introduced to Mutulu, who then arranged a meeting between her and Odinga. The two unlikely fugitives—the privileged White woman from Texas and the hardened former gang member and Black Panther leader from Jamaica, Queens—met at a hotel near Washington, D.C., in what amounted to something like a job interview. Odinga "kind of grilled her" over her knowledge of and commitment to the struggle. After a two- or three-hour conversation, during which Buck expressed her sincerity, related all she had done for the struggle, and instructed Odinga to "use me as you see fit," Odinga was satisfied. Buck was in.

One of Buck's first contributions to the new group was introducing what she termed "the White edge," in which the White women of the group—Buck, Baraldini, Rosenberg, Boudin, and Clark—used aliases and fake IDs to rent cars and serve as drivers after robberies, believing that police were less likely to notice the getaway car if it was driven by White women. This belief, unsurprisingly, turned out to be correct. Buck served as getaway driver during two early robberies: a holdup of a Livingstone armored truck and a holdup of a Coin Depot Corporation armored car on the morning of September 11, 1979, outside a Bamberger's department store in Paramus, New Jersey.

Mutulu, Odinga, Balagoon, Rison, and Sundiata—now calling themselves the "Action Five"—all took part in the holdup, afterward jumping into the back of a waiting Ford Fairmont station wagon, which had been provided by Boudin, who was working at a Manhattan rental car agency under an alias. The occupants of the wagon quickly abandoned the car and jumped into a waiting van and sped off. They made their way to Interstate 80, drove east for ten miles, and were approaching the George Washington Bridge when a police car pulled up alongside them. The officers inside had been notified of the robbery and were looking for Black men in a van but were confronted instead with a young White woman, Marilyn Buck, who proceeded to flirt with the officers. The cops went on their way, and the van continued on across the bridge and made it to a Mount Vernon safe house, where the group split the $105,000 yield.

Though each robbery had been perfectly executed, the group was by now eager for something more significant than stickups. They were seasoned radicals and veteran soldiers in an anti-imperialist struggle, after all, not common criminals and hoodlums. They needed to do something big, an action that would draw attention, earn respect, and stimulate the moribund movement. They needed to rescue one of their fallen soldiers—someone who had become one of the most famous political prisoners in the country, whose name itself represented defiance; someone who, over the last few years, had come to represent not only the Black liberation movement but the movement for anti-imperialist freedom fighters all over the world. It was time to free Assata Shakur.

The decision to liberate Assata didn't come naturally. It was true that her conviction for the shooting of New Jersey State Troopers Werner Foerster and James Harper was widely acknowledged by supporters as fraudulent and unjust, but she was one of many captured soldiers. Other comrades might've seemed like more deserving candidates to be freed. Sundiata Acoli, apprehended after the incident on the turnpike, had been an integral member of the Black Panther Party's Harlem chapter almost since its founding and was now sitting in a New Jersey state prison, serving out a life sentence. Geronimo "Ji-Jaga" Pratt, godfather to the clandestine Black liberation struggle and inspiration to the New York Panthers, was also serving a life sentence for what was clearly a deceptive, targeted COINTELPRO operation. An early leader of the New York Panthers and BLA organizer, Dhoruba bin Wahad was now on the eighth year of his life sentence, in what appeared to be another example of COINTELPRO harassment. So why did this group of fewer than a dozen soldiers decide that Assata was the one to be liberated from prison, with all the risks that this involved?

"In a way, we were tired of just doing robberies," Tyrone Rison later testified. "We were about more than just robbing money." Rison went on to describe how they'd drawn up a list of political prisoners whose escape would be widely publicized, and they landed on Assata because she "already had national coverage for being leader of the Black Liberation Army."

By 1979, after six years of numerous trials and accusations, Assata had grown into a symbol of resistance against the racist and patriarchal justice system. To liberate Assata would significantly raise the stature of this small group of veteran soldiers, who had thus far succeeded only in carrying out a handful of bank robberies. Though Odinga and Assata had known each other for only a brief time—a few months in 1973 between his return from Algerian exile and her capture on the turnpike—he would later describe her as "definitely one of my heroes."

The biggest advocates for Assata's liberation, however, probably came from the White women in the group, who had been the most active during her murder trial—demonstrating outside the courthouse, organizing fundraisers, and, in Rosenberg's case, being arrested and fined for hanging "Free Assata Shakur" signs in New Brunswick. Regardless of how the decision came about or who made the final call, Assata's escape could not have happened if not for a sequence of favorable events.

After her guilty verdict, Assata was first sent to the Clinton Correctional Facility for Women in New Jersey, but after ten days she was transferred to the all-male state prison in Yardville, New Jersey, where security was tighter. She was again transferred, on April 8, 1978, to the federal correctional facility for women in Alderson, West Virginia, where she was held in a maximum-security unit for inmates considered a flight risk. Alderson's maximum-security unit was soon declared unconstitutional, and on February 20, 1979, Assata was transferred back to the Clinton Correctional Facility.

Two hundred yards south of Interstate 78, in a rural, hilly area of New Jersey, near the scenic Spruce Run Reservoir and Recreation Area, the minimum-security facility was referred to by some guards and county residents as "the country club," due not only to its idyllic and unobtrusive setting, but for its less-than-stringent security. Many guards went unarmed. One dormitory in the prison, South Hall, was considered maximum security, but "security" at Clinton was more or less subjective.

Assata's mother, Doris, visited her at Clinton, bringing with her Assata's daughter. Kakuya was already four years old, and her relationship with Assata was strained. Raised by Doris, Kakuya could only interact with Assata during these brief visitations. Kakuya's first reaction was hesitation and aloofness, followed by anger. She cried and screamed and punched at her mother, accusing her of remaining in prison by choice. Overcome with emotion and feelings of powerlessness, Assata told Kakuya to go over and try to open the barred doors of the visitation room. Kakuya pulled at and attacked the bars until she fell defeated to the floor. Assata picked her up and consoled her. Soon the guard came in and announced visiting time was over. After one last hug, Assata watched her daughter turn to walk away.

"She waves good-bye to me, her face clouded and worried, looking like a little adult," Assata recalled. "I go back to my cage and cry until i vomit. I decide that it is time to leave."

Through a network of friends, Assata managed to get the word out to Odinga. Not only did she wish to escape, but the lax security at Clinton offered as close to a perfect condition for a jailbreak as they were going to get. They spent nine months preparing for the escape. The Paramus armored car robbery that September was carried out, in part, to finance Assata's escape.

The group kept their plans confidential to a small circle, referring to Assata by the code name "Cleo." She continued to receive visitors, but Odinga was the only Black member of the group to risk a visit to the prison. A brief moment of inattentiveness on October 29 almost ruined everything, including the escape plans. After visiting with Assata, Odinga was driving home on Interstate 78 when he was pulled over by a New Jersey state trooper. Trooper Gene Keith Ledder approached the driver of the car—a red 1979 Oldsmobile, acquired the year before by Marilyn Buck—requested his license and registration, and asked if he knew why he'd been pulled over. No stranger to police encounters and no doubt prepared for anything, Odinga replied diplomatically: "Why don't you tell me why you stopped me?"

Ledder said that he'd been driving seventy-three miles an hour.

"I thought I was going sixty," Odinga replied. He handed over a phony New Jersey driver's license with the name Edward Holmes and an address of 116 Prospect Street in East Orange. Ledder issued Odinga—or Edward Holmes—a speeding ticket and let him go, but this encounter was too close for comfort. Odinga would have to be more careful. But there wasn't much time for self-castigation. They were only four days away from the planned day of liberation.

On the afternoon of November 2, just before 3:00, a car stopped at a trailer near the prison entrance that was used as a reception area. After signing in with a fake name that Assata had approved earlier, Odinga waited for the arrival of the prison van, which transported visitors to and from the prison's maximum-security wing. The driver of the van, thirty-one-year-old Stephen Ravettina, collected Odinga without bothering to check him for weapons. Ravettina chaperoned the visitor through the prison grounds to South Hall, where the lone guard on duty was Helen Anderson, an elderly, kindhearted woman with a heart condition, known around Clinton as "Mama A." After

Anderson buzzed Ravettina and Odinga through the gate, Assata came up to hug Odinga, and, as the two embraced, he discreetly slipped her the .357 Magnum he'd concealed in the small of his back.

As Ravettina climbed back into the van, a message came over the radio from the lieutenant on duty: "Rav, there's more visitors at the gate for South Hall."

He drove back to the trailer and found two Black men in their midthirties patiently waiting. Again, Ravettina didn't search the men before they climbed into the van, one in the back seat, the other in the passenger seat. They had driven only a short distance up the road when the man in the passenger seat, Mtayari Shabaka Sundi-ata, pulled out a .45-caliber handgun, held it to Ravettina's neck, and ordered him out of the van. The man in the back seat, Kokayi, also withdrew a pistol. Born Winston Patrick Patterson, Kokayi was an acupuncture apprentice from Washington, D.C., who had been re-cruited only the night before, after Larry Mack had backed out. The three men walked the remaining distance up the road to South Hall, approached Anderson in the guard booth, and told her to open the gate. She hesitated for a moment but was then surprised to turn and see Odinga and Assata on the opposite side of the gate, pointing the .357 in her direction. She opened the gate.

The three men handcuffed Anderson and Ravettina together and ordered them to walk back down the road to the prison van. The small group jumped into the van and Kokayi took the wheel. Ner-vous and ill-prepared, Kokayi made a wrong turn down a dead-end road, then backed up, orbited the parking lot, and drove headfirst into a grassy knoll, jarring the van's occupants. Finally, Kokayi man-aged to steer the van to the switch point in the parking lot of the nearby Hunterdon State School. Two cars were waiting—a white Lin-coln Continental and a blue compact car—along with Buck, Barald-ini, and Rosenberg. Mutulu and Rison pulled up in a blue van, to be used as an auxiliary getaway vehicle, which proved unnecessary. As-sata and Odinga crawled into the trunk of the Lincoln and Baraldini and Buck peeled off onto the interstate, followed at a short distance by Mutulu in the van. The two hostages, Anderson and Ravettina, were left behind in the prison van, still handcuffed but unharmed.

Mutulu soon pulled into the Laneco Shopping Center parking lot, where he and Rison ditched the van and jumped into a new getaway car, piloted by Judy Clark. Seven minutes had passed before prison officials discovered the escape and set off an alarm. Roadblocks went up in neighboring counties and the prison was sealed off. State troopers raced across the interstate as police issued a forty-eight-state alarm. Their search would ultimately lead nowhere. In under ten minutes, without a single shot fired, this small, ragtag group had liberated Assata Shakur and disappeared into the night.

"It was such a dynamic act that went off without a real hitch," Odinga recalled years later. "It was well planned, and well carried out. At the time we had a pretty tight structure."

They still needed to coordinate safe houses, disguises, travel arrangements. They knew the FBI would very soon be kicking down a lot of doors, rounding up a lot of associates, friends, allies, relatives. But now wasn't the time to think about all of that. Now was the time to celebrate, and to announce their victory to the world.

16.
CRACKS IN THE FOUNDATION

THE SKY WAS clear and the air was crisp but not too cold on the afternoon of Monday, November 5, 1979. Hundreds of Black New Yorkers gathered in Harlem at the corner of 125th Street and Adam Clayton Powell Jr. Boulevard, before marching five miles to Midtown Manhattan, where they joined thousands of other demonstrators at Dag Hammarskjold Plaza, near the United Nations headquarters. The demonstrators carried red, black, and green liberation flags and large banners that read, "Free the Land," "Black People Charge Genocide," "Human Rights Is the Right to Self-Determination," and "Take Command: Fight for Human Rights." Some estimates put the crowd at up to five thousand attendees.

The occasion was the tenth-anniversary celebration of Black Solidarity Day, an annual event co-founded in 1969 by Afro-Panamanian activist and scholar Carlos E. Russell, intended as "a general protest against the intensifying repression that threatens the very existence of black people in America." Speakers articulated a list of demands to be presented to the secretary general of the United Nations and called for the international governing body to hold the United States accountable for committing "gross human rights violations and genocide" against Black Americans. This year's rally was co-organized by the National Coalition for Black Human Rights, with assistance from

Mutulu and Afeni Shakur, who were both national coordinators for the National Black Task Force for Cointelpro Litigation and Research.

Besides Russell, other speakers at the rally included such dignitaries as the esteemed reparations advocate and Garveyite elder "Queen Mother" Moore; civil rights activist and chairman of the National Black United Front Reverend Herbert Daughtry; and the Detroit-born Chokwe Lumumba, lawyer and Minister of Justice of the Provisional Government of the Republic of New Afrika.

The most notable moment of the rally came during Muntu Matsimela's speech. The Bronx-raised Black nationalist and activist took the stage and, before thousands of onlookers, read a communiqué prepared by the Coordinating Committee of the Black Liberation Army:

> Comrade-Sister Assata Shakur was freed from racist captivity in anticipation of Black Solidarity Day, November 5, and in order to express to the world the need to Free All Black Prisoners in the u.s. The Freedom of Black Political Prisoners is of fundamental importance to the protection of Black Human Rights in general. The brutal and callous Treatment by prison administrators of our captured comrades cannot be allowed to continue unnoticed by the Black Community. In freeing Comrade-Sister Assata we have made it clear that such treatment and the "criminal" guilt or innocence of a Black freedom fighter is irrelevant when measured by our people's history of struggle against racist u.s. domination.

The announcement of Assata's escape was greeted enthusiastically in progressive circles throughout New York. Reverend Daughtry published an opinion piece in the *Amsterdam News* with the headline "Run Hard Sister, Run Hard" and applauds Assata's anonymous liberators, writing that this "heroic deed will be told and retold around a million years to come . . . where Black people gather together to reminisce about heroes and heroines, great acts of courage and daring acts of courage and daring deeds, their exploits will be remembered."

Assata's escape also received international publicity, with the *South*

China Morning Post declaring, "Top terror woman escapes," and the *Times of India* reporting that "diehards" from the Black Liberation Army had engineered the prison break. In the January 5 edition of the *Amsterdam News*, a half-page advertisement, taken out by "the Black Community," wished "Peace to Assata Shakur (a.k.a. Joanne Chesimard)," encouraged her to "Stay Strong and Free," and closed with "Long Live Assata Shakur. Long Live the Black Liberation Struggle."

But while her escape was being hailed by supporters, the FBI and the NYPD had initiated a massive manhunt, raiding and ransacking the homes of anyone with even a marginal connection or resemblance to Assata. This collaboration between the FBI and local law enforcement led to the expansion of the Joint Terrorism Task Force, which would soon be implemented in numerous cities across the nation. In response to the manhunt, Black enclaves in New York were decorated with posters declaring, "Assata Shakur Is Welcome Here," with a large black-and-white photo of a young Assata smiling beneath a tall Afro.

As law enforcement searched in all directions for the escaped fugitive, following dead-end tips and reports that took them everywhere from New York and New Jersey to Florida and Mississippi to as far away as California, Assata was secured away in Sekou Odinga's safe house in Pittsburgh. She had been taken to Pittsburgh—hidden in the trunk of a Lincoln Continental driven by Marilyn Buck and accompanied by Odinga—after spending the first two nights immediately following her escape in Buck's own safe house in East Orange, New Jersey. While in Pittsburgh, Assata used the name Mary Davis, straightened her hair, and visited a dentist, Dr. Ralph Cato, to have her teeth fixed.

Members of the group that freed her, the so-called Family, gave her $50,000—half of the proceeds from the Paramus armored truck robbery—and asked her what she wanted to do next, if she'd like to be set up with an apartment somewhere in the United States. She said no, she wanted to leave the country for Libya, Angola, Cuba, or China. The Family purchased a ticket for her in August 1980 and created false identification for her, and one week later she was on a plane ferrying her from John F. Kennedy International Airport to the Bahamas, where she made the connecting flight that would take her to her new home in Havana, Cuba.

In the fall of 1980, a Lincoln Detox veteran and close friend of the Family, Nehanda Abiodun, was trusted with flying to Cuba for the first post-exile meeting with Assata. Assata's security detail met Abiodun at the airport and escorted her to the three-story home where Assata had been put up. Assata had regrown her Afro, and she carried a snub-nosed .38 for protection. She handed Abiodun a cassette tape, on which she'd recorded a message for her supporters back in the United States. Her recorded speech was transcribed, printed in a leaflet, and distributed among supporters, with the title, "From Somewhere in the World: Assata Shakur Speaks—A Message to the New Afrikan Nation." "Sisters and brothers, nobody on the face of this earth has more of a right to a nation than We do," she declares. She continues:

We are not citizens of amerika. We are victims of amerika. And We have a right to determine our own destiny. And anyone who says that We don't is either the worst kind of racist dog or the worst kind of Uncle Tom. When Black people, New Afrikans, get serious about our liberation there is nothing that can stop us.

While the 1970s had been a turbulent and disastrous decade for the Black liberation struggle as a whole—the violent dissolution of the Black Panther Party, and the incarceration and deaths of numerous leaders—Mutulu and his clique could at least claim a victory with Assata's liberation and close the decade on a triumphant note. But if Mutulu and his soldiers believed that by liberating Assata they would gain prestige for themselves while also recharging the moribund liberation struggle, they were soon disappointed. Few people outside of their immediate circle knew exactly who was responsible for the prison break. Even Kamau Bayette, who had been Mutulu's loyal acolyte since training under him at Lincoln Detox, was kept out of the loop. After the escape, Bayette showed Mutulu and Mtayari Shabaka Sundiata a newspaper article reporting on the prison break. "This is a big thing that happened. I'm sure it'll shake people up," Bayette excitedly told the two men, not knowing that each of them had taken part.

Responsibility for Assata's liberation was claimed by the Black Liberation Army, but this BLA bore little resemblance to the BLA that had been active nearly a decade earlier—not least because this new group consisted of several White people. Mutulu defended the use of Whites in the group. "Some of them are good people," he told the others. "Some of the crackers really do help us out with jobs."

The euphoria that followed Assata's liberation eventually tapered. The movement, despite Mutulu's efforts, was hardly rekindled. A new decade had arrived, bringing new demands, new challenges, a new president, and heightened subjugation. If any spark of the movement had remained by the end of the 1970s, it would be thoroughly extinguished in the 1980s. And just two years after the Family's greatest triumph, they would confront their greatest defeat.

Mutulu's first attempt at holding up an armored car, in Pittsburgh in 1976, had been a disaster, resulting in the arrest of Raymond Oliver and Chui Ferguson. But he had since recruited more experienced members to his team, including Sekou Odinga, Tyrone Rison, Mtayari Shabaka Sundiata, and Kuwasi Balagoon. These five men would be known as the "Primary Team" or the "Action Five." Their ace in the hole was the four White women who rented the cars and served as getaway drivers: Silvia Baraldini, Susan Rosenberg, Judy Clark, and Marilyn Buck. They were referred to as the "Secondary Team" or the "White edge." This specialized unit had successfully committed at least two expropriations of armored cars and one Chase Manhattan bank before liberating Assata from Clinton at the end of 1979.

On February 20, 1980, just three months after facilitating Assata's escape, they attempted another armored truck robbery, outside a Korvettes store in Greenburgh, New York. Though they beat and threatened to shoot one of the guards, a Black man named Terry Copeland, he stubbornly refused to unlock the door to the truck, and the thwarted robbers were forced to retreat empty-handed back to the Mount Vernon safe house.

After two months of licking their wounds, they attempted another armored truck robbery on April 22, outside a European American Bank branch in Inwood, New York, on Long Island. This attempt went much more smoothly, and, without a single shot fired, the group made off with $529,000, their largest haul. Much of the money they seized went toward BAAANA, while the rest was divided among the group and other close associates. Though the police and the media would later identify the Family as the Primary Team and Secondary Team members, there was an extended family of relatives, friends, and colleagues who depended on these expropriations. When a job was unsuccessful, mouths went hungry; bills went unpaid. A successful job meant money in everyone's pockets and people were fed.

Meanwhile, the immediate family was still growing. On May 16, 1981, inside the BAAANA clinic, Makini gave birth to a daughter, Nzingha Shakur. The father wasn't her husband Mutulu, but Kenneth "Dedon Kamathi" Carr, a member of the Pan-African organization All-African People's Revolutionary Party. Though Makini had been married to Mutulu, Makini explained that Mutulu wasn't troubled by the affair: "He understood the nature of our relationship." Mutulu took in Nzingha as his own child and, along with Mutulu's biological children, Maurice and Sekyiwa, and his adopted son, Tupac, Nzingha joined the young children of the Shakur family.

But now other, more worrying concerns were beginning to surface within the collective. Many dedicated people in the movement had for years been dabbling with cocaine. Seeing a surge of popularity in the 1970s, cocaine was considered a party drug, openly used by celebrities and entertainers. Even activists and militants who had so diligently crusaded against drug use, often going so far as to rob and threaten dealers, would sniff a little cocaine now and then. By the start of the 1980s, however, cocaine use among certain members of the Family had gotten out of control, contributing to its eventual undoing.

Some members of the group, particularly the White women, had been naive to Mutulu's increased cocaine consumption, attributing his hyperactivity to his longtime reputation as an energetic person. But it wasn't only Mutulu who had developed a dependency on the drug. Many members of the collective—Bayette, Balagoon, and Sundiata—had also become heavy users, as had Makini, who spent up to $50,000 on cocaine, missed mortgage payments on the brownstone, and lost their car after missing lease payments. Money also started to go missing from the clinic's safe. Mutulu and the others tried to hide their addiction from Odinga, who regarded such drug use as counterrevolutionary, but he had his suspicions, leading to heated confrontations with Mutulu. "Our purpose is to rob for Black people, as a mass of people," Odinga insisted, "to channel the money back into the neighborhoods." His admonitions increasingly fell on deaf ears.

At one point, the collective's drug use had gotten so bad that they asked their friend Bilal Sunni-Ali for help. A devout Muslim and the tenor saxophonist in singer Gil Scott-Heron's acclaimed Midnight Band, Sunni-Ali was a trusted comrade, respected in the movement for his self-discipline and piety. When people came backstage during a concert and offered the Midnight Band drugs, women, or any of the other trappings of a working musician, Scott-Heron would speak on behalf of Sunni-Ali, whom he called "the Spirit." "Oh, just give him a prayer rug," he'd say. "That's the Spirit. He doesn't want any of that other stuff." Sunni-Ali drafted a set of guidelines for drug use for the collective. This list consisted of eight rules, including: "No being under the influence of drugs while on family or operational business" and "Never spend money wastefully on intoxicants." These rules went largely unheeded, and more and more time and money continued to go toward feeding their cocaine addictions. The problem had gotten so severe that some members would secretly go out and rip off drug dealers or rob UPS truck drivers.

The Primary Team brought in two new members, recruited by Mutulu to assist with jobs in which Odinga and Rison refused to participate. The first was Chui Ferguson, whose muscle spasms had sabotaged the attempted armored car robbery in Pittsburgh five years earlier. Ferguson, now thirty-five years old, had recently been released from prison and was looking for a chance to redeem himself in front of Mutulu. The other new recruit was Jamal Joseph— the young Panther 21 defendant who had briefly been Dhoruba bin Wahad's acolyte until both men were arrested during the attempted robbery of the Triple-O Social Club in the Bronx. While bin Wahad had been circumstantially connected to the May 1971 machine-gunning of the two police officers on Riverside Drive and sentenced to twenty-five years, Joseph had been connected only to the April 1971 slaying of Panther newspaper distributor Samuel Napier, for which he pleaded guilty of attempted manslaughter and was given a four-year sentence.

Free since 1975, the twenty-seven-year-old Joseph drifted about New York, struggling to find purpose. He took odd jobs, taught martial arts classes, enrolled in acting classes at Brooklyn College, appeared in an off-Broadway production of a Lorraine Hansberry play, drove a jitney cab, and hung around street hustlers. He began self-medicating with alcohol, weed, and cocaine, suffering from "bouts of depression and guilt, feeling that I had fallen victim to some of the habits and behavior that I fought against as a young Panther." In fact, Joseph now found himself involved in the very activities that he had once crusaded so zealously against, not only peddling cocaine but also operating an escort service for teenage girls under the pseudonym Jay Daniels, or "J.D.," from his apartments in and around Greenwich Village. He was not making much money in either venture and he was looking for a new, big score. He eventually found his way to Mutulu.

By the spring of 1981, whatever prominence the Family had gained in the movement with the liberation of Assata Shakur had been squandered. Assata was free and had been whisked safely out of the country, but the remaining soldiers were still struggling for survival, fighting for the spoils of a lost war. Even the expropriations, which had become the group's essential fundraising source, were becoming increasingly desperate and disastrous.

On the morning of June 2, while robbing a Brink's armored truck outside a Chase Manhattan branch in the Bronx, Tyrone Rison impulsively fired his M-16 into the two guards lying down on the pavement, wounding forty-five-year-old guard Michael Schlachter and killing fifty-nine-year-old guard William Maroney. The robbers reconvened at the Mount Vernon safe house to divide the $292,000.

Odinga was outraged by the team's violence and carelessness. The White women, too, were appalled by the shooting, declaring that they wouldn't take part in any other jobs until the violence was addressed. By this point, however, it was too late to stop. Like the embattled desperado taking on one last job before retirement, Mutulu had been plotting a job so bold, so potentially lucrative, it eclipsed every job before it—one that would furnish him and his associates with enough money to keep BAAANA afloat, to purchase a homestead in Georgia, to provide for their growing families, and to give up the outlaw's life. If successful, the Family would walk away with $1.6 million. He called it The Big Dance. Odinga, who'd had reservations about the job from the beginning, viewed it differently. He called it "nothing but sure death."

17.
THE BIG DANCE

RONALD REAGAN WAS inaugurated as the fortieth president of the United States on January 20, 1981. A former movie actor and two-term governor of California, Reagan began his first term during a time of economic uncertainty, record inflation and unemployment, national malaise, and widespread mistrust of the government. In his inauguration speech, Reagan promised to shrink the size and influence of the federal government, declaring that the nation's "present troubles parallel and are proportionate to the intervention and intrusion in our lives that result from unnecessary and excessive growth of government." As president, Reagan introduced a set of "supply-side" or "trickle-down" economic policies, generating a large decrease in domestic social spending, including cuts to welfare, Social Security, and Medicaid; extensive tax cuts to higher earners; and the deregulation of markets, while also, paradoxically, increasing the defense budget at an exponential rate, more than doubling military spending over his first four years in office.

Reeling from the turbulence and radicalism of the 1960s and 1970s, Reagan's 1980s would also usher in a new era of conservatism, rabid consumerism, and materialism. While the previous two decades had seen numerous countercultural and social movements—from civil rights and Black Power to anti-war and anti-imperialist struggles—the new decade was marked by conformity and unrestrained greed. Gone were the marches, the sit-ins, and the free breakfast programs. What dissidents or revolutionaries remained by the beginning of the 1980s—those who hadn't yet been killed or incarcerated—now found themselves in an unfamiliar nation where the rules had changed virtually overnight. The revolution had given way to Reaganomics. Wealthy Americans devised means to become even wealthier, while the poor struggled merely to stay alive. "By any means necessary" was now "by any means available."

Nanuet is a small, suburban hamlet in New York's Rockland County, about thirty miles north of Manhattan and two miles from New Jersey. Rockland is a predominantly White county, but more Black and Haitian families had begun settling in the quiet community, particularly in the nearby village of Nyack. Thousands of visitors made the trip north each weekend, crossing the Tappan Zee Bridge over the Hudson River to visit Nyack's friendly craft stores and antique shops or to go shopping at the Nanuet Mall.

Mutulu had been planning this job for months, taking Family members with him on reconnaissance and surveillance missions of the target site: a small bank inside the Nanuet Mall, where the Primary Team planned to hold up a Brink's armored truck as it stopped on its afternoon pickup. Some on the team were not enthusiastic about this job—particularly Sekou Odinga and Tyrone Rison, who were concerned about being caught in traffic on Route 59 or stopped by a police roadblock on the Tappan Zee Bridge. There were few escape routes and not much hope of a Black man easily blending in with the White, suburban surroundings. As one of the most senior and experienced members of the group, Odinga tried to dissuade the others from attempting this robbery: "I told them, 'Don't do this. These are the weak points. If anything happens, this is what the police are gonna do and you're not gonna be able to get around,'" Odinga recalled. "They thought they had the secret, because it had worked [on other jobs]. It was eventually bound to happen. The weaknesses were there."

Mutulu couldn't be deterred. The payoff was too good; too many people were depending on this money. Here was an opportunity for the Family to score another big victory, which they hadn't had since Assata's liberation two years earlier. The job would proceed as planned.

Tuesday, October 20, 1981, nine months after Reagan's inauguration, began like any other day in Nanuet. Townsfolk went off to work or school, untroubled by big-city stresses, removed from the crime and other ills of their neighbors some thirty miles south. Three Brink's armored truck guards—James Kelly, Francis Joseph "Joe" Trombino, and Peter Paige—began their shifts early, at seven thirty in the morning, leaving from the Brink's office in Newark and continuing north up the New Jersey Turnpike, stopping for nineteen bank pickups along the way. Around 4:00 P.M., the guards arrived at the Nanuet National Bank branch at the Nanuet Mall, the final stop of the day.

Trombino and Paige entered the mall and reappeared five minutes later, guiding a pushcart weighted with three money sacks. They were loading the sacks into the back of the Brink's truck when a red Chevrolet van pulled up to a halt beside them. Three men wearing ski masks jumped out and, without warning, opened fire on the guards with automatic rifles and shotguns. At a nearby bus stop, Kuwasi Balagoon—who had moments ago been sitting on a bench, having a pleasant conversation with a woman waiting for the bus—jumped up and ran toward the melee, pulling out a pistol and joining the three men firing on the guards.

In under a minute, the shooting was over. The driver of the Brink's truck, James Kelly, lay unconscious after being struck by spraying glass and bullet shrapnel. Trombino was shot in the shoulder, nearly separating his arm from his body. Forty-nine-year-old Paige was struck in the neck with a bullet, killing him instantly.

The four assailants loaded the money sacks, containing almost $1.6 million, into the back of the van and sped off, with two men up front in the driver and passenger seats. Less than a mile later, the six-man team pulled into the rear delivery area of a Korvettes department store to make the switch into a waiting U-Haul truck and a Honda Accord. But the drivers of the U-Haul, a White man and a White woman who would serve as getaway drivers, arrived to the switch point thirty seconds late—a significant delay when every second matters. The man steering the U-Haul, moreover, had unknowingly parked in a spot within sight of a house at the end of Main Drive, an unpaved street behind the Korvettes store.

A White, twenty-year-old college student named Sandra Torgerson had been working on a paper for her economics course when she looked out the living room window and noticed a man with a rifle running back and forth between the van and the U-Haul while another man stood guard. Torgerson, unaware of the Brink's truck robbery that had taken place only minutes earlier, alerted her mother that there were men with guns behind Korvettes. Before she and her mother could take down the license plate numbers, the U-Haul and Honda sped off, leaving the van behind. Sandra called the police, who, at that moment, were only looking for a red Chevy van. Sandra told them about the U-Haul and the Honda, providing police with the tip that would soon prove both crucial and disastrous.

Odinga—who had been skeptical of this job from the beginning and had refused to participate—would later reflect contemptuously on this fatal misstep: "If it had went off perfectly, it wouldn't have been no problem. The problem was that it didn't go off perfectly. Somebody happened to look out of their window and see something that they thought looked strange and out of the ordinary. And being what somebody would call 'good citizens,' they called the police. Something that would never happen here [in Harlem] back in them days. People would've seen it and said, 'Oh, what the fuck,' and gone on, but nobody would've called the police. That's something White folks do. We don't do that. But she did do it. She thought it was strange. She told the police, 'It looks strange, I think something's wrong.' She didn't know. She's just being a good citizen, as they would call it, minding somebody else's motherfucking business."

Police units throughout Rockland County were alerted to the escaping U-Haul and Honda. Roadblocks were promptly set up at the Tappan Zee Bridge and other possible escape routes, and officers were told to be on the lookout for a U-Haul driven by Black men. Five minutes after the vehicle switch at Korvettes, Sergeant Edward O'Grady, Detective Arthur Keenan, Officer Brian Lennon, and Officer Waverly Brown—the only Black police officer in Nyack—stopped a U-Haul near the New York Thruway, at the intersection of Route 59 and Mountainview. They drew their guns and ordered the occupants out of the truck, but the officers were confused when a White man stepped out from the driver's side, followed by a White woman exiting the passenger's side. The woman reacted fearfully to Lennon's shotgun, raising her arms and pleading for him to lower his weapon. "Put the shotgun back," O'Grady told Lennon. "I don't think it's them."

Lennon followed orders, returning to his patrol car and waiting inside. But Keenan remained suspicious. He attempted to open the rear door of the U-Haul, which was locked. He grabbed the frightened woman and demanded, "I want to know what's in there." Before she had time to think of a response, Keenan heard a metallic object strike the floor of the truck, which turned out to be a dropped ammunition clip. A split second later, the door flew open and six men with automatic weapons began spraying bullets.

Keenan was grazed in the leg before diving for cover behind a tree. Thirty-two-year-old O'Grady was struck repeatedly in the chest, back, and abdomen. He later died from his wounds. Forty-five-year-old Brown was hit in the thigh, chest, and shoulder, killing him almost instantly. In the ensuing confusion and disorder, some of the assailants managed to escape by foot into a nearby wooded area, others jumped into a white Oldsmobile, others carjacked a silver BMW from a mother and daughter, and the rest got away in the Honda. An off-duty New York City corrections officer, Michael Koch, spotted a White woman sprinting across the Thruway, ran after her, and apprehended her. "He shot him, I didn't shoot him, he shot him," the woman screamed with panic at Koch. "I didn't shoot him, he shot him."

Meanwhile, scores of police cars were speeding toward the scene as the Thruway ramp became jammed with stuck or abandoned cars. Twenty-nine-year-old South Nyack Police Chief Alan Colsey saw the tumult on the Thruway and turned around, realizing the getaway vehicles were likely trying to find another escape route. Colsey soon spotted the Honda and Oldsmobile speeding down a rural road and gave pursuit, leading to a high-speed chase through Nyack's quiet residential streets. At the intersection of Sixth Avenue and North Broadway, the Oldsmobile made a quick and deft turn, narrowly avoiding hitting a concrete wall. The Honda wasn't as lucky, sideswiping a pole before skidding out of control across the road and crashing hard into the wall.

Colsey jumped out of his patrol car and pointed his gun at the wrecked Honda, ordering the occupants out. A White man crawled out of the passenger seat and raised his hands, followed by the driver, a White woman who also had her hands raised. A third passenger, a Black man in the back seat, had been injured in the crash. When backup officers arrived at the scene, they dragged him out of the car and put him in an ambulance to Nyack Hospital. The injured Black man, who gave his name as Solomon Bouines, was forty-one-year-old Samuel Brown, former car thief and ex-convict. The White man was thirty-seven-year-old David Gilbert, a former member of the Weather Underground. The White woman who had been driving the Honda was thirty-one-year-old Judy Clark, a former member of the Weather Underground and the May 19 Communist Organization.

It was 4:30 P.M. Only thirty minutes had passed since the Brink's truck robbery outside the Nanuet Mall, and three men were dead, with four suspects in police custody. The identity of the woman apprehended earlier on the Thruway by the off-duty corrections officer would prove to be the biggest surprise for authorities. Giving her name as Barbara Edson, she was identified the next morning as thirty-eight-year-old Kathy Boudin, the former Weather Underground member who had been a fugitive from the FBI for the last eleven years.

Though the other participants in the robbery managed to escape that day, police recovered all of the stolen money from the Honda and the abandoned U-Haul. Authorities traced the license plate on the getaway Oldsmobile to an apartment in East Orange, New Jersey, rented and occupied by a woman listed as Nina Lewis. When police arrived at the vacated apartment the next morning, they discovered bomb-making materials, shotguns and automatic weapons, floor plans for New York City police stations, and "Black Liberation Army documents." Information in these documents led police and FBI agents to another apartment in Mount Vernon, New York, also hastily evacuated, where they found ski masks, an air pistol, ammunition, a bank bag seal, and bloodied clothing; and to an apartment in the Bronx, where they found ammunition, weapons, and disguises. All three apartments had been listed as being rented and occupied by Nina Lewis or Carole Durant. By the afternoon of Thursday, October 22, authorities determined Lewis and Durant to be the same woman: Marilyn Jean Buck. The bloodied clothing found in the Mount Vernon apartment was discovered to belong to Buck, who had apparently shot herself in the leg during the shoot-out on the Thruway as she attempted to pull her gun out from her boot.

The remaining members of the group convened after the botched robbery to debrief, count their losses, and pass the blame around. Odinga was furious that the unstable and untrustworthy Samuel Brown had been recruited for this job; he was now in police custody and liable to say anything. But much of the immediate blame was placed on the White getaway drivers, the so-called "White edge." If David Gilbert and Judy Clark hadn't messed up the switch at the Korvettes, they would've gotten away undetected. If they hadn't crashed into the wall during the police chase, they wouldn't have been apprehended. But the Whites weren't the only ones to blame. Some of the robbers had been too hotheaded, too ready to shoot. In the end, no one wanted to take responsibility for the disaster in Nyack.

"'T' got carried away with his shooting," reported the alleged ringleader of the group, using a nickname for a comrade. "The crackers fucked up driving . . . one of us got shot in the leg."

Members of the group fanned out, abandoning safe houses and skipping town. But a joint task force composed of local police and the FBI had been staking out apartments, running license plates on cars coming and going from the apartments, and wiretapping phones, and authorities eventually drew up a list of the alleged participants in the disastrous October 20 robbery. To their astonishment, they discovered that this group wasn't an ordinary gang of armed bandits, but a close-knit team consisting of former Black Panthers, Black liberation movement veterans, and White radicals. Many had taken part in earlier actions and were already familiar to law enforcement: Chui Ferguson, Mtayari Shabaka Sundiata—the "T" who "got carried away with shooting"—Nehanda Abiodun, Jamal Joseph, and Kuwasi Balagoon. Of the four Whites who directly participated in the robbery, only one had escaped: Susan Rosenberg, who was alleged to have been the driver of the Oldsmobile that got away during the high-speed chase through Nyack.

Meanwhile, the supposed ringleader of the Family—the one who was said to call the shots and organize the jobs—was believed to be Mutulu Shakur.

▬

Things went from bad to worse for the Family. On Friday, October 23, at twelve thirty in the afternoon—only three days after the botched Brink's robbery—NYPD detectives in the South Ozone Park neighborhood in Queens noticed a gray 1978 Chrysler LeBaron with two Black men inside and the same New Jersey license plate that had been seen the day before on a different car, circling outside Buck's Mount Vernon apartment. The car belonged to Yaasmyn Fula. The detectives followed the LeBaron in their unmarked patrol car, and when the driver of the LeBaron began picking up speed, trying to evade them, the detectives radioed for backup. Additional cars immediately joined the pursuit, leading to a high-speed chase north on the Van Wyck Expressway, then onto Northern Boulevard in Flushing. The driver jumped the road's concrete center divider, spun around, and now sped west toward Shea Stadium and onto the Flushing Avenue bridge, at which point the passenger in the LeBaron leaned out the car window and began shooting from a 9mm handgun at the pursuing officers.

A tire blew out on the LeBaron, and the driver screeched to a halt in a warehouse district near Northern Boulevard and 127th Street. The two men, both wearing bulletproof vests, sprang out of the car and squeezed off a few rounds at the advancing officers, then turned and ran into the rear area of a construction company and split off running in different directions. The man who had been in the passenger seat of the LeBaron, Mtayari Shabaka Sundiata, scrambled up and over a chain-link fence, but when he landed on the other side, he was met by Detective Irwin Jacobson. Jacobson hit Sundiata with one bullet in his neck and one bullet in his head. He died instantly.

The driver of the LeBaron had meanwhile run into a yard behind the Willets Point Contracting Corporation and dived underneath a parked van. He pointed a 9mm at the advancing officers but, a moment later, tossed the gun aside.

"I give up," said Odinga.

After more than a decade underground, the veteran soldier was finally captured.

Police took Odinga to the 112th Precinct, where they beat him for hours. They struck his face and body with fists, burned him with cigarettes, and flushed his head in a toilet. Days later, he was taken to the prison ward of King's County Hospital to await charges. His pancreas was so damaged from the beating that he had to be fed intravenously for the next three months.

As early as December 15, federal agents had been surveilling BAAANA via wiretaps on the acupuncture clinic's phones. By that point, however, Mutulu had already gone into hiding, laying low in an apartment in Washington, D.C., using the alias Donnelle Johnson.

Odinga bitterly remembered the Brink's robbery as the dissolution of whatever had remained of the group and its actions, blaming the tragic incident on the group's hubris and lack of preparedness. "That was the beginning of the end. First of all, it never should've happened," he explained. "And once it did happen, it exposed a lot of our weaknesses. Not just [Mutulu's], but organizational weaknesses, structural weaknesses. It really exposed it. A lot of it, we knew we were weak in them areas and were trying to deal with it at the time, and some of it we didn't even know. The action just exposed it because it brought the pressure on us that we wasn't ready to absorb and sustain. It just showed us that we wasn't ready."

After three months in Washington, Mutulu returned to New York and stayed in a Greenwich Village apartment at 85 Barrow Street, which had been earlier occupied by one of Jamal Joseph's female escorts. On February 2, Mutulu's wife Makini received a phone call from her friend Asha Sundiata. "He's back," Asha told Makini. "Everything is in position if you want to touch base." Makini, however, wasn't the only one listening to this call. When she traveled from BAAANA to Barrow Street to be reunited with her husband, she was trailed by federal agents. The FBI received court authorization to install a hidden microphone in the Barrow Street apartment, as well as wiretaps on nearby pay phones, to gather evidence against Mutulu.

Finally, in the predawn hours of March 26, after a 169-day surveillance involving fifty agents and at a cost of $2 million, the FBI made its move.

"I had put Nzingha to bed and I was just about to go to sleep, when I heard a boom and all the lights went out," Makini recalled. Her and her ten-month-old daughter's room was on the top floor of the brownstone, and Makini ran out to the balcony to see what was happening. "All I could see was guns and the lights [on the guns], because they had blown the lights. And the riot squad was coming up the stairs."

Susan Rosenberg was on her way to work, walking down an uncharacteristically empty 139th Street, when she noticed federal agents in riot gear perched on surrounding rooftops. She then saw a tank pushing down the street, approaching the clinic. "I ran out of there," she remembered. "I did a wheel-about and went down the block and got in the subway and was like, 'This is it, they're going to take down this building.' And it wasn't a question of going there to defend it. It was like, 'No no no.'" Rosenberg went underground and was subsequently placed on the FBI's "Most Wanted" list.

On the same morning of the raid on BAAANA, task force agents also raided an apartment on West 110th Street, where they apprehended Chui Ferguson, and a ground-floor apartment on 14th Street, where they found Jamal Joseph in bed with his pregnant wife, Joyce. Both men were taken into custody without incident. But their primary suspect and target—whom agents had been hoping above all to capture that morning—slipped away just in time.

Mutulu Shakur had disappeared.

In the months and years that followed the fatal Brink's robbery, charges and convictions were meted out against anyone tenuously affiliated with the perpetrators. The prosecution in each case was aided considerably by the statements of Tyrone Rison and Kamau Bayette, who would each cooperate with the government and testify against their compatriots.

Judith Clark, David Gilbert, Samuel Brown, and Kuwasi Balagoon were convicted of murder and robbery and sentenced to the maximum seventy-five years to life. Kathy Boudin pleaded guilty to the same charges and was sentenced to twenty years to life. Jamal Joseph and Chui Ferguson were each convicted for being an accessory after the fact, for harboring Mutulu, and were sentenced to the maximum twelve and a half years.

In addition to these criminal convictions, more than a dozen people were jailed for lengthy sentences for refusing to testify before a grand jury, including Yaasmyn Fula and Bilal Sunni-Ali's wife, Fulani. Alan Berkman—the White doctor who had worked at BAAANA and was said to have treated Marilyn Buck after the shoot-out—spent a year in jail before jumping bail and going underground. Nehanda Abiodun—alleged to have taken part in Assata Shakur's liberation and the Brink's robbery—fled to Cuba and, like Assata, was granted political asylum. After moving back home to Texas in 1982, Makini Shakur was allowed to refuse to testify before the grand jury only because she was still married to Mutulu, but that didn't stop FBI agents from continuing to follow and harass her.

In November 1982, Bilal Sunni-Ali was apprehended in Belize. He was extradited to the United States to face charges related to the Brink's robbery and an earlier armed robbery. During closing arguments, Sunni-Ali's attorney, Chokwe Lumumba, played a song from the 1975 record by Gil Scott-Heron and the Midnight Band, *The First Minute of a New Day*. "The Liberation Song" featured Sunni-Ali playing an extended and powerful tenor saxophone solo. Sunni-Ali explained how he and his attorney entered the record into evidence "as an example of why there would be an effort to silence me, why would there be an effort to put me in jail." They wanted to show the jury that it was through music "that we made our contribution to the liberation struggle."

Sunni-Ali watched the eight Black jurors in the jury box "slapping their hands and bobbing their heads."

"Oh man, the jury loves you," Chokwe Lumumba told his client. "They're not going to convict you of anything."

Sunni-Ali was acquitted of all charges.

The final two captured defendants, however, didn't fare as well. Odinga and Italian activist Silvia Baraldini were tried together—on racketeering and conspiracy charges from earlier, unconnected robberies and for aiding in the 1979 liberation of Assata. Choosing to represent himself in court, Odinga denied taking part in the Brink's robbery but supported the actions of the Revolutionary Armed Task Force and the Black Liberation Army. He refused to disavow the robbing of banks and armored cars, stating that these "expropriations" had been intended "to take back some of the wealth that was robbed through the slave labor that was forced on them and their ancestors."

In his opening statement on April 19, 1983, Odinga vehemently defended his actions in the liberation movement and the actions of his fellow captured soldiers. "I am a New Afrikan soldier, and we have an absolute right to fight for our freedom," Odinga declared. "That is a human right. That is not a right your oppressor gives you. That is not a right you have to ask and beg for. Like all people who want to be free, what is necessary to exercise that right is to stand up like men and women and exercise it. If it calls for fighting, then we fight."

On Saturday, September 3, Odinga and Baraldini were found guilty. Manhattan Federal Court Judge Kevin Duffy imposed the maximum sentence of forty years and recommended Odinga serve the entire sentence. "Rub it on your chest, sucker," Odinga shouted at the judge.

The final three remaining suspects, Susan Rosenberg, Marilyn Buck, and the alleged ringleader, Mutulu, were still fugitives. For all intents and purposes, the struggle was over. What had begun in the late 1960s—with young Black students and activists from Oakland to New York picking up the gun and teaching self-defense and self-determination; with community healthcare workers taking over a Bronx hospital in the early 1970s and introducing a revolutionary form of holistic drug addiction treatment; with the daring jailbreak of a highly revered thinker and activist—had come to an ignoble end in October 1981, in the small, quiet, and otherwise unexceptional town of Nyack, New York.

But though the Black liberation movement, as it had once been, was now effectively crushed, its tenets and creeds would soon find a renewed voice with a young spokesman—one who would take the passion, zeal, and fire of the early movement and translate it for a younger generation. As the son of a Black Panther and raised by movement veterans, he was uniquely qualified for this role. He was, he would later reflect, groomed for this role all his life: "I used to sit outside by the streetlights and read the autobiography of Malcolm X . . . And it changed me, it moved me. And then of course my mother had books by people like . . . Patrice Lumumba and Stokely Carmichael, *Seize the Time* by Bobby Seale, and *Soledad Brother* by George Jackson. And she would tell these stories of things that she did or she saw or she was involved with and it made me feel a part of something. She always raised me to think that I was the Black Prince of the revolution."

He had grown up witnessing the government repression of Black freedom fighters. His own family had been targeted, jailed, and killed by the U.S. government, but the Shakur name would defiantly live on, finding fame and notoriety in ways no one before him could have anticipated.

Tupac Amaru Shakur would soon enough discover the unendurable weight and responsibility of his name.

PART III

18.
YOUNG BLACK MALE

U.S. HIGHWAY 59 stretches in a straight, nearly vertical line from the Canadian border to the Mexican border, only bending slightly west when it reaches southeast Texas. In Texas, the highway travels through Texarkana, Marshall, and Houston, ending at the border town of Laredo, a distance of more than six hundred miles. Trooper Bill Davidson—forty-three years old and an eighteen-year veteran of the Texas Department of Public Safety—was patrolling U.S. 59's Jackson County on the night of April 11, 1992. At twenty minutes past 8:00 P.M., five miles south of the town of Edna, Davidson spotted a 1986 GMC Jimmy with a broken headlight. He hit the lights.

The driver of the GMC was eighteen-year-old Ronald Ray Howard, a native of South Park, a notoriously crime-ridden and distressed neighborhood in Houston. Raised by an abusive father, shuttled around at a young age from school to school, Howard finally dropped out when he was fifteen or sixteen and began selling drugs and stealing cars. With a number of run-ins with the law, including two arrests for car theft and burglary, Howard was on probation at the time he was stopped on U.S. 59; he'd been on his way to Port Lavaca, a two-hour drive from Houston, where he allegedly sold his drugs. After pulling over Howard, Davidson learned that the GMC had been reported stolen two days earlier from Port Lavaca.

Davidson got out of his patrol car and approached the GMC. As he neared the driver's side window, the trooper addressed Howard amiably: "How you doing?"

Howard immediately lifted a 9mm handgun and shot the trooper in the neck. He then sped off, leaving Davidson bleeding on the highway. Witnesses alerted the police, who pursued Howard in a chase south down U.S. 59. Howard crashed the GMC and attempted to flee on foot, but he was soon apprehended near Victoria and confessed to the shooting. Davidson died three days later from his wound.

At first, the trooper's murder didn't receive much press besides a few brief mentions in Texas media outlets, slipped in somewhere in the middle sections of the local newspapers. Within weeks, the incident all but disappeared from the public. But by the end of the year, details of the shooting would spread far beyond the Texas border, attracting national media attention from the *Los Angeles Times* to the *Washington Post*, as well as the attention of the vice president of the United States. What brought about this sudden, sweeping interest was the recently disclosed existence of a cassette tape police had recovered from the GMC. The cassette was a dubbed copy of *2Pacalypse Now*, the debut album by a young rapper named Tupac Shakur.

Howard confessed that he'd been listening to the album, released the previous year, at the time Davidson pulled him over: "The music was up as loud as it could go with gunshots and siren noises on it and my heart was pounding hard," he said. "I watched him get out of his car in my side view mirror, and I was so hyped up, I just snapped."

Howard's court-appointed attorney, Allen Tanner, argued that his client was psychologically affected by the album's lyrics, which addressed police brutality in Black communities, with characters who responded aggressively against police repression. "Without the music riling him up," Tanner said, "I do not think that this incident would have occurred."

Newspapers across the country followed this story, printing excerpts of lyrics from the album, particularly "Soulja's Story," in which the narrator boasts about shooting a cop who'd pulled him over while driving, asking the fallen officer if he remembers Rodney King, the Black man who'd been brutalized by the Los Angeles Police Department in the same year of the album's release. A jury had already and easily convicted Howard of capital murder, but Tanner sought to use the lyrics on *2Pacalypse Now* during sentencing to argue for life imprisonment rather than the death penalty. Emboldened in part by public outrage over the relatively new genre of music derided in the press as "gangsta rap," the slain trooper's widow, Linda Davidson, hired her own attorney and filed a civil lawsuit against Time Warner, the parent company of Interscope Records, which had released *2Pacalypse Now*. Her suit charged the record label and its artist of gross negligence in manufacturing and distributing music that promoted "imminent lawless action." Davidson's attorney, Jim Cole, grumbled that Tupac's lyrics read like "pages out of a cop-killing manual." Davidson and Cole were promised support from disgraced Reagan White House aide Oliver North, of the Iran-Contra scandal, and soon Vice President Dan Quayle also waded in, calling for Time Warner to pull *2Pacalypse Now* from shelves. "There is absolutely no reason for a record like this to be published by a responsible corporation," he said, adding that the record "has no place in our society."

This wasn't the first time rap music or Black artists had been maligned and accused of inciting violence against law enforcement. Only months earlier, the rapper Ice-T had bowed to mounting pressure to pull the song "Cop Killer" from the debut album of his thrash-metal project Body Count. But the outcry over *2Pacalypse Now* was believed to be the first time a civil suit had been brought against a music company alleging that one of its products led to murder. It was also the first time a jury would have to consider whether song lyrics should determine a condemned man's fate. By the start of the 1990s, it seemed as though not only rap music but the grievances of Black America were on trial.

"This suit isn't just about some storyteller spouting militant rhetoric here," said the attorney Jim Cole. "Tupac is dangerously serious."

Tupac himself issued no public comment on these accusations. This wasn't the first time the emerging young rapper would find himself at the center of controversy, nor would it be even close to the last.

The lawsuit against Time Warner ultimately failed. The jury in Howard's criminal case, composed of only one Black juror, also wasn't persuaded by the defense's arguments. On July 14, 1993, after a six-day deliberation, Ronald Ray Howard was sentenced to die by lethal injection.

"Where I come from, people hate the police," Howard told a reporter two weeks before his sentencing. "They harass you for nothing there, just because you're a young black male, like Tupac says . . . To me, rap never glorified violence. It just told the truth."

During the national debate over *2Pacalypse Now,* journalists and critics frequently referred to Tupac Shakur as a San Francisco Bay Area rapper or an Oakland rapper. When the album was released in November 1991, however, Tupac had been living in the Bay Area for only three years. Tupac's journey to becoming not only a nationally recognized rapper but an ambassador for West Coast hip-hop began years earlier and thousands of miles away, on the opposite end of the country.

Tupac's mother, Afeni, had been having a difficult time in the years following the Panther 21 acquittal in 1971. The Black Panther Party she'd believed in and for which she'd sacrificed so much was coming apart at the seams, and her Party comrades were in jail, turning against each other, or going underground to engage in guerrilla warfare. Afeni, like many other movement leaders and soldiers, was suffering from effects of post-traumatic stress, though she might not have yet recognized it as such, and had begun to self-medicate with alcohol and drugs.

The first few years after her acquittal, Afeni stayed busy. She was invited to speak at colleges and universities, including Harvard and Yale. She and Mutulu worked together as national coordinators for the National Task Force for Cointelpro Litigation and Research, helping inmates obtain their FBI files for their legal defense. She worked as a paralegal at Bronx Legal Services, helping tenants organize rent strikes against exploitative or negligent landlords and providing legal assistance to prisoners inside New York's penal institutions. But Afeni's prospective law career and promising future as a legal and housing advocate were suddenly ruptured following the fatal robbery of the Brink's truck on October 20, 1981.

After authorities alleged Mutulu had been the ringleader, he disappeared underground, leaving behind Afeni; his biological children, Maurice and Sekyiwa; and his stepchildren, Nzingha and Tupac. Though Mutulu was legally married only to Makini, and his marriage to Afeni had been more or less ceremonial, Afeni's connection to the fugitive suspect would soon entangle her directly, affecting the lives of her and her children. When she was let go from her job at Bronx Legal Services, she believed it was because of her association with Mutulu. She tried to find new employment, but many employers in New York remembered the criminal accusations leveled against her and remained suspicious. As she struggled to find employment, to make ends meet, and in need of help raising her two young children, Afeni began a relationship with a street hustler named Kenneth "Legs" Saunders. His impact on the lives of Afeni and her children would carry lifelong repercussions, as he was allegedly the one to introduce Afeni to crack cocaine.

Though Afeni and others in the movement had freely dabbled in powdered cocaine, marijuana, and occasionally LSD, the arrival of crack was catastrophic, particularly in Black communities. Unlike powdered cocaine, crack could be purchased more cheaply, produced an immediate and much more intense high, and was extremely addictive. Also unlike powdered cocaine, crack was linked to the increase in criminal activity in America's cities. Overlooking how these cities were suffering from economic disinvestment and a reduction of social welfare programs under President Ronald Reagan, the government and media alike blamed the rise in crime and addiction on America's so-called crack epidemic. Reagan significantly expanded Nixon's "War on Drugs" campaign, passing draconian and disproportionate drug laws and flooding prisons with young Black men.

Saunders entered Afeni's life at a moment when the pressures of being a newly unemployed single mother to two young children was too much to endure, though their relationship was built less on love than on the use of crack cocaine. "That was our way of socializing," Afeni later recalled. "He would come home late at night and stick a pipe in my mouth." Saunders left a more favorable impression on Tupac, bringing home clothes and toys for the young boy.

Not yet a teenager, Tupac had been, in his own words, "quiet, withdrawn. I read a lot, wrote poetry, kept a diary." After cooking himself dinner, he'd sit alone in front of the television for hours, watching the actors and pretending his family was no different from the families on the screen. Other kids his age teased him for his soft looks, his long eyelashes, his effeminacy. He "didn't feel hard," cried often, and wished he could fit in. He knew the expectations his mother and her movement friends had of him—that he would be the "Black Prince of the revolution"—but at that time all he wanted was to be less alone and to find his own way.

In the summer of 1984, Afeni enrolled twelve-year-old Tupac in free acting classes, and he was cast in the role of Travis Younger in Lorraine Hansberry's *A Raisin in the Sun,* produced by the 127th Street Repertory Ensemble and directed by visionary alumnus of the Black Arts Movement Ernie McClintock. Right away, Tupac realized he had found his calling: "When the curtain went up, I just caught that bug that everybody talks about," he later recalled. "I was like, 'Whoa, this is it.' It was better than sex and anything, money, everything. It was like, 'Whoa, I want this.'"

But he would have to put his newfound calling on hold while he and his family addressed more pressing concerns. Saunders was arrested and jailed for credit card fraud, and the Shakurs were without a home or any source of income. Newly homeless, the family crashed with friends and relatives in Harlem and the Bronx, staying at times with Sekou Odinga, Yaasmyn Fula, or Afeni's sister, Gloria, and her husband, Tommy. Gloria soon learned of an apartment owned by a cousin in Baltimore, Maryland. The cousin agreed to let Afeni and her children move in. Afeni took thirteen-year-old Tupac and nine-year-old Sekyiwa and what little money she had and made the nearly two-hundred-mile journey south to Baltimore, where they hoped for a new beginning, a clean slate, and a better life.

The new arrivals moved into a one-bedroom apartment at 3955 Greenmount Avenue, in North Baltimore's Pen Lucy neighborhood. Sekyiwa attended fourth and fifth grades at a private school and Tupac began eighth grade at Roland Park Middle School, as Afeni attended a computer-training program and received welfare assistance.

"The first two years in Baltimore were good," Afeni recalled. "I didn't do drugs there. Baltimore was a heroin town, and my drug of choice was cocaine. So, I just smoked weed in Baltimore, and I was just a mom for the first two years. I just took care of the kids. Got them settled in school and all."

As they were still settling into their new home, grief visited the family. When Afeni phoned New York to let Saunders, who'd been recently released from jail, know where they could be found, she learned he'd died, at age forty-one, of a heart attack after using crack cocaine. Tupac, who considered Saunders to be his father, or at least the closest thing he'd had to a father after Mutulu had gone underground, was distraught. "It was three months before he cried," Afeni later recalled. "After he did, he told me, 'I miss my daddy.'"

Tupac was also affected by his family's desperately impoverished living situation. Supporting herself and her children while on welfare, Afeni struggled to pay the bills, and the cramped apartment was often without lights. At school, Tupac's new classmates teased him for his raggedy clothes, lopsided haircut, skinny frame, and unfinished braces. But he soon forged a close friendship with a boy named Dana Smith, who went by the nickname "Mouse Man" and was a skilled beatboxer. The two boys bonded over their shared enjoyment of a somewhat new style of music called hip-hop. Tupac had just begun writing his own rap lyrics, and the two boys performed together in school hallways, playgrounds, out in the neighborhood streets, anywhere they could, for anyone who would listen. As homage to his hometown, Tupac gave himself the name "MC New York."

In February 1985, the two boys were offered their first official performance, opening for New York electro hip-hop group Mantronix and Brooklyn rapper Just-Ice at Baltimore's Cherry Hill Recreation Center. Performing under the name "the East-Side Crew," the young group's debut was favorable though not especially earth-shattering. "I mean, we really didn't get any boos or nuthin'," remembered Smith.

Their next public performance was better received. That November, the Enoch Pratt Free Library held a rap competition, open to anyone under the age of eighteen. "Calling All Rappers!" the flier announced. Tupac composed "Library Rap," persuading people to get library cards and telling kids to stay in school. The submission earned them an invitation to perform in person at the semifinal competition, held at the library branch on Pennsylvania and North Avenues. After an impressive performance for the modest, seated audience, the East-Side Crew advanced to the finals, held in a larger room at the library's downtown branch. The two boys, now fourteen years old, won first place.

The East-Side Crew didn't last much longer, as the two boys finished eighth grade and went off to different high schools—Tupac to Paul Laurence Dunbar High School and Smith to Northern High School—but they remained in touch and continued to hone their rap skills. After one unhappy year at Paul Laurence Dunbar, Tupac auditioned for the Baltimore School for the Arts. For his audition, he recited lines from *A Raisin in the Sun*.

"It was so good," remembered the head of BSA's theater department, Donald Hicken, "and the first thing I noticed was that he was extremely charismatic. From the very beginning, we all sensed he was the real deal."

Tupac was accepted into BSA and was cast as Walter Lee in *A Raisin in the Sun* for the school's annual "Spring Fever" student showcase. Though he struggled academically, he took acting seriously, studying playwrights and dreaming of one day becoming a Shakespearean actor. Only a couple of years later, Tupac would denigrate Baltimore as "total ignorance town," but his time at BSA, at least, was beneficial and gratifying. He was "exposed to everything. Theater, ballet, different people's lifestyles—rich people's lifestyles, royalty from other countries and things, everything." He became friends with many of his classmates, both Black and White, forming a lifelong bond with a young aspiring actor named Jada Pinkett.

Despite his crushing poverty and the occasional ridicule from his peers—for being poor, for being sensitive, or for being, as he referred to himself, a "skinny kid with a funny name"—Tupac stayed active in his adopted city. He continued to write lyrics and perform in competitions with his rap partner Mouse Man, and he soon befriended another young rapper named Darrin Keith Bastfield, who, along with a DJ named Gerard Young, joined Tupac and Mouse Man to form a new rap crew they called Born Busy. One of Born Busy's central performance pieces, which they recorded a cappella onto a cassette tape in 1988, was a song Tupac had written a year earlier called "Babies Having Babies." Three years later, Tupac would revisit and expand upon this theme in another song, "Brenda's Got a Baby."

Tupac was now beginning to dabble in local activism, becoming briefly involved in a campaign, "Yo-No," in which he and his girl-friend, a White dance student named Mary Baldridge, canvassed door to door, participated in rallies, gave talks, rapped, and performed a self-composed, half-hour-long operetta, spreading the word about the damages of gun violence and teen pregnancy. Throughout this nascent organizational work, Tupac made it a point to credit his social and political awareness to the influence of his mother, Afeni. Bastfield remembered Tupac schooling him on the history of the Black Panther Party and the Panther 21 trial and how the police had, in April 1969, ignited a fire outside the door of Afeni and Lumumba's Harlem apartment. "They set your shit on *fire*?" Bastfield asked, astounded. When Tupac brought his friend home and introduced him to his mother, Bastfield was struck by the "powerful, radiant woman," who was "strong and bounding with life, almost otherworldly."

"Tupac and his mother communicated openly and unashamedly," Bastfield later recalled, "that's why he wasn't afraid to express himself. The once intriguingly, even mystically blurred picture was becoming more and more clear. Ms. Shakur spoke like a prophet with her words of wisdom and sobering perspectives on reality. She was the burning fire behind his red-hot personality and the guiding light leading him to question, always more deeply, in his times of quiet contemplation. She meant everything to him."

Despite the rosy domestic picture, however, not all was well at home. Afeni had relapsed and had again begun using crack cocaine, while Tupac and his sister Sekyiwa often had to escape from their mother's frightening episodes, crashing on friends' couches and finding their own meals. And though Afeni wouldn't mention it publicly, she had been privately dealing with another family loss.

On February 3, 1986, Lumumba Shakur was found in a New Orleans apartment, dead from multiple gunshot wounds. Afeni's first husband and founder of the Harlem chapter of the Black Panther Party, Lumumba had since moved to New Orleans with his children from his first marriage to Sayeeda. He'd followed in his father Salahdeen's footsteps, selling goods and clothing brought in from West Africa, and he was a regular vendor at the annual New Orleans Jazz & Heritage Festival, often working side by side with the elder Shakur. When assailants entered his apartment and shot him in his head and neck, Lumumba was somehow able to stumble to the home of his neighbor, who called the police.

Some, like Lumumba's oldest friend, Sekou Odinga, believed his murder was an attempted robbery gone wrong; others, like Lumumba's closest friend during the last years of his life, Bilal Sunni-Ali, believed Lumumba was killed "because of his connections to the movement" and that it had been "a vendetta by the police to retaliate for things that had happened to policemen over the years." Lumumba's murder was never solved.

Salahdeen arrived in New Orleans from his home in New Jersey and flew his son's body north, to be buried in the Oak Grove Cemetery in Hammonton, New Jersey, in the Black Sunni Muslim community of Ezaldeen Village. This was the second time the Shakur patriarch had had to bury a son. Lumumba Abdul Shakur was forty-four years old.

Misfortune continued to fall on the Shakurs, as though earthly or supernatural forces were conspiring against the fragmented family. Only one week after Lumumba's death, on a quiet street corner in West Los Angeles, after evading authorities for four years, Mutulu Shakur was captured.

19.
NEW AFRIKAN
PANTHER

AS AFENI AND her children were in Baltimore, trying to get a new start on their lives, authorities across the country were busy pursuing the remaining fugitives from the Brink's robbery, extinguishing whatever small cinders still remained from the radical movement. In November 1984, Susan Rosenberg was arrested by police in Cherry Hill, New Jersey, after she and a companion were discovered unloading firearms and 740 pounds of explosives into a storage unit. In May 1985, FBI agents arrested the activist doctor Alan Berkman and a companion near Doylestown, Pennsylvania, and he, too, was convicted of possession of explosives, firearms, and false identification. That same month, police also captured Marilyn Buck in Dobbs Ferry, New York.

The subject of a nationwide manhunt since 1982 and one of the FBI's "Ten Most Wanted Fugitives," Mutulu Shakur was discovered in West Los Angeles on February 12, 1986. Acting on information from materials seized after the earlier arrests, FBI agents, local law enforcement, and NYPD officers traced Mutulu to Los Angeles and tailed him throughout the city for a month. He was standing on the corner of Packard Street and Spaulding Avenue at just after 9:00 p.m. when two undercover NYPD officers approached him. Mutulu fled but was soon tackled to the ground by the officers.

The morning after his arrest, a group of supporters demonstrated peacefully outside the West Los Angeles police station where he was held, and later that week, during Mutulu's extradition hearing, three dozen supporters crowded into the courtroom, applauding and shouting the New Afrikan refrain, "Free the land!" On Friday, March 7, when Mutulu was brought to the U.S. District Court in Manhattan, he was again met by about forty supporters, who stood and applauded when he entered the courtroom. Mutulu raised his fist. "Free the land, you all," he said.

"Free the land," they called back.

Mutulu noticed his mother, Delores Williams, sitting in the gallery. "Hi, Ma," he said, before going on to chat with supporters.

Reading from a one-page prepared statement, Mutulu declared himself a "New Afrikan freedom fighter" and a prisoner of war. He apologized for being captured and pleaded not guilty. He and Buck were tried together on charges of racketeering, conspiracy, armed robbery, and murder, connecting the pair to the Brink's robbery and to additional bank robberies, and assisting with Assata Shakur's escape. By charging Mutulu with violating the Racketeer Influenced Corrupt Organizations (RICO) Act, enacted by the federal government to prosecute organized crime and Mafia figures, prosecutors didn't need to place Mutulu physically at the scene of the crime; they only needed to argue that he had conceived of the Brink's robbery and had furthermore been the leader of the alleged "Family" of Black and White armed revolutionaries. On May 11, 1988, after a six-month trial, the jury found Mutulu and Buck guilty on all charges.

"I am here for advocating change and justice," Buck told Judge Charles Haight Jr. during the sentencing hearing on August 2, adding that she remained committed to fighting "the cancer of white racism and supremacy."

"I am not guilty of any criminal act," Mutulu declared. "I am guilty of conspiring to be a revolutionary. I am not guilty of a criminal enterprise. I want to be recognized as a political prisoner and as a prisoner of war. I am a freedom fighter."

The crowd of about 150 supporters inside the courtroom stood to their feet and applauded, shouting, "Freedom fighter!"

Buck was sentenced to fifty years. Mutulu was given sixty years. With Mutulu's incarceration, authorities had effectively neutralized the final active leader of the Black liberation movement and delivered a decisive blow to the troublesome Shakur family. Zayd was dead, Lumumba was dead, Assata was in exile, Afeni was struggling with drug addiction and PTSD, and Mutulu was now behind bars. In only three short years, however, local and national law enforcement would again find themselves contending with the younger and even more hot-tempered Tupac Shakur, whose fame and influence would reach far beyond those of any of his forebears.

Back in June 1988, only one month after Mutulu's conviction and two months before his sentencing, Tupac arrived in Marin City, California. He was still in his junior year and he was heartbroken to have to leave the Baltimore School for the Arts, but between the family's untenable poverty, the city's high and rising rates of violent crime, and Afeni's growing drug dependency, Afeni made the difficult decision to send her children to California to stay with a family friend, Linda Pratt, wife of Geronimo "Ji-Jaga" Pratt. Former Southern California Black Panther leader, decorated Vietnam War veteran, and Tupac's godfather, Geronimo was at the time held at Mule Creek State Prison in Northern California. He was serving out a life sentence after his 1972 murder conviction.*

As Pratt was busy fighting his murder conviction, his wife, Linda, was fighting her own personal battles with alcoholism. She berated Tupac and Sekyiwa, taking out her anger and frustrations on the two children. Eventually she sent word to Afeni that she was entering rehab and had deposited the children at a neighbor's home. Afeni had planned to join her children in California when she'd gotten the money together, but this sudden crisis hastened her plans. She gave away her possessions, boarded the next bus, and soon reunited with her children in Marin City.

---

* Pratt's conviction was vacated in 1997 after his attorneys—including Johnnie Cochran, who became famous during the O.J. Simpson trial—proved that he had been targeted by the FBI and had in fact been hundreds of miles away from the scene of the murder.

Five miles north of San Francisco, Marin City had been a destination for many Black Southern migrants, who came to work on the shipyards during World War II. Marin City in the 1980s was a predominantly Black community, afflicted by high rates of poverty and crime and known by locals as "the Jungle." Once again the new kid in an unfamiliar town, Tupac struggled to be accepted. He "dressed like a hippie," wrote poetry, and read Shakespeare, and he often found himself harassed by neighborhood gangs and bullies. "I was the outsider," he remembered, a recurring theme throughout his adolescence. "I was the target . . . for street gangs. They used to jump me, things like that."

Tupac enrolled at Tamalpais High School, a majority-White school in the relatively affluent Mill Valley, took menial jobs at pizza joints and as a grocery store bagger, and sneaked off any chance he could to write raps. During his first year at Tamalpais, in the fall of 1988, he volunteered to be interviewed on camera about life as a teenager. In his first known interview to be filmed, seventeen-year-old Tupac—sporting the Gumby fade that he would keep for a few more years—demonstrates a calm and contemplative maturity, talking at length about income inequality in America, criticizing school curricula that don't address urgent community needs, and criticizing his male peers who disrespect women. After sharing a story about a recent night when local skinheads caused mayhem at a house party, Tupac tells the interviewers that he and his friends are "starting the Black Panthers again, in Marin City." As someone who grew up among Panthers and was intimately familiar with the Panthers' missteps, Tupac said he and his friends would be "doing it more to fit our views, less violent and more silent," and their central focus would be to "get the pride back in the Black community, because I feel like if you can't respect yourself, then you can't respect your race and you can't respect another's race . . . it just has to do with respect, like my mother taught me."

But what Tupac didn't mention in the interview was that he and his sister had been experiencing periodic stretches of homelessness, crashing on friends' couches or on floors, as Afeni waited for subsidized housing and descended even further into her addiction to crack cocaine. "I was broke, nowhere to stay," Tupac recalled later. "I smoked weed. I hung out with the drug dealers, pimps, and the criminals. They were the only people that cared about me at that point. And I needed a father—a male influence in my life, and these were the males. My mom, she was lost at that particular moment. She wasn't caring about herself. She was addicted to crack. It was a hard time, because she was my hero."

Tupac dropped out of Tamalpais in his senior year and tried to make money by selling drugs in Marin City. He wasn't a natural hustler, however, and two weeks after he'd started, the supplier demanded his drugs back and told Tupac to stay out of the game. He went on to connect with other local rappers and formed a group they called Strictly Dope, who performed around the Bay Area and self-recorded a handful of songs. On the song "Panther Power," Tupac and rapper Ray Luv trade verses about America's history of racism and hypocrisy, while Tupac declares that "my mother never let me forget my history" and that "Panther power is running through my arteries." Tupac's rhyming skills at this point were rudimentary. He was still honing his craft, while also navigating his future path.

By 1989, Tupac was at a crossroads. He was clearly passionate about music and acting, but his mother and other movement veterans still expected him to take up his family's mantle and become the voice of a new generation of Black Panthers. On one side of the divide was the potential for celebrity and riches, of becoming a famous entertainer and lifting his family out of poverty. On the other side were his ancestors who sacrificed their lives in America's war against the Black liberation movement. Though his few friends and rapping buddies in Marin City and the Bay Area only superficially knew of Tupac's political sensibilities and how deep his radical roots were, they had no way of knowing that, at the same time he was considering a rap career, he was receiving political mentorship by close family comrades and associates. When Tupac visited Pratt in prison and told him of his wish to rebuild the Black Panthers, Pratt told him to go to Los Angeles to meet a New Afrikan scholar, activist, and friend of the family, a man named Watani Tyehimba.

Born in Los Angeles in 1951, Tyehimba met Mutulu and Afeni in the early 1970s and became the Southern California representative for the National Task Force for Cointelpro Litigation and Research, working on the campaign to overturn Pratt's murder conviction.

After Mutulu's arrest in Los Angeles, authorities accused Tyehimba of harboring Mutulu and another fugitive from the Brink's robbery, Nehanda Abiodun. When Tyehimba declined to testify before a grand jury and refused to provide fingerprints and handwriting samples, the thirty-six-year-old father of three was jailed. "I will not betray the memories of all those who have struggled before me," Tyehimba said in a sworn declaration with the court, "and I will not endanger those who struggle now. I will not collaborate with the grand jury."

Tyehimba was sent to the federal prison at Terminal Island, where he said he was kept in solitary confinement for his first forty-five days, then held in lockdown twenty-three hours each subsequent day. "They put me in lockdown conditions like they would do hardened criminals," he recalled years later. "It was because of how we're perceived. We're part of the New Afrikan Independence Movement and the assumption was, if people got Assata out of prison, if Mutulu stayed underground all that time, then maybe there were elements that were gonna come."

Tyehimba was jailed from August 21, 1986, to October 6, 1987. His incarceration, he told the court, "actually made me more resolved . . . The only thing it made me do is reflect on the things our people have gone through."

After his release he remained active in the movement, going on to lead a Los Angeles–based community program, the Center for Black Survival, which hosted a local youth group called the New Afrikan Panthers, who performed politically themed plays and skits to encourage young people to become involved in social issues. On Pratt's recommendation, Tupac traveled to Los Angeles to help the New Afrikan Panthers with their performances, staying with Tyehimba and his family. When Tyehimba moved to Atlanta, Georgia, in August 1989, Tupac followed, often staying in Atlanta for long stretches of time, either with Tyehimba or with another friend of the family, Akinyele Umoja.

Like Tyehimba, Umoja was born and raised in Los Angeles. He met Mutulu and Afeni in 1973 when the couple traveled to Los Angeles in support of Pratt's campaign and also in hopes of re-creating a radical, holistic treatment center similar to Lincoln Detox. Umoja was eighteen years old and remembered being starstruck by Afeni. "I would tell people, if that sister told me to run into a wall or jump off a cliff, I would've did that, during that time," Umoja recalled. "She was that dynamic of a speaker, that passionate, that motivational."

Umoja moved to Atlanta in 1984 to pursue his master's degree at Emory University, later becoming a professor of the Department of African American Studies at Georgia State University. While in Atlanta he co-founded, with Tyehimba, the New Afrikan People's Organization (NAPO) and the Malcolm X Grassroots Movement (MXGM). In 1989, when he and Tyehimba decided to grow the New Afrikan Panthers into a national organization, Tupac enthusiastically volunteered to be its national chairman.

"He wasn't gonna be a follower. He was gonna have to take a leadership position," explained Tyehimba. "That's just Pac's personality. He said, 'Yeah, I'll be the chair.'"

Tyehimba and Umoja were skeptical. "We said, 'OK, if you're going to be the chairman of this organization, you can't be getting drunk no more, you can't be getting into silly fights with people,'" Umoja recalled telling Tupac, "because he was getting into fights a lot in Marin City. I'm not sure if we told him he can't smoke weed, but we might have. 'In other words, you got to be the public face of this group, so you really got to think about how you behave.'"

Tupac took his new responsibility seriously, organizing local youth meetings, canvassing Atlanta's HBCU campuses, and selling copies of the NAPO newspaper, *By Any Means Necessary*, throughout Atlanta and back home in Marin City. "He was all over the damn place selling that newspaper," recalled Umoja.

Atlanta radio host Bomani Bakari, of WRFG's Radio Free Georgia, invited the eighteen-year-old, newly confirmed national chairman of the New Afrikan Panthers to be a guest on his *Round Midnight* show. With a zeal and articulateness that belied his age, Tupac talks about the importance of embracing African names and African consciousness, encouraging unity in the Black community, and challenging sexism within the movement. He talks about COINTELPRO, the Last Poets, and the recent murder of a young Black man, Yusef Hawkins, by a White mob in Brooklyn. He goes on to answer calls from young listeners on how to get involved with the New Afrikan Panthers. Tupac is manifestly serious about his role not only as spokesperson for the fledgling organization but as a promising leader of the movement. He was preparing to move permanently to Atlanta, staying between Tyehimba's and Umoja's homes until he got on his own feet, while continuing his work with the New Afrikan Panthers.

One late night in 1990, he called Umoja from Marin City, crying and hysterical. Something was wrong at home and, though Tupac wouldn't go into details, Umoja suspected it had to do with Afeni, who was sinking deeper into her addiction. On top of that, Tupac was homeless and desperately poor. He wanted to fly to Atlanta as soon as possible and leave California behind for good.

A few weeks went by before Umoja heard again from Tupac. He sounded better now, electrified, even. He told Umoja he had just been hired by an Oakland-based rap group called Digital Underground.

Tupac wasn't an obvious choice for Digital Underground. It didn't make much sense, considering Tupac's reputation in the Bay as a serious-minded and politically conscious rapper and Digital Underground's popularity as a party rap group with a leader known for wearing an oversized novelty nose and singing about having sex in a Burger King bathroom. It certainly wasn't the direction in which Tupac imagined himself heading. The path that led Tupac to Digital Underground had been put into motion one year earlier, by a chance encounter between Tupac and a young woman named Leila Steinberg.

Born in Los Angeles, raised in Watts, and of mixed Jewish, Mexican, and Turkish descent, Steinberg had been raised to be politically engaged and race conscious. She moved to Northern California after finishing college and hosted spoken word and poetry workshops for students. She was also known around the Bay Area as a music industry insider, someone who could recognize young talent, foster their skills, and, more important, make the right connections.

One afternoon, in the fall of 1989, Steinberg visited Marin City to lead a workshop at a local school. She had some time to kill, so she walked to a park, took a seat on the grass, and opened up the book she'd brought with her: *Part of My Soul Went with Him*, by Winnie Mandela.

"Give me a break," said a male voice above her. "What do you know about Winnie Mandela?"

The skinny, smiling teenage boy standing above Steinberg told her he had recently finished reading the book and went on to quote passages from it. Steinberg and Tupac struck up a conversation and, despite their age difference—Steinberg was twenty-six and Tupac was seventeen—were pleased to discover a close connection between them and a shared desire to use art to promote social justice issues. "He came from a family that was driven by this movement across the board," Steinberg remembered. "His creativity early on was driven by political activism."

Steinberg agreed to become Tupac's manager, though her managerial duties consisted at first of encouraging his writing and sharing and discussing literature with him. When the situation at Tupac's home became untenable, Steinberg brought Tupac to her house to stay with her husband and children. But Steinberg was unable to find anyone interested in taking on the young and untested rapper. Not until the summer of 1990—almost a year after their first meeting—was Steinberg able to attract the interest of Atron Gregory, Digital Underground's manager. Gregory introduced Tupac to Digital Underground's leader, Gregory "Shock G" Jacobs, who agreed to give him an on-the-spot audition in the recording studio, where he was working on the group's debut album, *Sex Packets*. Jacobs liked what he heard from Tupac, but the group, which already had a full roster of rappers, didn't have much need for another. Jacobs and Gregory hemmed and hawed about taking Tupac on, not committing either way.

Meanwhile, Tupac was still a penniless high school dropout with no immediate prospects for the future. Nothing was holding him to Marin City. His bag was all but packed to relocate to Atlanta and lead the New Afrikan Panthers. Steinberg realized she was close to losing Tupac for good. "That was a deciding factor, and what I had to use to get Atron to sign the deal and really get to work," Steinberg recalled. "Because Tupac was gonna move out there and run the youth chapter if he didn't get a record deal and get that going."

Tupac felt he could most effectively reach out to and connect with other young, struggling Black men through his music, but if the music wasn't happening, another opportunity was waiting for him in

Atlanta: "He felt like he could advance his mission faster and further if he got a deal," Steinberg explained, "but he didn't want to sit around if it didn't happen, because he felt like he could go out there and do the work."

Finally, that August, recognizing how close everyone was to losing him, Jacobs agreed to take Tupac on tour with the group—not as a rapper, however, but as a roadie and backup dancer. Tupac didn't seem to care. It was money in the pocket and a chance to see the world. But more important, it was a foot in the door. While loading musical equipment and dancing in zebra-print bikini briefs on stage hadn't been his original plan, once he got his own career going, he would continue to do what he'd always set out to do: represent the underprivileged members of society and, as he explained, to speak for "the young Black males in America in the ghettos."

"That was the intention, to stay on a social-political path and use the music as leverage, and to bring the fans to the mission and the work," Steinberg recalled years later, "but the industry has a way of co-opting people's plans and visions, because it's so unhealthy.

"In hindsight," she continued, "now that I'm older and I understand all these other dynamics, I wish he would've gone to serve the New Afrikan Panthers and gotten out of the business in LA and the Bay."

Tupac was a rising star. His star would soon be extinguished, but until then he would burn brighter and hotter than anyone could've dreamed.

20.
THUG LIFE

BILAL SUNNI-ALI WAS home in Atlanta one day in early 1993, working on music in his office, when he was interrupted by abrasive sounds coming from the other room. "I heard my children playing some music," Sunni-Ali remembered. "It was all, 'Motherfuckin' this and motherfuckin' that and motherfuckin' this and motherfuckin' that.' I told them, 'Turn that shit off.' And they said, 'That's Tupac, Daddy.' And I said, 'I don't give a fuck who it is, turn that shit off in this house.' And then I said, 'Tupac? That's Tupac? Turn that shit back on, let me hear what the fuck he's talking about.' So they turned it on and I listened, and I've been a fan ever since."

Sunni-Ali, who'd known Tupac when he was still a boy in New York, identified with the political themes in Tupac's music. "It wasn't a surprise for me to hear him singing those lyrics," Sunni-Ali remembered. "That's what *I* was doing. That's what those who were in the *family*, who were entertainers, were doing. When I played with Gil Scott-Heron and the Midnight Band, that's what Gil was doing, that's what Brian was doing, so it wasn't a surprise for me to hear a younger person in the family doing the same thing that the elders were doing. It was only natural."

"I always thought he'd end up being some sort of political leader," remembered Sekou Odinga, who had also known Tupac as a young boy in New York. "He was just sharp. He was a sharp kid. You could talk to him and he would show you his intelligence by talking back to you."

Like Sunni-Ali, Odinga hadn't been a fan of rap music until he, too, listened more closely to Tupac's lyrics. Odinga came to recognize Tupac's potential to spread the message of Black empowerment, self-determination, and liberation—everything Odinga had fought and sacrificed for decades earlier—to a younger generation. "Once I heard that Tupac was doing it and becoming kind of famous for it," Odinga recalled, "I was always hopeful that that's what he was gonna do with it. Because he knew the message. He had grown up with the message."

Sonia Sanchez had a more visceral reaction upon hearing Tupac's music for the first time. The acclaimed poet and longtime activist was mother to twin sons and, like Sunni-Ali, her children were fans of rap music and often fought with their mother when they played the stereo too loud. One day Sanchez came home and heard the familiar sounds blasting from the stereo, but something this time made her stop.

"I was pouring some water to drink," she remembered, "and I said, 'Who is that?' And one of my sons said, 'That's Tupac Shakur,' and I dropped the glass. It shattered on the floor."

The boys asked what was wrong.

"Shakur?" she said. "Do you know that all the Shakurs are in jail, dead, or in exile? Does that young man know he's at risk?"

By 1993, Tupac had become a national star. After gaining entry into the industry with Digital Underground, he soon released his debut album, *2Pacalypse Now*, in November 1991, followed by his sophomore album, *Strictly 4 My N.I.G.G.A.Z.*, in February 1993. He'd also starred in two movies, 1992's *Juice* and 1993's *Poetic Justice* alongside Janet Jackson. Though neither of his albums achieved the commercial and critical success of the biggest rap stars at the time, like Dr. Dre and Ice Cube, Tupac's music gained notice for his melding of sociopolitical themes with contemporary sounds and topical issues. Hip-hop magazine *The Source* praised his music as being "a combination of black political thought and '90s urban reality."

While many critics and politicians would denigrate rap music, particularly abhorring what was dubbed "gangsta rap," Tupac likened his work to that of wartime reporters in Vietnam, when horrifying images were broadcast regularly into American homes, shifting public approval of the war and ostensibly hastening its end. "So I thought, that's what I'm going to do as an artist, as a rapper," he said. "I'm going to show the most graphic details of what I see in my community and hopefully they'll stop it quick."

With explicit and illustrative language, Tupac's lyrics address police brutality, child pregnancy, and gang violence. He fantasizes about taking up arms against racist police officers, bringing America to trial for its history of crimes against Black people, and—in tribute to his roots as a child of the movement—gives shoutouts to Assata, his stepfather Mutulu, and his godfather Geronimo "Ji-Jaga" Pratt.

"It was like their words with my voice," Tupac said of his predecessors. "I just continued where they left off. I tried to add spark to it, I tried to be the new breed, the new generation. I tried to make them proud of me."

Unlike other politically conscious rap acts at the time, like Public Enemy and Paris, Tupac also didn't hesitate to demonstrate his lighthearted and lascivious side, which is why he chose to follow the sympathetic "Brenda's Got a Baby" with a self-aggrandizing track like "Tha' Lunatic," or why he would place "I Get Around," a bawdy celebration of promiscuity, on the same album with "Keep Ya Head Up," a tribute to Black women and a support of women's reproductive rights. For Tupac, this wasn't a contradiction. He wanted to reach his audience—specifically young Black men—where they were, to speak the language of the streets, the jails, the barber shops, the clubs. This was how any entertainer or leader most effectively connected with his audience. The Black Panthers certainly didn't shy away from crude language. Even Huey P. Newton had at one time been a sex symbol.

But few things Tupac did would cause as much confusion and consternation as when he, in 1992, got "THUG LIFE" tattooed in giant letters across his abdomen. What was thug life? Was Tupac now promoting wanton criminal behavior? The media wasn't alone in its puzzlement. Watani Tyehimba was particularly appalled by the provocative tattoo. He had mentored Tupac to be a New Afrikan Panther, not a "thug." Tyehimba arranged a meeting with Tupac to discuss the meaning behind the tattoo, but he was disappointed to learn

Tupac didn't yet have an immediate defense for it. "You put some shit on you, you don't even have an explanation for it?" Tyehimba asked.

Tupac faced more interrogations from Mutulu. Interned at federal prisons in Lompoc, California, and Lewisburg, Pennsylvania, Mutulu kept in touch with Tupac and periodically imparted practical advice to his suddenly famous stepson. So when Mutulu learned that Tupac was now running around with his buddies screaming "thug life," he, too, sought some clarification.

"What do you mean by 'thug life'? What are you talking about?" Mutulu demanded to know. "Are you and the thugs gonna beat up an old lady and take her pocketbook? Is that what you're talking about?"

"No," Tupac replied, "that's not what we're talking about."

"Well, what is it?" Mutulu asked. "I know that's not what you're talking about, but you have to define it, Pac."

Tupac would retroactively define THUG LIFE as an acronym for "The Hate U Give Little Infants Fucks Everybody"—or, the neglect and violence children experience has damaging and far-reaching impacts on society. He, Mutulu, and veteran gang members developed what they called "the Code of THUG LIFE," a list of twenty-six guidelines for gang members and drug dealers to observe, in hopes of bringing an end to the violence plaguing urban Black communities. The Thug Code had little in common with other social programs, such as the Black Panther Party's Ten-Point Program. Rather than demanding fair housing, full employment, and free healthcare for all Black people, the Thug Code was designed specifically for hustlers, dealers, and gangbangers, "the true dwellers in the thug life," with such rudimentary demands as "No slinging in schools," "No slinging to pregnant Sisters," "Senseless brutality and rape must stop," and "Control the Hood, and make it safe for squares."

"It was a set of bylaws to ensure the survival of our community," explained Tupac's stepbrother and Mutulu's son, Mopreme, who'd become Tupac's close ally. "That's who we were talking to— the thugs, primarily."

But as fans and critics were still trying to figure out exactly what "Thug Life" was, Tupac found himself in a position of having to constantly defend it. "I don't understand why America doesn't understand Thug Life," he said. "America is Thug Life."

In Tupac's definition, a thug wasn't "a criminal, someone who beats you over the head," but "the underdog"—those who Karl Marx called "the lumpenproletariat" and Huey Newton called "the brothers on the block."

"Young Black males out there identify with Thug Life because I'm not trying to clean them up," Tupac said. "I am, but I'm not saying come to me clean. I'm saying come as you are. Everybody come as you are, and they feel my genuine love for the street elements."

"He was a griot. He was a messenger," Tyehimba explained. "He wanted to be the voice of young Black men . . . so he spoke their language. He spoke to their issues."

The desire to speak for the abandoned and misunderstood brothers and sisters on the street became Tupac's priority. He often brought up his own upbringing as an example, as someone who'd grown up in the movement and had witnessed its leaders either fall victim to drugs or form into exclusive fraternities, leaving his generation—the children of the movement—to fend for itself. He felt the movement had betrayed the people.

In February 1992, only three months after releasing his debut album, Tupac came to Atlanta, on Tyehimba's invitation, to be a guest speaker at the annual Malcolm X memorial banquet, hosted by the Malcolm X Grassroots Movement. In a banquet room with dozens of New Afrikan elders, adorned in colorful dashikis, kufis, and *geles*, Tyehimba introduced Tupac as a "second generation revolutionary." Twenty-year-old Tupac stood before the lectern in a baggy red hooded sweatshirt and a backwards red baseball cap. He began his six-minute, unscripted speech by paying tribute to the influence and sacrifices of his mother, Afeni—whose name continued to inspire a level of respect in movement circles—before launching into a fiery and profanity-laced condemnation of movement elders who had dismissed Tupac's generation, abandoning them to the streets. He rebuked those who were less concerned about reaching vulnerable young Black men and women than they were about "who got the baddest dashiki on."

"Before we can be New Afrikans, we gotta be Black first," Tupac told the audience. "We gotta get our brothers from the street, like Harriet Tubman did. Why can't we look at that and see exactly what she was doing? Like Malcolm did—the real Malcolm, before the

Nation of Islam. You gotta remember, this was a pimp, a pusher and all that. We forgot about all that. In our striving to be enlightened, we forgot about all our brothers in the street, about all our dope dealers, our pushers and our pimps, and that's who's teaching the next generation. Because y'all not doing it. I'm sorry, but it's the pimps and the pushers who's teaching us. So if you've got a problem with how we was raised, it's because they was the only ones who could do it."

Despite his criticisms, Tupac remained close to many movement elders. He hired his mentor Tyehimba as his security manager. He collaborated with Sunni-Ali on a musical project, though it was ultimately shelved. In 1992, during a visit to New York to celebrate the release of *Juice* with his family on the East Coast, he paid his respects to the Shakur family patriarch, Salahdeen Shakur.

Salahdeen remained a highly regarded merchant of African goods, dividing his time among Pennsylvania, New Jersey, and New Orleans, where he was a distinguished presence at the annual Jazz & Heritage Festival. After recovering from a stroke in early 1993, he was honored by the festival as a pioneer of the African marketplace. Only a few weeks later, on May 21, 1993, El-Hajj Salahdeen Shakur—father of Lumumba and Zayd, and mentor to Sunni-Ali, Sekou Odinga, Mutulu Shakur, and an entire generation of radical Black activists and leaders—passed away. He was seventy-three years old.

As Tupac's fame grew in the first few years of the 1990s, he became more adept and articulate in both his art and his message. His records were selling well, and his acting had earned critical praise. But even as his star was steadily rising, Tupac was receiving regular media attention not only for his music or his movies but for his many confrontations and legal troubles.

On October 17, 1991—one month after releasing his first single, the anti–police brutality anthem "Trapped"—Tupac was stopped by two White police officers in downtown Oakland and accused of jaywalking. Tupac alleged that, after asking for his identification, the officers mocked his name and told him he had "to learn your place." He argued with the officers, at which point they slammed him to the pavement, handcuffed him, and accused him of resisting arrest. He was released from jail several hours later with a bloodied and scarred face. Tupac called them his "learn-to-be-a-nigga scars." This was only the beginning of Tupac's many headaches to come.*

After eighteen-year-old Ronald Ray Howard fatally shot Texas trooper Bill Davidson during a traffic stop on April 11, 1992, the trooper's widow filed a civil suit against Tupac and his record label, alleging his lyrics inspired Howard to kill her husband.

On August 22, following a concert in his former hometown of Marin City, Tupac got into a heated altercation with some local residents who were angry about disparaging comments he had made in the press about his time living there. In the ensuing skirmish, gunshots were fired and a six-year-old boy, Qa'id Walker-Teal, was fatally struck by a stray bullet.

On March 13 of the following year, Tupac was arrested in Hollywood after he and a member of his entourage assaulted a limousine driver during a break while taping an episode of the television show *In Living Color*. A few weeks later, Tupac was arrested again and sentenced to ten days in jail after threatening another rapper with a baseball bat during an April concert at Michigan State University. Several days after that, Tupac and his entourage were accused of physically assaulting film director Allen Hughes in Los Angeles following an argument after Hughes dropped Tupac from a starring role in the film *Menace II Society*. Tupac was convicted of battery and assault and sentenced to fifteen days in jail.

Despite all of these arrests and charges, Tupac entertained a stubborn sense of invincibility. In the early morning hours of October 31, Tupac was back in Atlanta, where he'd been living at the time, and had just performed for Clark Atlanta University's homecoming celebration. He and his sizable entourage were heading from the concert to the Sheraton Hotel in a long caravan of cars, with Tupac behind the wheel of his new BMW. In addition to his rap crew and other assorted hangers-on, the caravan also included his security man-

---

* Tupac later brought a $10 million civil lawsuit against the Oakland Police Department, which was eventually settled for $42,000.

ager, Tyehimba, and Akinyele Umoja. Tupac's BMW was stopped at a traffic light on the corner of Peachtree and 14th Streets when he noticed a Black motorist arguing with two visibly intoxicated White pedestrians, whom Umoja had sized up as "just two drunk crackers." Tupac and his passengers got out of his car and, according to Umoja, "the White guys see these Black guys get out the car, they pull their guns out, they're cursing everybody, and fired a round off. Then shooting starts. I didn't see anybody pull the trigger, for the record, but shooting starts. I didn't see anybody get hit. I only knew somebody got hit because the police came and told us later on that one of them was shot in the behind and one of them was shot in the side."

The two White men, Mark Whitwell and his brother, Scott, turned out to be off-duty Atlanta police officers. Tupac was arrested and charged with two counts of aggravated assault. Like Umoja, Tyehimba has also never acknowledged who actually fired the shots that hit the men. "The mythology is out there, where people saw Tupac as being the shooter," Tyehimba explained, while admitting that the shooting "raised his profile." Charges against Tupac were eventually dropped, after it was proven that the Whitwells had been acting belligerent prior to the shooting, they had been the first to brandish a firearm, and the gun in their possession was stolen from a police evidence locker.

Regardless of who fired the shots that struck the men, Tupac emerged from the incident with greater street cred and an almost fabled status. He was believed to have achieved the impossible: a Black man not only shot two police officers, but he got away with it. A writer from the British periodical *New Musical Express* reported that Tupac was viewed by many in the Black community as "a black hero in the tradition of blues archetype Stagger Lee, who created a system for himself based on his own perceptions."

"These disenfranchised—the young blacks who are poor and hopeless—have no leader," Mutulu recalled years later. "Their heroes are cultural and sports heroes. No one—not Jesse Jackson, not Ben Chavis, not Louis Farrakhan—has as much influence with this segment as rappers. So when Tupac stands up to a white cop, shoots it out, wins the battle, gets cut free, and continues to say the things he's been saying—the decision to destroy his credibility is clear."

Tupac Shakur fought the law and won—for now.

By Tupac's side during nearly all of these incidents was his older step-brother, Mopreme. Tupac and Mopreme's relationship began many years earlier, when they were still boys in New York. Mopreme's father, Mutulu, and Tupac's mother, Afeni, used to bring their boys with them throughout New York, hanging "Fuck the Pigs" posters on walls and lampposts. The year he turned seventeen, Mopreme enlisted in the military. He had just finished high school. His father had been underground for three years. "One of the last things I remember him always saying was, 'You my little soldier,'" Mopreme recalled. "So I went to learn how to be a soldier."

After three years in the Army, Mopreme moved to Oakland to pursue a music career. Soon after his arrival in the Bay Area, he was invited to contribute a rap verse to a song by Oakland-based R&B group Tony! Toni! Toné! Calling himself "Mocedes the Mellow," he was given only three bars, or less than twelve seconds, but the song, "Feels Good," was a hit for the group.

By then, Tupac had also relocated to the Bay, and the two es-tranged stepbrothers soon reconnected. Inspired by the gangster and drug dealer from Queens Kenneth "Supreme" McGriff, Tupac began calling Maurice "Mopreme." The name stuck.

In 1993, Mutulu arranged to lead a Black cultural workshop for inmates at Lompoc penitentiary, and Tyehimba pressed Tupac to visit. Instead of a routine meet-and-greet, Tupac decided he wanted to put on a concert at Lompoc. He brought with him Mopreme and female R&B group YNV (or Y?N-Vee). He also used the occasion to debut a new rap collective he and Mopreme had named Thug Life. Tupac hoped Thug Life, as a performing and recording collective, would help his goal of connecting with marginalized communities, using the music as a lodestar for his greater mission.

"That's who Pac wanted to talk to," Mopreme explained. "That's who we were reaching: the poor, disenfranchised people in the hood . . . If you get their attention, you can deliver the message. If you don't get their attention, you can't deliver shit."

Thug Life released its first and only album, *Thug Life: Volume 1*, in September 1994—the same month that a controversial crime bill, drafted by then-senator Joe Biden of Delaware, was signed into law by President Bill Clinton, contributing to the mass incarceration of young Black men. The timing of the album was deliberate, Mopreme said, explaining how "the people who were directly in danger from the crime bill were the ones we needed to talk to: the thugs."

But though Tupac was as famous as he'd ever been—his albums sold well and his third film, *Above the Rim*, had come out earlier in the year to decent reviews—by the summer of 1994 his finances had become increasingly precarious, owing in large part to his near-constant legal expenses and ostentatious lifestyle. He was behaving erratically, getting into unnecessary fights, drinking too much liquor, and smoking weed all the time. A production assistant who'd worked with Tupac on *Juice* commented later that there might've been something "chemically unbalanced about him," while a rap executive disparaged Tupac as "a full-fledged, motherfuckin' nut." A February 1994 *Vibe* cover story asked, "Is Tupac Crazy or Just Misunderstood?"

"He was the most intelligent stupid dude that I know," Tyehimba recalled. "He was intelligent, but he did some stupid shit."

Whether he was suffering from undiagnosed trauma from his unstable childhood or he was desperate to prove to the world that he was no longer the sensitive former drama student who used to write poetry and study Shakespeare and cry himself to sleep at night, Tupac was fighting a battle between motivation and fatalism, between self-determination and self-destruction. This inner conflict would come to be reflected even more in his music.

"His music was always that pure," Mopreme remembered. "It was always coming from a real place, all of it. There's a realness to all of it. The key was in the music. People didn't listen close enough. He was telling people the whole time he was gonna die early. It's like, 'Why your young ass keep talking about death, nigga? I know it's around, but do you have to talk about it all the time?'"

"Pac was chasing death," Tyehimba recalled. "He didn't think he was gonna live beyond twenty-five."

21.
GUIDED BY STRUGGLE

IN 1981, WHILE still living in New York, Afeni took her ten-year-old son Tupac and his younger sister Sekyiwa to attend Sunday service at the House of the Lord Pentecostal Church in Brooklyn. Presided over by civil rights activist Reverend Herbert Daughtry, the large and imposing church on Atlantic Avenue was known for attracting young Black community campaigners and political leaders and scholars, including Cornel West and former Harlem Black Panther member and future New York Congressmember Charles Barron. It was a fitting church for someone of Afeni's prominence.

During service this Sunday, Daughtry brought Tupac up to the front of the church, stood him before the congregation, and asked the young boy what he wanted to be when he grew up. Tupac, who had been raised in the movement and reared by veteran movement leaders, answered right away: "A revolutionary."

Fourteen years after that Sunday, Tupac was back in New York, the place of his birth and early years, but now he was behind bars, facing up to four and a half years in prison. Coincidentally, the prison where he was held, Clinton Correctional Facility, in upstate New York, shared a name with the last institution to hold Assata Shakur, the Clinton Correctional Facility for Women. Tupac, however, wasn't locked up for revolutionary purposes, and his eventual freedom would come not from a team of armed radicals but from a menacing businessman with gang ties.

Tupac's incarceration was the culmination of a tumultuous two years in a life that had already faced numerous storms. While 1993 and 1994 were productive years for Tupac, they were also a time of increasingly reckless behavior and mounting legal trouble. He was verbally or physically attacking other rappers, film directors, critics, and politicians, and these outbursts often resulted in criminal convictions and jail time. For someone who had once been positioned as the spokesperson of a new generation of politically conscious Black activists and thinkers, Tupac was now, by all appearances, vying to be the spokesperson for gangbangers and hustlers. Those closest to him believed he had been transformed by the characters he'd portrayed in film: the sociopathic nihilist Bishop from *Juice* or the shot-caller Birdie from *Above the Rim*, whom Tupac had modeled on the real-life New York City hustler Jacques "Haitian Jack" Agnant. Hoping to get Tupac back on track, Watani Tyehimba gave him a book to read by gangbanger turned Black nationalist author Monster Kody.

Born Kody Scott in 1963, Monster Kody joined Los Angeles's Eight Tray Gangster Crips at an early age and quickly became infamous for his brutality, earning him his nickname. While in prison, he was introduced to the nationalistic tenets of the Republic of New Afrika, became politically conscious, and, influenced by one of the most respected family names in radical Black liberation, changed his name to Sanyika Shakur. His memoir, *Monster: The Autobiography of an L.A. Gang Member*, was published in 1993 and became a bestseller, giving readers the first insider's look at gangbanging culture in Southern California.

Tyehimba gave Tupac the book in 1994, hoping it would provide an example of the pitfalls of gang culture and the redemptive qualities of New Afrikan consciousness. He wanted Tupac to remember who he really was, who he'd been brought up to become, who he still was in his heart. Tupac read the book in one night, Tyehimba remembered, but he took a different message from it. "I gave him the book because I wanted to show him somebody who came from Monster Kody and became a Shakur," Tyehimba recalled. "But he took it the other way."

Tupac's preoccupation with gangbangers and street life only deepened, and though he was never affiliated with either side, Bloods or

Crips, he would mimic gang culture, adorning himself head to toe in red on one day and in blue on another day, getting gang-associated tattoos, and hiring both Bloods and Crips to work his security detail. When he would get into trouble with one set or another, Tyehimba and Mutulu, who each held some influence over certain gang members, would step in and put out the flame Tupac had kindled. For Tupac, who had spent the majority of his life bouncing from community to community—from New York City to Baltimore to Marin City to Atlanta to Oakland to Los Angeles, struggling to fit in with and be accepted by his more streetwise peers—gangs were not only a community in which to belong; they also were a way for him to prove his authenticity, his realness, in an industry that is built upon largely manufactured conceptions of "realness."

"If you're rapping this hard stuff, you have to live it," said Tyruss "Big Syke" Himes, a member of the Thug Life group. "Otherwise people check your résumé and say, 'You don't look like you're hard from your résumé, let's see if you are.' Pac always felt he had to prove something to his homeboys."

According to his first manager and creative mentor, Leila Steinberg, Tupac believed his alliance with gangbangers would further his original mission of reaching young Black men where they were, helping to inspire political engagement and pride in themselves, which had always been his foremost concern. "He was drawn to where he felt he could have an impact and where he was needed," Steinberg recalled. "I wouldn't say that he was drawn to gang culture because he wanted to participate. He was drawn to the streets because he believed that's where his service was required . . . He always wanted to be able to go into any hood and be embraced by gang members of every set, including Mexican gangs." But even with the best of intentions, Steinberg explained, Tupac "did not understand the beast that he stepped into."

Tupac would soon be betrayed by the company he kept, setting into motion the events that would lead to his ultimate ruin.

In the fall of 1993, Tupac was in New York City co-starring in the film *Above the Rim* when he made the acquaintance of Jacques

"Haitian Jack" Agnant. A well-known hustler and industry power broker with a penchant for expensive clothing, jewelry, and guns, Agnant lived the life Tupac only portrayed in his work, and Tupac followed Agnant and his entourage at the heel. "They took me shopping, and that's when I bought my Rolex and my jewels," Tupac said. "They made me mature. They introduced me to all these gangsters in Brooklyn. They was showing me all the guys who I needed to know to be safe in New York."

Despite warnings from friends and colleagues, Tupac courted Agnant's favor, still seeking approval from those with more street hustling experience than he'd had. On November 14, Tupac accompanied Agnant to a New York nightclub and was introduced to a young woman, Ayanna Jackson. The two danced and made out inside the club before leaving together, going to Tupac's hotel, the Parker Meridien, and having consensual sex. Jackson returned to the hotel four days later to meet Tupac but found three additional men inside the suite: Agnant; Tupac's road manager, Charles "Man Man" Fuller; and an unidentified man. Jackson followed Tupac into his bedroom and began giving him a massage on his bed. Soon after, Agnant, Fuller, and the unidentified man entered the room.

Accounts of what happened next vary between accuser and defendant, but only slightly. Both Tupac and Jackson agree that sometime after the three men entered the room, Tupac stood up and left, passing out on the couch. But while Tupac would admit that his only error was not doing more to stop what was happening, Jackson maintained that he had actively participated, forcing her to perform oral sex on him. After leaving the hotel room, Jackson called the police, who arrived at the hotel and arrested Tupac, Agnant, and Fuller. The unidentified man had already disappeared.

Tupac was indicted on charges of sex abuse, sodomy, and—because two guns were discovered by police in the hotel room—possession of weapons. When Agnant's lawyer successfully severed his client's case from the other two defendants, Tupac suspected that Agnant had been secretly working for the government. His suspicions, though doubtful, were not entirely without precedent. As a child of the movement, where stories of agents provocateurs and informants had been like bedtime stories, Tupac was well aware of the threats that surrounded him and his family at all times. Moreover,

Agnant had introduced Jackson to Tupac only two weeks after the shooting of the off-duty police officers in Atlanta. Law enforcement agencies across the country, Tupac believed, had good reason to conspire against him.

Nevertheless, he reserved most of the contempt for himself, particularly for not standing up for Jackson as Agnant and the other man took advantage of her. He would later reflect how "even though I'm innocent of the charge they gave me, I'm not innocent in terms of the way I was acting . . . I'm just as guilty for not doing nothing as I am for doing things." To certain politicians and media outlets, however, the sexual assault accusation confirmed the worst-held beliefs about Tupac—of being not only a misogynist and a thug, but also a rapist. He wept when he spoke with friends, distraught that his aspiration to be seen as a champion of Black women had become irreparably damaged. He felt misunderstood, distrustful, and, worst of all, betrayed. "Pac called me crying. Pac wasn't afraid to cry," Steinberg remembered. "That [rape charge] crushed him. You know, sometimes it's about the company you keep. Pac's company was his downfall."

His feelings of betrayal and distrust deepened throughout the next year, culminating in what he perceived to be the ultimate betrayal.

One year after the incident at the hotel, Tupac was back in New York, facing trial for the sexual assault charges. The rape accusation, in addition to the spate of lawsuits over the last couple of years, had nearly bankrupted him. He'd been dropped from concerts and film opportunities. His extended family—his mother, sister, and various aunts and uncles and cousins—all depended on him for financial support. So when New York City hustler and music mogul James "Jimmy Henchman" Rosemond offered Tupac $7,000 to contribute a verse on a track by rapper Little Shawn, Tupac was compelled to accept.

Tupac arrived at Quad Recording Studios in Times Square with three associates at half past midnight on Wednesday, November 30. He buzzed to be let inside the studio, and one or two men who'd been standing outside the door followed them inside. As the group entered into the secured building, Tupac saw another man sitting inside the lobby, reading a newspaper. The men suddenly pulled out guns.

"Don't nobody move. Everybody on the floor," the men commanded. "You know what time it is. Run your shit."

Tupac hesitated, failing to get down fast enough, and the men rushed him. During the scuffle, Tupac was shot five times: twice in the head, twice in the groin area, and once in the hand. The robbers made off with $45,000 worth of their victims' jewelry.

After the assailants fled, Tupac's friends dragged his bleeding body to the elevator, went up to the eighth-floor recording studio, and were met by a large crew, including Jimmy Henchman, the Notorious B.I.G., rapper Lil' Cease, and Bad Boy Entertainment CEO and record producer Sean "Puffy" Combs. Tupac asked for someone to pass him a blunt. An ambulance soon arrived, and as Tupac was loaded onto the gurney, he summoned just enough strength to lift his arm and give the finger to a waiting photographer.

As he lay in his hospital bed at Bellevue Hospital Center, recuperating from surgery, Tupac opened his eyes and saw a strange but oddly familiar face hovering above him. The man introduced himself as Billy Garland, Tupac's biological father. For most of his life, Tupac considered the street hustler Kenneth Saunders, who'd died a decade earlier, to be his father. But Tupac now learned his father was in fact alive. "I thought my father was dead all my life," he later recalled. "After I got shot, I looked up, there was this nigga that looked just like me. And he was my father; that's when I found out."

The family reunion was brief, though Garland would continue to check in with Tupac intermittently in the following months. Hours after his surgery, Tupac checked out of the hospital against the advice of his doctors, fearing whoever had shot him might try to come back and finish the job. He was taken by wheelchair out of the hospital by Afeni, flanked by Tyehimba and the Nation of Islam's security wing, the Fruit of Islam. He convalesced at the house of a family friend, the actor Jasmine Guy, while Afeni, who had since stopped using drugs, helped feed and care for him. Afeni, Guy, and family friend Yaasmyn Fula talked a distraught Tupac out of taking his own life, convincing him that he likely wouldn't face hard time. The case was "very weak," in the opinion of one lawyer.

The following day, December 1, Tupac was wheeled into the Manhattan courtroom, wrapped in bandages, for the jury's verdict.

He was acquitted of sodomy and weapons possession, but convicted of two counts of sexual abuse, for "forcibly touching Ayanna Jackson's buttocks." His codefendant, Charles Fuller, received the same verdict, though Jackson would years later admit Fuller hadn't assaulted her.

On February 7, Tupac returned to the courthouse for sentencing by State Supreme Court Justice Daniel Fitzgerald. The judge took the opportunity to berate and publicly condemn Tupac for his pattern of appalling behavior. Holding back tears, Tupac apologized to Jackson but maintained his innocence. He turned to the judge: "My name is Tupac Shakur," he said, "and like other Shakurs I stand before an unsympathetic judge." Like his mother and Lumumba and Assata and Mutulu before him, Tupac doubted he would receive fair or impartial treatment in a court of law. He wasn't mistaken. Citing Tupac's "arrogance," Justice Fitzgerald sentenced him to a prison term of up to four and a half years.

Tupac was further incensed when he learned that, later that year, Agnant pleaded guilty to two misdemeanors and was fined $1,000 and given a three-year probation. The enormous disparity in their punishments, as well as Agnant's case being split from Tupac's, gave Tupac another reason to believe Agnant had in fact been working with the federal government; he later recorded a song calling Agnant a "snitch" who was "working for the feds."

But Tupac reserved most of his vitriol for Combs and B.I.G., claiming they had purposefully set him up to be ambushed at Quad. Though Combs and B.I.G. maintained their innocence, and Tupac had no proof of their involvement, he held firm to his convictions, verbally attacking them and everyone affiliated with them as orchestrating the attempt on his life.

After the shooting, Tupac often woke up sweating and screaming in his jail cell. He grew increasingly paranoid and suspicious. He not only believed he'd been betrayed by his alleged friends and colleagues; he now felt he'd been abandoned by the Black community he'd defended and championed throughout his adult life.

"I really did believe, at one point, up until I got shot, that no Black person would ever shoot me," he said during an interview from prison. "I was their representative. I believed that I didn't have to fear my own community. I represent them, I'm their ambassador to the world. They would never harm me, they would never rob me, they would never do me wrong."

Just over one month after he was sent to the maximum-security Clinton Correctional Facility, Tupac's third solo album was released. Recorded in the weeks before his conviction, *Me Against the World* was the most personal, confessional, introspective, and somber record of his career, reflecting on themes of isolation, mortality, and disillusionment. The record's first and most popular single, "Dear Mama," was a tribute to Afeni, praising her strength and resilience and confronting her long battle with drug addiction. The album also introduced Tupac's new group Dramacydal (later changed to Outlawz), which included Tupac's childhood friend Yafeu "Yaki Kadafi" Fula, the only son of Sekou Odinga and Yaasmyn Fula. *Me Against the World* received extensive critical praise and debuted at number one on the *Billboard* 200, making Tupac the first musician to debut a number one album while incarcerated.

Speaking with *Vibe* magazine's Kevin Powell, Tupac announced his intention to collaborate with Sanyika "Monster Kody" Shakur and create a community program called Us First. He then goes on to renounce thug life, calling it "ignorance" and stating that "Thug Life to me is dead. If it's real, then let somebody else represent it, because I'm tired of it.

"I'm going to show people my true intentions, and my true heart," Tupac continued. "I'm going to show them the man that my mother raised. I'm going to make them all proud."

While *Me Against the World* was a critical and commercial success, Tupac reaped little financial benefit, with most of the royalties going to lawyers and paying off other legal fees. His attorneys filed an appeal, but he couldn't be released from prison without putting up more than a million dollars in bail, which he couldn't afford, despite having the number one album in the country. After eleven months in prison with no end in sight, Tupac was lost, afraid, and desperate, with his thoughts turning often to suicide.

And then Suge Knight arrived.

A six-foot-four, 315-pound Compton native and former defensive end for the LA Rams, Marion "Suge" Knight Jr. had already earned a reputation for using strong-arm tactics to build his record label, Death Row Records, whose biggest stars at the time were the chart-topping Dr. Dre and Snoop Doggy Dogg. Knight had long been angling to sign Tupac to Death Row, and he now saw a ripe opportunity to seal the deal. Visiting Tupac in prison with his lawyer in tow—a White criminal attorney named David Kenner—the Death Row CEO offered Tupac an offer he couldn't refuse: sign with Death Row and not only would his bail be covered but Knight would make Tupac his top priority and would make him a bigger star than he'd ever dreamed of. More than that, he agreed to buy Afeni a house. Kenner scrawled out a handwritten three-page contract. Tupac felt like he had no other option than to sign the contract.

Allegedly affiliated with the Bloods, Knight was typically seen clad head to toe in red, cutting a menacing figure, adding to his already diabolical presence. Tupac knew he was entering into a Faustian bargain. Shortly before signing the contract, a tearful Tupac hugged Tyehimba and said, "I know I'm selling my soul to the devil."

Knight put up $250,000, while Interscope and Time Warner put up the remainder of Tupac's $1.4 million bond, though Tupac either was led to believe or chose to credit Knight with paying the entire bond himself. "Pac got out and said Death Row bailed him out, because that's who he is," Tyehimba explained. "He's gonna ride with whoever he's with at that time. But he knew better than that."

On October 12, 1995, after nearly a year incarcerated, Tupac was a free man, pending appeal. Knight arranged for Tupac to be picked up in a white stretch limousine, and he was soon on a private jet, which whisked him away from New York and back to California. He went straight into the Can-Am recording studio in Los Angeles and got to work. Fueled by copious amounts of weed and Hennessy, Tupac operated at a fever pitch, writing and recording in nineteen-hour stretches, working nonstop into the early morning hours.

Tupac's first record for Death Row, the double album *All Eyez on Me*, was released February 13, 1996. Like his previous album, it was an immediate success, garnering widespread critical praise, selling more than half a million copies in its first week, and again reaching number one on the *Billboard* 200. But unlike any of his earlier

albums, *All Eyez on Me* featured hardly any politics, social consciousness, or personal introspection. It was a party record, an incontest-
able West Coast record, with chest-thumping swagger and libidinous
anthems, with beats by some of the biggest producers in the game.
And where previously he'd reserved his indignities for crooked police officers and racist judges, he now had scores to settle with all
those who had supposedly betrayed and deceived him.

Music journalists were now reporting on an alleged rivalry between West Coast and East Coast rappers, with Tupac and Death
Row on one side and Combs, B.I.G., and Bad Boy on the other. Tupac
fanned the flames, launching spiteful tirades and threats against any
New York rapper who dared speak his name. For someone who was
undoubtedly familiar with the history of the fatal rift in the Black
Panther Party, which pitted Huey Newton's Oakland-based Panthers
against Eldridge Cleaver's loyalists in New York, Tupac should have
been aware of the divide-and-conquer strategies used against successful Black organizations. But his feelings of anger and desire for
vengeance, compounded with depression and paranoia, were encouraged by his new boss and benefactor.

Knight kept Tupac close. Tupac was now Death Row's biggest star,
and Knight took care of his star, buying him cars and jewelry and
clothes. Tupac, in turn, felt indebted to Knight for getting him out
of prison and resurrecting his career. He promised Knight he would
make Death Row "the biggest label in the whole world."

Leila Steinberg continued to stay in touch with her friend and former pupil, but she watched helplessly as Tupac dug himself deeper
and deeper into Death Row's predatory trenches.

"I don't think he realized how over his head he was," Steinberg
recalled. "I think that, in his heart and in his intention every day,
he wanted to make the world better for Black people primarily, but
all oppressed people. He believed he was a warrior and a soldier for
the oppressed. But your behavior contradicts your fight for the oppressed when you're hanging out with Suge. Suge was not fighting
for the oppressed. He was fighting for power and control and his
pockets. So Tupac was a very valuable pawn in Suge's game of power
and chess."

Tupac didn't admit to any contradiction. "Tupac the son of the

Black Panther, and Tupac the rider. Those are the two people inside of me," he said.

Though he continued to promote Death Row, privately Tupac was looking for a way out. The culture of gang violence and intimidation surrounding the record label was becoming overwhelming, and he began to suspect he was being ripped off by Knight, who was treating his star client more like an indentured servant. By the summer of 1996, Tupac was pursuing his own interests outside of Death Row. He was set to star in two more feature films; he was engaged to be married to producer and arranger Quincy Jones's daughter Kidada; he and Yaasmyn Fula established a new production company, Euphanasia; and he was providing financial support to youth programs in vulnerable communities. Steinberg believed Tupac had only been temporarily sidetracked, and once he'd fulfilled his contractual obligations to Death Row, Tupac would return to fight in the struggle for Black liberation.

"On the surface it looks like he abandoned his principles, but I know he didn't," Steinberg recalled. "He got caught up in this fucked-up industry, and he never got to show people what was brewing and what his plans were . . . We know that he was a deep thinker, he was a critical thinker, and his underlying intention was the liberation of Black people, oppressed people. We know that he was following the Shakur thread."

Tupac felt the world closing in around him. He had few people he could trust, and it was proving impossible—disastrous, even—to try to keep carrying the burdensome weight of his name. For the first time, he chose to release his next album, *The Don Killuminati: The 7 Day Theory*, not under his own name but as his alias, Makaveli, after the Renaissance-era Italian philosopher Niccolò Machiavelli, whom Tupac discovered while in prison. The cover of the album shows Tupac naked and crucified. Mopreme believed the image and some of the darker themes of the album were deliberate. "I think Pac always knew he was going to die soon, die early," Mopreme remembered, "and that was his goodbye."

Whatever Tupac's next intentions were—leave Death Row and strike out on his own, pursue his acting career more seriously, write his life story—they would never have a chance to materialize. On the night of September 7, 1996, Tupac was shot in Las Vegas, Nevada, in a drive-by ambush as he and Knight were stopped at a red light, two hours after attending a Mike Tyson boxing match at the MGM Grand. The first officer to arrive at the scene of the shooting, Sergeant Chris Carroll of the Las Vegas Metropolitan Police Department, claimed Tupac was unconscious when he pulled his bleeding body from Knight's bullet-riddled BMW. Carroll said he attempted to get a response from Tupac by asking the same question again and again: "Who shot you? Who did this?"

Tupac eventually regained consciousness long enough to breathe out a response to the officer's question. "Fuck you," he said.

He was rushed to the University Medical Center for emergency surgery, but six days later, on the afternoon of Friday the thirteenth, with his mother, Afeni, by his bedside, Tupac was taken off life support. His murder has yet to be solved. Tupac Amaru Shakur was twenty-five years old.

Inside the federal penitentiary in Florence, Colorado, Mutulu learned of Tupac's death on the night it happened. Immediately upon hearing of his passing, Mutulu sat down and wrote a letter to his stepson. What follows below are excerpts from his letter:

I love you whenever . . . forever. Tupac, so much I needed to say, so much you wanted to say. Many conversations between us within the ether, whenever . . . forever.

The Shakurs have been guided by struggle, prepared or not, whenever . . . forever. We've exposed our existence, naked from fear, to those who would hear the positive. Who would witness the stress, wear and tear of this lonely path. You couldn't have evaded the effect or the changes. You inherited it, it was in your genes.

Please give my love to our family. Ask them to help you on the other side. Tell Zayd, Lumumba, Abu, Brother Leggs, Mtaryi, Attallah,

that they are to continue to help us down here. Shakur's love is
strong. Whenever . . . forever.

Your family will keep the spirit high, for we are Shakurs. We are
thankful for what life gives us. Through the pain and the struggle we
are blessed by the victory. Go forward, Tupac.

The story of the Shakurs might well have ended on that September night in Las Vegas. Tupac was, after all, the appointed heir to the movement, the "Black Prince of the revolution," but he, like so many other Shakurs before him, was defeated before he could finish his work.

But though the Shakur family has endured countless losses and heartbreaks, the story doesn't end with one person. The Shakurs have been guided, prepared or not, by the struggle. They have suffered, lost, and grieved, but, against all odds, they have survived—which is all they demand of us.

"Our ride wasn't like everybody else's ride in this game," Mopreme explains. "Our ride was unique. Our lives were here to be an example for the youth, for the ones coming up after us, for example, what to do and what not to do. We went through a number of scenarios and situations, going through the game. We made a mark, and if those coming up after us could use our lives, could use our legacy, to better themselves, that's what it is."

EPILOGUE

ON TUESDAY, NOVEMBER 25, 2014, Sekou Odinga walked out of prison a free man. The New York Black Panther leader, Panther 21 fugitive, and Black Liberation Army strategist was paroled from Clinton Correctional Facility in Dannemora, New York—the same prison that held Tupac Shakur twenty years earlier—after thirty-three years of incarceration. The seventy-year-old Odinga celebrated that evening at the National Black Theater in Harlem, surrounded by supporters, friends, and family, including his wife, children, and more than a dozen grandchildren. One of his children, however, wasn't there to welcome him home. His son, the rapper Yafeu "Yaki Kadafi" Fula, a member of Tupac's Outlawz group, was shot to death in a New Jersey apartment building on November 10, 1996, only two months after Tupac's murder. He was nineteen years old.

A few months after Odinga's release, on Sunday, February 22, a formal homecoming celebration was held for him at the Malcolm X and Dr. Shabazz Memorial and Education Center, formerly the Audubon Ballroom, where Malcolm X was assassinated nearly fifty years earlier. Activists and movement veterans traveled from New York; Washington, D.C.; Philadelphia; and Newark to attend the celebration. In front of a sizable crowd, Odinga addressed his supporters: "Don't forget those that are still behind the wall," he said. "They deserve to be remembered. They paid the price and continue to pay the price to be remembered, to be supported and to be released, to be free. We need to free our political prisoners."

Living in Cuban exile for more than forty years, Assata Shakur was added to the FBI's "Top Ten Most Wanted Terrorists" list in 2013, with a reward of $2 million for her capture. Despite numerous extradition requests by United States politicians, Cuba continues to provide unequivocal harbor to Assata. The excessive bounty on Assata, however, has compelled her to remain largely silent and concealed, effectively creating an exile-within-exile status.

Years earlier, she had already begun to pull away from the militant tactics she once espoused. In her *Autobiography*, published in 1988, Assata recounts a memory, when her companions in the movement came to visit her in Cuba. She was grateful for the visit and remained sympathetic to the struggle, but she had evolved during her years in exile. "I was no longer the wide-eyed, romantic young revolutionary who believed the revolution was just around the corner," she writes. "I still appreciated energetic idealism, but i had long ago become convinced that revolution was a science. Generalities were no longer enough for me. Like my comrades, I believed that a higher level of political sophistication was necessary and that unity in the Black community had to become a priority."

Interviewed for the 1997 documentary *Eyes of the Rainbow*, Assata, approaching her second decade in exile, acknowledges that her long separation has been difficult on her family, while acknowledging her responsibility to her supporters and followers back home. "I hope I can live up to my ancestors' expectations of me," she says, "because I really believe that I have a duty to all those who have come before me, to all those who lie at the bottom of the ocean, to all those who lost their lives—whether it's in the cane fields or the cotton fields or hanging off some tree—to continue this struggle, and to continue to love, and to continue to believe, and continue to try to be human, to be giving, to be loving."

The acupuncture drug detoxification techniques Mutulu Shakur helped pioneer at Lincoln Detox in the 1970s have since been standardized as the National Acupuncture Detoxification Association (NADA) protocol. With an estimated six hundred programs in the United States and at more than 25,000 healthcare providers in forty countries, NADA has trained more than ten thousand health professionals in the use of acupuncture as a method of addiction recovery.

Seventy-two years old, Mutulu suffered from numerous critical health complications, including Type 2 diabetes, hypertension, glaucoma, and advanced bone marrow cancer, and he was infected with COVID-19 multiple times. On November 10, 2022, just as this book was going into production, Mutulu was granted parole after more than thirty-five years in prison. He transitioned on July 6, 2023.

After Tupac's murder, Afeni successfully sued Suge Knight, Death Row Records, and Death Row lawyer David Kenner over the rights to her late son's master recordings and royalties. She then became administrator of Tupac's estate and created Amaru Entertainment, which oversaw the posthumous releases of his unreleased music. Using the proceeds from those albums—which sold in the millions and consistently topped music charts—she launched the Tupac Amaru Shakur Foundation, an annual performing arts day camp in Atlanta, preserving her son's commitment, toward the end of his life, to provide support and community resources for young people interested in the arts. In 2005, the Tupac Amaru Shakur Center for the Arts opened its headquarters on nine acres of land in Stone Mountain, Georgia.

Like she had in the 1970s, following her acquittal in the Panther 21 trial, Afeni was again invited to speak at conventions, colleges, and universities across the country, including Vanderbilt University's Black History Month Commemoration in 2007 and 2008's Dream Reborn convention in Memphis, Tennessee, recognizing the fortieth anniversary of the assassination of Martin Luther King Jr.

In May 2014, Afeni was the keynote speaker at the Circle of Mothers retreat in Florida, a two-day summit for grieving mothers who have lost children to violence. The retreat was initiated by Sybrina Fulton, whose seventeen-year-old son Trayvon Martin was killed two years earlier, while walking home from a convenience store, by an armed neighborhood watch volunteer. Trayvon's death and his killer's subsequent acquittal launched what would become the nationwide Black Lives Matter movement for racial justice. Though they came from different backgrounds, these two strong-willed mothers, Afeni and Sybrina, shared in common the agony and grief of having sons taken violently from them at a young age. Afeni implored the mothers in the audience not to become overwhelmed by anger and a yearning for retribution. They had a responsibility to help make sure that all children in the country today are provided for, supported, and protected. "All change begins with the choices we make," Afeni said. "It is imperative that we as a community make better choices that benefit the whole, not just the individual parts. Justice will not come in the form of a mob; justice will be felt when every mother knows that her child is safe walking the streets of America."

Afeni looked out at the sixty gathered mothers in the room and offered compassion, advice, and the wisdom that comes from a life of service and anguish—a life dedicated to the betterment of all struggling people. "Think of the least thing you can do that will benefit your community," she said. "Start as small as a mustard seed if you have to. I guarantee that the seed you plant in love, no matter how small, will grow into a mighty tree of refuge. We all want a future for ourselves, and we must now care enough to create, nurture and secure a future for our children."

Afeni Shakur joined the ancestors on May 2, 2016, after suffering a cardiac arrest at her home in Sausalito, California. She was sixty-nine.

Her homegoing celebration was on Saturday, June 18, at the House of the Lord Pentecostal Church in Brooklyn, where, thirty-five years earlier, ten-year-old Tupac had declared he would grow up to become "a revolutionary." More than one hundred people filled the church for Afeni's memorial, including her former Panther 21 comrades Sekou Odinga, Dhoruba bin Wahad, and Jamal Joseph, as well as Black Panther leader Kathleen Cleaver, activist poet Sonia Sanchez, and New York Assemblyman Charles Barron, who brought the crowd to its feet chanting, "Long live Afeni Shakur."

The Tupac Amaru Shakur Center for the Arts closed in 2015, one year before Afeni's passing, but the Foundation continues to operate as a nonprofit organization, under the leadership of Afeni and Mutulu's daughter, Sekyiwa "Set" Shakur. Concentrating particularly on the creative arts and issues surrounding mental health and wellness, the Foundation provides support and resources to individuals and communities that have been impacted by trauma, a subject with which the Shakur family has long been intimately familiar. In 2021, the Foundation welcomed a new member to its leadership team: Sekyiwa's son, Malik Shakur.

Malik is a musician and actor in his midtwenties with starring roles in two independent films. When he first set out on his own, he felt encumbered by his surname as he sought to make a reputation for himself without being immediately associated with his late uncle Tupac. At first, he would only introduce himself by his first name, leaving his famous surname unspoken, but over time he came to accept his inheritance, remarking that "you can't run away from who you are."

After Trayvon Martin's killing, Malik became more politically engaged, joining and organizing protests for social justice. When he began attending these protests—first in Los Angeles and then in New York, where he now lives—his mother was apprehensive. Still healing from the trauma of growing up in a family that was constantly persecuted and harassed by law enforcement, Sekyiwa was afraid of her son suffering a similar fate. "She associates it with police repercussions and the CIA," Malik said. "She's terrified every time I go to a protest. She doesn't like it. But she knows we have to do it. She knows this is who our family is."

What remains today of the Black liberation movement is not immediately evident. Often, today's activists and organizers seem to be bound by a nostalgia for the past, a mythic reverence for the revolutionaries who came before. The Black Panther Party is hailed by many today for its community service programs, like the Free Breakfast for School Children program—which has since been adopted by the USDA, providing breakfast to millions of children across the country—while influential Black Power leaders and thinkers like Huey P. Newton, Fred Hampton, and Assata Shakur are venerated by younger generations of activists. But these important figures are often revered and quoted without an understanding of how much they sacrificed. They lived as fugitives, went into exile, served long prison sentences, or lost their lives. They abandoned families and children, many of whom are still suffering from trauma and loss. They knew that standing up against the twin pillars of racism and imperialism requires more than a signature on a petition or a post on social media. It requires more than slogans and yard signs.

Dismantling hundreds of years of racist oppression is not an easy task, of course—and there is no single, correct approach. But while we are working toward that ultimate goal, there is plenty that can be done in our communities right now. Though the images of shotgun-wielding Panthers will always capture our imagination, the real work is done quietly, without sensationalism or fanfare. It's offering holistic healthcare to the community, organizing tenants against exploitative landlords, or advocating for better education opportunities. It's feeding hungry people. It's challenging all instances of racism, sexism, ableism, transphobia, and homophobia, especially within our own circles.

The Shakur name today represents many things to many different people all over the world. To music fans, it might represent the talent and rebellion of Tupac. To younger activists, it might represent the sagacity and defiance of Assata. To movement elders, it might represent Afeni or Mutulu. To American law enforcement, the Shakur name might symbolize insubordination, radicalism, terrorism.

But regardless of what words or sentiments you immediately associate with the Shakur name, one word is indisputable: resilience. The legacy of the Shakur family can be seen today anywhere people are organized, committed, and dedicated to the struggle to improve the lives of Black people here and now. After more than fifty years and numerous attempts to pacify them, the Shakurs remain an eminent, essential, and everlasting part of our Amerikan story.

ACKNOWLEDGMENTS

An Amerikan Family is the result of hundreds of hours of interviews and research: poring over dozens upon dozens of books, digging through decades-old newspaper archives, and, most important, holding many face-to-face conversations. While researching this book, I was fortunate to meet and speak with several Shakur family members, friends, and comrades, from New York City and Los Angeles to Memphis and Atlanta. I would soon come to discover not only how deep the roots of the Shakur family extend, but how richly they have cultivated the soil of the radical Black liberation movement.

That being said, there are several members of the Shakur family tree who have gone unmentioned in this book. Though they carry the Shakur surname, these many sons, daughters, brothers, sisters, fathers, mothers, and grandparents have lived quiet, largely anonymous lives with their families. I did not feel it was in anyone's interest to track down and interview every person in the world who calls themselves Shakur. At any rate, *An Amerikan Family* is not just about one particular family. It is not a complete genealogy, nor does it attempt to be. This book is, more than anything, an exploration of the times in which this family lived, the revolutionary people who inspired them, and the repressive, institutional forces that produced them.

For taking the time to speak with me and share their stories, I'm immensely grateful to Mopreme Shakur and Talia Rodriguez-Shakur, Makini Shakur, Malik Shakur, Sekou Odinga, Bilal Sunni-Ali, Watani Tyehimba, Akinyele Umoja, Cleo Silvers, Walter Bosque del Rio, Yaasmyn Fula, Richard Fischbein, Susan Rosenberg, Brother Bullwhip, Matt Meyer, Margie Navarro, and Leila Steinberg. I'd also like to give a special thanks to the filmmaker Mia Donovan, who facilitated my introduction to the family and put the wheels for this book in motion.

Thanks to Stephen Shames, David Fenton, Lely Constantinople, Lily Noonan, Tricia Gesner, and Brynn Krause for tracking down and sharing with me the stunning photos included in this book, many of which have never been published.

Many thanks to my literary agent, Kerry Sparks, and editor, Rakia Clark. Thank you both for your confidence in this project and your enthusiasm from the beginning. I couldn't have asked for a better team. Thanks to the immensely helpful and ever-patient Ivy Givens at Mariner Books, and thanks to Kelly Shi, Tavia Kowalchuk, and everyone at HarperCollins/Mariner Books. Thanks also to Martha Cipolla, Katie Shepherd, and Laura Brady for the close attention to detail in copy editing, and Kerry Rubenstein for the stunning cover design.

Thanks to Lance Cleland for being a supportive friend and dependable sounding board since way back when we were both cashiers at Powell's Books, with low morals but high literary aspirations.

To Tony Perez, Jon Raymond, Cheston Knapp, Alex Morris, Kyle von Hoetzendorff, Thomas Ross, Alex Laskowski, Jeremy Okai Davis, Kevin Sampsell, Bradley Glenn, Annae Nichelson, Jacob Schraer (thanks for letting me use your library card in a pinch), Kevin Maloney, Aubrey Lenahan, Matt Best and Jessica Mallare-Best, Drew and Laura Holguin, and the rest of my Portland folks: I appreciate you and I miss y'all.

Thanks to James Spooner and Lisa Nola for offering a warm welcome to Los Angeles.

Thanks to Sergio De Barros (Serge Severe) and Reyna Mallare for the support. Keep rocking the mic.

Thanks to Nathaniel and Shannon Finley, for being there for me over many years.

And thanks to the Sou'Wester Lodge in Seaview, Washington, for offering me an artist residency in which to begin writing this book. I hope to see you again for the next one.

A special note of gratitude is reserved for Megan Irwin, who was the first to listen to my idea for this book and encouraged me to continue throughout the entire process, even when it felt like I had gotten in way over my head. Thank you for believing in this project and in my ability to write it. Thank you for being my travel companion, for always being in my corner, for reading an early draft of the manuscript, and for your honesty, support, and love. I couldn't have done this without you.

It is my hope that this book serves as a record, to preserve this essential history and to give the revolutionary Shakur family its long-overdue recognition. I hope the stories inside this book offer inspiration—and caution—to present and future generations who bravely carry on the fight for Black Americans and for all oppressed people worldwide. If this book succeeds, it is thanks to everyone named above. Any mistakes or shortcomings are mine alone.

SELECTED BIBLIOGRAPHY

BOOKS

Ahmad, Akbar Muhammad. "RAM: The Revolutionary Action Movement." In *Black Power in the Belly of the Beast*, edited by Judson L. Jeffries. Urbana and Chicago: University of Illinois Press, 2006.

Ahmad, Muhammad. *We Will Return in the Whirlwind: Black Radical Organizations 1960–1975*. Charles H. Kerr Publishing Company, 2008.

Austin, Curtis J. *Up against the Wall: Violence in the Making and Unmaking of the Black Panther Party*. University of Arkansas Press, 2006.

Baldwin, James. "To Be Baptized." In *No Name in the Street*. Vintage International, 2007.

Bastfield, Darrin Keith. *Back in the Day: My Life and Times with Tupac Shakur*. Da Capo Press, 2003.

Bloom, Joshua, and Waldo E. Martin Jr. *Black Against Empire: The History and Politics of the Black Panther Party*. University of California Press, 2016.

Burrough, Bryan. *Days of Rage: America's Radical Underground, the FBI, and the Forgotten Age of Revolutionary Violence*. Penguin Books, 2016.

Carmichael, Stokely. "Toward Black Liberation." *The Massachusetts Review*. September 1966. Reprinted in *Stokely Speaks: From Black Power to Pan-Africanism*. Lawrence Hill Books, 2007.

Castellucci, John. *The Big Dance: The Untold Story of Weatherman Kathy Boudin and the Terrorist Family That Committed the Brink's Robbery Murders*. Dodd, Mead & Company, 1986.

Churchill, Ward, and James Vander Wall. *The Cointelpro Papers: Documents from the FBI's Secret Wars against Dissent in the United States* (2nd Ed.). South End Press, 2001.

Cleaver, Kathleen Neal. "Back to Africa: The Evolution of the International Section of the Black Panther Party (1969–1972)." In *The Black Panther Party Reconsidered,* edited by Charles E. Jones. Black Classic Press, 1998.

Cunnigen, Donald. "The Republic of New Africa in Mississippi." In *Black Power in the Belly of the Beast,* edited by Judson L. Jeffries. Urbana and Chicago: University of Illinois Press, 2006.

Daley, Robert. *Target Blue: An Insider's View of the N.Y.P.D.* Delacorte Press, 1973.

Donner, Frank. *Protectors of Privilege: Red Squads and Police Repression in Urban America.* University of California Press, 1990.

Dyson, Michael Eric. *Holler If You Hear Me: Searching for Tupac Shakur.* Basic Books, 2006.

Ferguson, Iyaluua. *An Unlikely Warrior: Herman Ferguson, the Evolution of a Black Nationalist Revolutionary.* Black Classic Press, 2011.

Fernández, Johanna. *The Young Lords.* University of North Carolina Press, 2019.

Foner, Philip S., ed. *The Black Panthers Speak.* Da Capo Press, 2002.

Fula, Yaasmyn. *Spirit of an Outlaw: The Untold Story of Tupac Amaru Shakur and Yaki "Kadafi" Fula.* Bearded Dragon Books, 2020.

Grady-Willis, Winston A. "The Black Panther Party: State Repression and Political Prisoners." In *The Black Panther Party Reconsidered,* edited by Charles E. Jones. Black Classic Press, 1998.

Guy, Jasmine. *Afeni Shakur: Evolution of a Revolutionary.* Atria, 2005.

Hilliard, David, and Lewis Cole. *This Side of Glory: The Autobiography of David Hilliard and the Story of the Black Panther Party.* Little, Brown and Company, 1993.

Hoye, Jacob, and Karolyn Ali, eds. *Tupac: Resurrection 1971–1996.* Atria Books, 2003.

Joseph, Jamal. *Panther Baby: A Life of Rebellion & Reinvention.* Algonquin Books of Chapel Hill, 2012.

Joseph, Peniel E. *The Black Power Movement: Rethinking the Civil Rights–Black Power Era.* Routledge, 2006.

———. *Waiting 'Til the Midnight Hour: A Narrative History of Black Power in America.* Owl Books, 2007.

Kempton, Murray. *The Briar Patch: The People of the State of New York v. Lumumba Shakur Et Al.* Notable Trials Library Special Ed., 1998.

Kioni-Sadiki, Déqui, and Matt Meyer, eds. *Look for Me in the Whirlwind: From the Panther 21 to 21st Century Revolutions.* PM Press, 2017.

Malcolm X and Alex Haley. *The Autobiography of Malcolm X.* Grove Press, 1965.

Marable, Manning. *Malcolm X: A Life of Reinvention.* Penguin Books, 2012.

———. *Race, Reform, and Rebellion: The Second Reconstruction in Black America, 1945–1990* (2nd Ed.). University Press of Mississippi, 1991.

McQuillar, Tayannah Lee, and Fred L. Johnson III, PhD. *Tupac Shakur: The Life and Times of an American Icon.* Da Capo Press, 2010.

Newton, Huey P. *Revolutionary Suicide.* Penguin Books, 2009.

Onaci, Edward. *Free the Land: The Republic of New Afrika and the Pursuit of a Black Nation-State.* The University of North Carolina Press, 2020.

O'Reilly, Kenneth. *Racial Matters: The FBI's Secret File on Black America, 1960– 1972.* The Free Press, 1991.

Payne, Les, and Tamara Payne. *The Dead Are Arising: The Life of Malcolm X.* Liveright Publishing Company, 2020.

Shakur, Assata. *Assata: An Autobiography.* Lawrence Hill Books, 2001.

Strain, Christopher B. "The Deacons for Defense and Justice." In *Black Power in the Belly of the Beast,* edited by Judson L. Jeffries. Urbana and Chicago: University of Illinois Press, 2006.

Umoja, Akinyele O. "The Black Liberation Army and the Radical Legacy of the Black Panther Party." In *Black Power in the Belly of the Beast,* edited by Judson L. Jeffries. Urbana and Chicago: University of Illinois Press, 2006.

Williams, Evelyn A. *Inadmissible Evidence: The Story of the African-American Trial Lawyer Who Defended the Black Liberation Army.* Iuniverse.com, Inc., 2000.

PERIODICALS AND WEBSITES

"(1963) Malcolm X, 'Message to the Grassroots.'" *Blackpast,* August 16, 2010.

"(1964) Malcolm X's Speech at the Founding Rally of the Organization of Afro-American Unity." *Blackpast,* October 17, 2007.

"135 Militants Seized in Detroit Cop Killing." *Daily News,* March 31, 1969.

"2 Radicals Get Terms in Slay-Thefts." *Philadelphia Daily News,* February 15.

"20 Years after Tupac Shakur's Death, Remembering His Baltimore Beginnings." *Baltimore Sun,* September 13, 2016.

"3,000 at Funeral of Slain Trooper." *New York Times,* May 6, 1973.

"A Suspect in Panther's Death Here Is Slain by F.B.I. in South." *New York Times,* January 1, 1972.

"Acupuncture Believed Useful in Treatment of Drug Addiction." *Courier-Post,* March 13, 1975.

"Afeni Shakur, Former Black Panther, Mother of Slain Rapper, to Headline Black History Month Events at Vanderbilt University." Vanderbilt University News, February 1, 2007.

"An Interview with the Chief of Staff David Hilliard." *The Black Panther— Black Community News Service,* Vol. 2, No. 30, April 20, 1969.

"Armed Negroes Protest Gun Bill." *New York Times,* May 3, 1967.

"Bail Hiked to 100gs for Antiwhite Speaker." *Newsday,* February 28, 1968.

"Black 'Assault Squad' Takes Credit for Ingleside Attack." *Sun Reporter* (1968–1979), September 4, 1971.

"Black History: The History of Freeman Beach." *WWAY News,* February 22, 2019.

"Black Lib Chief Is Indicted for Murder." *Atlanta Constitution,* May 12, 1973.

"Black Liberation 'Priestess' Fights Court Photos." *Ithaca Journal,* January 1, 1975.

"Black Pig Instrumental in Frame-Up of N.Y. 21." *The Black Panther—Black Community News Service,* Vol. 3, No. 8, June 14, 1969.

"Brink's Fugitive Oks Extradition." *Morning Call,* February 19, 1986.

"Busting RAM." *Time,* June 30, 1967.

"Chesimard Trial Opens in Death of Trooper." *Courier-Post,* October 9, 1973.

"Civil Rights: The New Racism." *Time,* July 1, 1966.

"Convict Claims He Helped Plot Failed Brink's Holdup." *Daily Record,* November 24, 1982.

"Defense Hails Verdicts in Brink's Case." *Philadelphia Inquirer,* September 5, 1983.

"End of the Love-In." *Newsweek,* Vol. 73, Is. 15, April 14, 1969.

"False Note on Black Panthers." *New York Times,* January 16, 1970.

"FBI Arrests Fugitive Sought in Killings of N.Y. Policemen." *Washington Post,* September 3, 1973.

"FBI Hunt for Escaped Murderer." *Times of India,* November 5, 1979.

"FBI Informant Claims He Helped Chesimard Escape from Prison." *Courier-News,* May 3, 1983.

"Final Conviction in Brink's Case." *Newsday,* June 15, 1984.

"Former Friend of Tupac Shakur Sues Rapper's Estate for $200 Million." *New York Beacon,* April 16, 1997.

"Fugitive in Slayings of 4 Policemen Here Is Seized." *New York Times,* June 9, 1973.

"Harlem Public School Speech: Go Get a Gun." *Newsday,* February 22, 1968.

"Hong Kong Doctors Use Acupuncture to Relieve Addicts' Withdrawal Symptoms." *New York Times,* April 5, 1973.

"Hoover Links Carmichael to Negro Leftist Group." *New York Times,* May 17, 1967.

"Hospital Bows to 35 Addicts." *Daily News,* November 11, 1970.

"Hot Summer." *New York Times,* July 26, 1964.

"Inside the Mind of Shakur." *Vibe,* June 1996. In *Tupac Shakur,* edited by Alan Light. Three Rivers Press, 1998.

"IS 201 Project Faces Halt in Ford Support." *Daily News,* March 1, 1968.

"Joanne Chesimard Is Acquitted in Robbery of a Bank in Queens." *New York Times,* January 17, 1976.

"Judge Draws Criticism for Releasing Subjects." *Los Angeles Times,* April 1, 1969.

"N.A.A.C.P. Leader Urges 'Violence.'" *New York Times*, May 7, 1959.

"N.Y. 21—Letters from Jail." Afeni Shakur. Reprinted in *The Black Panther—Black Community News Service*, Vol. 3, No. 8, June 14, 1969.

"NY Comrades Celebrate Sister Afeni's Life." *New York Amsterdam News*, June 23, 2016.

"Oceanside Divide." *Our State*, November 2013.

"On the Assassination of Deputy Field Marshall Robert Webb." *Right On!*, April 3, 1971.

"On the Purge of Geronimo from the Black Panther Party." Huey P. Newton. *The Black Panther—Black Community News Service*, Vol. 5, No. 30, January 23, 1971.

"Panthers Seeking New Constitution." *New York Times*, June 20, 1970.

"Panthers Urge Change." *Hartford Courant*, September 7, 1970.

"Police Kill a Gypsy Cab Driver in Shootout with Bar Robbers." *New York Times*, August 5, 1971.

"Prison Racial Fight Injures 23 Upstate, 450 Join in Melee." *New York Times*, September 28, 1963.

"Profiles of Brink's Case Defendants." *Journal-News*, September 4, 1983.

"Profiles of Other Brink's Case Figures." *Journal-News*, April 27, 1984.

"Rap Artist Tupac Shakur Shot in Robbery." *New York Times*, November 30, 1994.

"Rapper Sentenced to 10 Days in Jail." *Morning Call*, November 2, 1994.

"Revolutionary Doctor Convicted of Conspiracy." *Morning Call*, March 27, 1987.

"Riot in Gallery Halts U.N. Debate." *New York Times*, February 16, 1961.

"Sekou Odinga, after 33 Years, Is Now Free." *New York Amsterdam News*, December 4, 2014.

"Shift Slayer of Trooper to Clinton Center." *Daily News*, February 25, 1979.

"Stokely on King." *Los Angeles Free Press*, April 12, 1968.

"Submachine Gun Hits 2 Patrolmen." *Evening Press*, May 20, 1971.

"To My People." Joanne Chesimard. *The Black Scholar*, October 1973.

"To the Black Community and the Black Movement Special Communique—(Joanne Chesimard)." *Breakthrough*, Vol. IV, No. 1, Winter 1980.

"Top Terror Woman Escapes." *South China Morning Post*, November 4, 1979.

"Two Rappers Held in Assault." *Los Angeles Times*, March 14, 1993.

"Twymon Myers Buried in N.J." *New York Amsterdam News*, November 24, 1973.

"Woman Is Jailed as a Gunrunner." *New York Times*, October 28, 1973.

"Woman Shot in Struggle with Her Alleged Victim." *New York Times*, April 7, 1971.

Adofo, Salim. "Harlem Welcomes Home Sekou Odinga." *New York Amsterdam News*, February 26, 2015.

Allyn, Bobby. "1969, a Year of Bombings." *New York Times,* August 27, 2009.

Anderson, Joel. "The Moment Tupac Became America's Most Dangerous Rapper." Slate, November 6, 2019.

Anson, Robert Sam. "To Die Like a Gangsta." *Vanity Fair,* September 3, 2013.

Asbury, Edith Evans. "16 Black Panthers Go on Trial Tomorrow in State Court Here." *New York Times,* February 1, 1970.

———. "Battle of Algiers Is Presented at Black Panthers' Trial Here." *New York Times,* November 6, 1970.

———. "Black Panther Party Members Freed after Being Cleared of Charges." *New York Times,* May 14, 1971.

———. "Detective Joined Panthers in 1968." *New York Times,* February 3, 1971.

———. "Detective Tells of Panther Role." *New York Times,* February 17, 1971.

———. "Ex-Policeman Describes Shoot-Out to Panther Jury." *New York Times,* January 12, 1971.

———. "Fragments at Blast Sites Linked to Panthers' Office." *New York Times,* January 6, 1971.

———. "Panther Pursues Her Own Defense." *New York Times,* March 30, 1971.

———. "Trial Told of Panthers' Chagrin after Police Foiled Sniper Plan." *New York Times,* March 4, 1971.

———. "Undercover Agent Tells of Panther Drills and Plots." *New York Times,* November 11, 1970.

Avery, Ron. "Explosives Cache Seized in Cherry Hill." *Philadelphia Daily News,* November 30, 1984.

Baldwin, James. "A Negro Assays the Negro Mood." *New York Times,* March 12, 1961.

Barner, George. "FBI Harlem Brink's Raid Called Terror." *New York Amsterdam News,* April 3, 1982.

Barron, Charles. "Afeni Shakur Smiling down from Heaven." *New York Amsterdam News,* June 23, 2016.

Bates, Josiah. "The Enduring Mystery Surrounding Malcolm X's Assassination." *Time,* February 20, 2020.

Blair, William G. "Two Brink's Suspects Seized in Dawn Raids in Manhattan." *New York Times,* March 27, 1982.

Blumenthal, Ralph. "Fugitive Trapped in Brooklyn Stake-Out." *New York Times,* June 8, 1973.

Bracelin, Jason. "Remembering Tupac." *Las Vegas Review-Journal,* September 7, 2021.

Bradley, Johnathan. "Maxwell Curtis Stanford Jr. (A.K.A. Muhammad Ahmad) (1941–)." *Blackpast,* January 12, 2001.

Broder, John. "Quayle Calls for Pulling Rap Album Tied to Murder Case." *Los Angeles Times*, September 23, 1992.

Browne, J. Zamgba. "5,000 Blacks Observe Solidarity Day." *New York Amsterdam News*, November 10, 1979.

Bruck, Connie. "The Takedown of Tupac." *The New Yorker*, June 29, 1997.

Burnham, David. "3 in Black Panther Party Win Hearing over Bail." *New York Times*, August 24, 1968.

———. "Off-Duty Police Here Join in Beating Black Panthers." *New York Times*, September 5, 1968.

———. "Panthers to Seek Voice over Police." *New York Times*, September 11, 1968.

Caldwell, Earl. "Black Panthers: 'Young Revolutionaries at War.'" *New York Times*, September 6, 1968.

———. "Internal Dispute Rends Panthers." *New York Times*, March 7, 1971.

———. "Suspects in Police Deaths Seen Likely to Be Indicted." *New York Times*, September 24, 1971.

Carmichael, Stokely. "What We Want." *The New York Review of Books*, September 22, 1966.

Castellucci, John. "Brink's Case Wiretaps Revealed." *Journal-News*, July 14, 1982.

———. "Chesimard Fled to Cuba, FBI Report Says." *Sunday Journal-News*, October 2, 1983.

———. "Gang Leader's Path: Medicine to Murder?" *Journal News*, July 25, 1982.

———. "Suspect Tied to Radical Group." *Journal-News*, October 21, 1981.

Celizic, Michael. "Shakur Mourned as 'Warrior.'" *Home News*, May 8, 1973.

Clendenin, Michael, and Robert Carrol. "500 Teachers Brave Threat." *Daily News*, September 29, 1967.

Conlon, Edward. "The Undercover Lives of NYPD's Black Officers." *Esquire*, March 21, 2017.

Corinealdi, Kaysha. "Dr. Carlos E. Russell and the Origins of Black Solidarity Day." *Black Perspectives*, September 14, 2021.

Crouse, Timothy. "Stranger in Harlem, Part One: Where the Prisoners Come From." *Village Voice*, December 25, 1978.

Cruse, Harold. "Revolutionary Nationalism and the Afro-American." *Studies on the Left*, Vol. 2, No. 3, 1962. Reprinted in *The Brotherwise Dispatch*, Vol. 2, Is. 1, December 2009–February 2010.

Cruz, Gloria. "Murder at Lincoln." *Palante*, Vol. 2, No. 8, July 31, 1970.

Cummings, Judith. "2 of 3 Black 'Army' Suspects Are Held without Bail." *New York Times*, September 19, 1973.

———. "Angela Davis Asks Support for 'Political Prisoners.'" *New York Times*, October 8, 1973.

Daley, Robert. "Target Blue: The Story behind the Police Assassinations." *New York,* February 12, 1973.

Daly, Michael. "Confessions of an Accused Cop Killer." Daily Beast, January 13, 2016.

Darnton, John. "7 Panthers Indicted in Slaying of a Party Official in Corona." *New York Times,* July 30, 1971.

Daughtry, Rev. Herbert. "Run Hard Sister, Run Hard." *New York Amsterdam News,* December 1, 1979.

Dawn, Randee. "Sex and Thugs and Bulletholes." *New Musical Express,* December 1994.

Delaney, Paul. "Black Separatists Raided in Jackson, Miss., 3 Lawmen Wounded." *New York Times,* August 19, 1971.

———. "Panthers to Reconvene in Capital to Ratify Their Constitution." *New York Times,* September 8, 1970.

Elkins, Jeanmaire, Robert Marino, Jack Lutton, and Mike Celizic. "Trooper's Killing Spurs Massive Manhunt." *The Home News,* May 2, 1973.

Everett, Arthur. "Police Guard against Ambushes." *Morning Call,* February 1, 1973.

Faso, Frank, and Paul Meskil. "Alarm out for 4 as Killers of 2 Cops in East Village." *Daily News,* February 9, 1972.

———. "Cops Go All Out in Hunt for 6 Black Libbers," *Daily News,* January 30, 1973.

Faso, Frank, James Duddy, and Henry Lee. "90g Bandits Escape Cops, Girl at Wheel." *Daily News,* March 17, 1972.

Feron, James. "Last Defendant in Brink's Trials Given 75 Years to Life in Prison." *New York Times,* June 27, 1984.

Finkelstein, Ileen. "Militants Charged with Two Murders." *Courier-News,* March 4, 1973.

Flood, Joe. "Why the Bronx Burned." *New York Post,* May 16, 2010.

Fosburgh, Lacey. "Panther Gets Life Term in Attack on 2 Policemen." *New York Times,* April 27, 1973.

Fox, Tom. "Panther Road Material." *Philadelphia Daily News,* September 1, 1970.

Fraser, C. Gerald. "Black Panther Fugitive in Algiers Charges That Huey P. Newton Is Seeking to Split Party." *New York Times,* March 12, 1971.

———. "Panther Buried in U.S. Cemetery." *New York Times,* May 8, 1973.

Fried, Joseph P. "2 Patrolmen Who Are Brothers Shot in a Brownsville Attack." *New York Times,* January 26, 1973.

———. "2 Policemen Slain by Shots in Back; 2 Men Are Sought." *New York Times,* May 22, 1971.

Gansberg, Martin. "Abortion Death Reported by City." *New York Times,* July 21, 1970.

Garrity, Bronwyn. "The Music Is the Message." *Los Angeles Times,* April 2, 2002.

Gearty, Robert. "Sentence a Crying Shame for Rapper Tupac." *Daily News,* February 8, 1995.

Gladwell, Malcolm. "Rapper Tupac Shakur Robbed, Shot in N.Y." *Washington Post,* December 1, 1994.

———. "The Rapper's New Rage." *Washington Post,* December 17, 1993.

Graczyk, Michael. "'Gangsta Rap' Killer Executed for Trooper's Death." *Houston Chronicle,* October 7, 2005.

Greene, Mel, and Edward Kirkman. "2 Killed, 2 Cops Shot in Brooklyn." *Daily News,* January 24, 1973.

Gross, Daniel A. "The Eleventh Parole Hearing of Jalil Abdul Muntaqim." *The New Yorker,* January 25, 2019.

Grutzner, Charles. "Bronx Is Deadliest of Teen War Areas." *New York Times,* May 10, 1950.

Gupte, Pranay. "Joanne Chesimard Pleads Not Guilty in Holdup Here." *New York Times,* July 21, 1973.

Hammer, Richard. "Is There a War against the Cops?" *New York Times,* May 23, 1971.

Hand, Judson. "Teacher Held in Rights Plot Freed on Bail." *Daily News,* March 8, 1968.

Hevesi, Dennis. "Alan Berkman, 63, Activist Doctor, Dies." *New York Times,* June 15, 2009.

Hicks, James L. "Another Angle." *New York Amsterdam News,* February 2, 1974.

Hightower, Charles. "A Year of Panther Struggle." *Daily World,* January 2, 1970.

Holley, Santi Elijah. "How Acupuncture Became a Radical Remedy in the Bronx." Atlas Obscura, November 9, 2020.

Howell, Ron. "Mutulu Shakur: A Father of Revolution." *Newsday,* April 6, 1994.

———. "On the Run with Joanne Chesimard." *Newsday,* October 11, 1987.

Huysman, Fritz. "3 Fail in Armored Car Holdup." *Pittsburgh Post-Gazette,* December 7, 1976.

Janson, Donald. "Panthers Raided in Philadelphia." *New York Times,* September 1, 1970.

———. "Release Is Denied to 14 Seized in Philadelphia Raids." *New York Times,* September 2, 1970.

Johnson, Cory. "Sweatin' Bullets." *Vibe,* February 1995. In *Tupac Shakur,* edited by Alan Light. Three Rivers Press, 1998.

Johnson, Rudy. "Joan Bird and Afeni Shakur, Self-Styled Soldiers in the Panther 'Class Struggle.'" *New York Times,* July 19, 1970.

Johnson, Thomas A. "Black Panthers Picket a School." *New York Times,* September 13, 1966.

Johnston, Richard J. H. "Squire Sentenced to Life for Killing State Trooper." *New York Times*, March 16, 1974.

———. "Trooper Recalls Shooting on Pike." *New York Times*, February 14, 1974.

Juravich, Nick. "Community Control and the 1968 Teacher Strikes in NYC at 50: A Roundtable." The Gotham Center for New York History, October 18, 2018.

Kahler, Kathryn. "The Capture: 'Stay Back.'" *Journal-News*, October 21, 1981.

Kaplan, Morris. "9 Allegedly in Black Army Indicted Here." *New York Times*, August 24, 1973.

Kaufman, Michael T. "Evidence of 'Liberation Army' Said to Rise." *New York Times*, February 17, 1972.

———. "Seized Woman Called Black Militants' 'Soul.'" *New York Times*, May 3, 1973.

Kavanaugh, Reginald. "Chesimard Convoyed to B'klyn Arraignment." *Home News*, July 20, 1973.

Kennedy, John. "Listen: Afeni Shakur Consoles Sybrina Fulton at Trayvon Martin Foundation Retreat." *Vibe*, May 22, 2014.

Khazan, Olga. "How Racism Gave Rise to Acupuncture for Addiction Treatment." *The Atlantic*, August 2, 2018.

Kifner, John. "FBI Sought Doom of Panther Party." *New York Times*, May 9, 1976.

———. "Ferguson Convicted in Death Plot Trial." *New York Times*, June 15, 1968.

Kirkland, Dennis, and James Lintz. "Panthers Open Headquarters, Vow to Hold Convention; 14 Suspects Lose Appeal." *Philadelphia Inquirer*, September 2, 1970.

Kirkman, Edward, and Lester Abelman. "'Top Suspect' Cleared in Slaying of 2 Cops." *Daily News*, May 25, 1971.

Kirkman, Edward. "In Black Lib Diary: 'More Bad News.'" *Daily News*, January 10, 1974.

———. "To Militants, She's a St. Joanne." *Daily News*, May 3, 1973.

Kitchen, Travis. "Unfortunate Son: The Roots of Tupac Shakur's Rebellion." *Baltimore Sun*, November 29, 2016.

Knight, Michael. "Death Here Tied to Panther Feud." *New York Times*, March 10, 1971.

Lake, Katherine, Stuart Marques, and Larry Cole. "Sentence 4 in Brink's Case." *Daily News*, February 16, 1984.

Langer, Gary. "Brink's Suspect Pleads Innocent." *Journal-News*, March 8, 1986.

Lassiter, Matthew D., and the Policing and Social Justice History Lab. "'New Bethel Incident,' Detroit under Fire: Police Violence, Crime Politics, and the Struggle for Racial Justice in the Civil Rights Era." University of Michigan Carceral State Project, 2021.

Ledbetter, Les. "Huey Newton Seized on Intent to Murder." *New York Times*, May 12, 1978.

Lee, Christina. "What Happened to the Tupac Amaru Shakur Center for the Arts?" *Rolling Stone*, July 6, 2016.

Lee, Vincent, and Henry Lee. "100 Hunting Cop Shooters; Murphy Asks Gun Control." *Daily News*, May 21, 1971.

Lewis, John. "Tupac Was Here." *Baltimore*, September 2016.

Lissner, Will. "Panthers Admit Guilt in Robbery." *New York Times*, September 25, 1971.

Llorens, David. "Black Separatism in Perspective: Movement Reflects Failure of Integration." *Ebony*, September 1968.

Lubasch, Arnold H. "Barnes Guilty in Drug Case; Could Get Life." *New York Times*, December 3, 1977.

———. "Brink's Witness Tells of Robbery in Bronx in 1981." *New York Times*, May 5, 1983.

———. "Brink's Witness Testifies on the Chesimard Escape." *New York Times*, May 4, 1983.

———. "Witness Says He Aided 2 Brink's Robbery Suspects." *New York Times*, June 19, 1983.

Maniace, Len. "Brink's Guard Recalls Afternoon of Horror." *Journal-News*, October 23, 1981.

Manley, Howard. "2 Guilty in 1981 Brink's Robbery." *Newsday*, May 12, 1988.

Marino, Robert, and Christopher Guidette. "Telephoned Tip Led Police to Quarry Who Was Ready to Quit." *Home News*, May 4, 1973.

Marriott, Michel. "Shots Silence Angry Voice Sharpened by the Streets." *New York Times*, September 16, 1996.

Martin, Douglas. "Elmer G. Pratt, Jailed Panther Leader, Dies at 63." *New York Times*, June 3, 2011.

Matthews, Les. "Gunplay Alerts Police." *New York Amsterdam News*, April 24, 1970.

———. "How Did She Get Pregnant in Jail?" *New York Amsterdam News*, February 2, 1974.

McCormack, Ned. "One Dead in Queens Shootout." *Journal-News*, October 24, 1981.

McDonnough, Maxine. "Sister Samad: Living the Garvey Life." *Jamaica Journal*, Vol. 20, No. 3, August–October 1987.

McFadden, Robert D. "4 Panthers Admit Guilt in Slaying." *New York Times*, May 22, 1973.

———. "Man Killed in Queens Car Chase; Plate Tied to Armored-Car Gang." *New York Times*, October 24, 1981.

———. "Patrolman Slain, Partner Is Shot." *New York Times,* January 28, 1972.

———. "Police-Black Panther Scuffles Mark Brooklyn Street Rally." *New York Times,* August 2, 1968.

———. "Police Force of Hundreds Hunts Comrades' Killers." *New York Times,* May 23, 1971.

McFadden, William. "Panther Leader Faces Arms Rap." *Daily News,* September 20, 1970.

McMorris, Frances. "Brink's Robbers Sentenced." *Daily News,* August 3, 1988.

McQuiston, John T. "Fugitive Black Militant Killed, 4 Wounded in Bronx Shootout." *New York Times,* November 15, 1973.

Meddis, Sam. "Observer Says Confusion Reigned following Escape." *Courier-News,* November 3, 1979.

Medsger, Betty. "Remembering an Earlier Time When a Theft Unmasked Government Surveillance." *Washington Post,* January 10, 2014.

Melvin, Tessa. "Fund for Inmates Celebrated." *New York Times,* June 26, 1983.

Moritz, Owen. "When the Teachers Union Shut Down NYC Schools for Two Months over Racially-Charged Community Control." *Daily News,* August 14, 2017.

Morrison, Micah. "Did an FBI Call Accidentally Kill an NYPD Officer?" *New York Post,* April 19, 2015.

Mulvaney, Kieran. "How the Ali-Frazier 'Fight of the Century' Became a Proxy Battle for a Divided Nation." *History,* March 5, 2021.

Murphy, Kim. "Activist's Bid for Freedom Blocked." *Los Angeles Times,* August 12, 1987.

Narvaez, Alfonso A. "Young Lords Seize Lincoln Hospital Building." *New York Times,* July 15, 1970.

Nicholas, JB. "August Rebellion: New York's Forgotten Female Prison Riot." *Village Voice,* August 30, 2016.

O'Malley, Daniel, Patrick Doyle, and John Murphy. "Machine Gun Rips 2 Cops of Guard on Hogan's Home." *Daily News,* May 20, 1971.

Oser, Alan S. "Rent Strikes Grow Widespread in the South Bronx." *New York Times,* March 19, 1972.

Pastor, Carl. "Seize the Hospitals!" *Palante,* Vol. 2, No. 16, December 11, 1970.

Perlmutter, Emanuel. "16 Negroes Seized; Plot to Kill Wilkins and Young Charged." *New York Times,* June 22, 1967.

———. "Extra Duty Tours for Police Set Up after 2d Ambush." *New York Times,* January 29, 1973.

Philips, Chuck. "Music to Kill Cops By? Rap Song Blamed in Texas Trooper's Death." *Washington Post,* September 20, 1992.

———. "Rap Defense Doesn't Stop Death Penalty." *Los Angeles Times,* July 15, 1993.

———. "Texas Death Renews Debate over Violent Rap Lyrics." *Los Angeles Times*, September 17, 1992.

Porzig, Molly. Interview with Vicente "Panama" Alba. "Lincoln Detox Center: The People's Drug Program." *The Abolitionist*, March 15, 2013.

Powell, Kevin. "All Eyez on Him." *Vibe*, February 1996. In *Tupac Shakur*, edited by Alan Light. Three Rivers Press, 1998.

———. "Ready to Live." *Vibe*, April 1995. In *Tupac Shakur*, edited by Alan Light. Three Rivers Press, 1998.

———. "This Thug's Life." *Vibe*, February 1994. In *Tupac Shakur*, edited by Alan Light. Three Rivers Press, 1998.

Pugh, Thomas, Gerald Kessler, and Henry Lee. "Nab 16 in Rights Assassination Plot." *Daily News*, June 22, 1967.

Reed, Roy. "Armed Negro Unit Spreads in South." *New York Times*, June 6, 1965.

Riesel, Victor. "'Black Labor' Threat." *Burlington Free Press*, September 20, 1968.

Roos, Dave. "The 1969 Raid That Killed Black Panther Leader Fred Hampton." *History*, February 3, 2021.

Rosen, Jane. "Black Lib Woman Shot in Battle." *Guardian*, May 4, 1973.

Rule, Sheila. "On Solidarity Day, Blacks Say 'We Are Still Slaves.'" *New York Times*, November 6, 1979.

Russell, Judy. "Joanne Is Found Guilty of Murder of a Jersey Cop." *Daily News*, March 26, 1977.

Rustin, Bayard. "'Black Power' and Coalition Politics." *Commentary*, September 1966.

Ryan, Hugh. "The Queer History of the Women's House of Detention." *The Activist History Review*, May 31, 2019.

Sackett, Russell. "Plotting a War on 'Whitey.'" *Life*, June 10, 1966.

Santangelo, Mike, and Stuart Marques. "Top Terror Figure Grabbed." *Daily News*, May 12, 1985.

Saunders, D. J., and Henry Lee. "Judge Warns Joanne She May Be Gagged." *Daily News*, December 5, 1973.

Saunders, D. J., and Paul Meskil. "Tells of Chesimard Jailbreak." *Daily News*, May 3, 1983.

Sayles, Justin. "A Deal with the Devil: The Triumph and Tragedy of 'All Eyez on Me.'" *The Ringer*, February 12, 2021.

Scott, Cathy. "Shakur Shooting Witness Found Dead in N.J." *Las Vegas Sun*, November 13, 1996.

Seem, Mark. "Montreal, South Bronx and the Early Days." Mutulushakur .com, March 14, 2016.

Seiler, Michael. "Suspect in N.Y. Brink's Holdup, Three Killings Caught in L.A." *Los Angeles Times*, February 13, 1986.

Senna, Danzy. "Violence Is Golden." *Spin*, April 1994.

Sherrod, Lena. "Brinks Robbery Trial Goes to the Jury." *New York Amsterdam News*, May 7, 1988.

Sinclair, Abiola. "Tupac Shakur in New Fracas; This Time He's in LA Jail." *New York Amsterdam News*, April 2, 1994.

———. "Tupac Tied to Murder?" *New York Amsterdam News*, January 1, 1994.

Slack, Sara. "The Inside Story of the Malcolm X IS 201 Memorial." *New York Amsterdam News*, March 2, 1968.

Slotnik, Daniel E. "Nehanda Abiodun, 68, Black Revolutionary Who Fled to Cuba." *Philadelphia Tribune*, February 12, 2019.

Smothers, Ronald. "Suspect in Queens Shootout Says That Officers Beat Him." *New York Times*, October 28, 1981.

Solis, Gustavo, and Murray Weiss. "Black Panther Convicted of Trying to Kill 6 Officers Released from Prison." *DNAinfo*, November 26, 2014.

Stanford, Max. "We Are at War with White America." *Black America*, Fall 1964.

Stephens, Ronald J. "Freeman Beach-Seabreeze, Wilmington, North Carolina (ca. 1885–)." *Blackpast*, March 9, 2014.

Sullivan, Joseph F. "Chesimard Asks Clarification of Assault Charges." *New York Times*, March 25, 1977.

———. "Doctor Testifies on Bullet Scars in Chesimard Trial." *New York Times*, March 18, 1977.

———. "Mrs. Chesimard, on Stand, Denies Having Weapon in Turnpike Shooting." *New York Times*, March 16, 1977.

———. "Panther, Trooper Slain in Shoot-Out." *New York Times*, May 3, 1973.

Sullivan, Ronald. "Bronx Drug Program Called a 'Ripoff.'" *New York Times*, November 28, 1978.

———. "Leaders of Drug Unit at Lincoln Removed on Orders from Koch." *New York Times*, November 29, 1978.

Surgens, Carol. "Convicted Murderess Flees Jail." *Courier-News*, November 3, 1979.

Taylor, Rebecca. "Seabreeze—A History Part I—The Freeman Family." Federal Point Historic Preservation Society, April 15, 2016.

Tolchin, Martin. "150 Hunt Ambushers Who Shot Policemen." *New York Times*, August 3, 1968.

———. "Rage Permeates All Facets of Life in the South Bronx." *New York Times*, January 17, 1973.

———. "South Bronx: A Jungle Stalked by Fear, Seized by Rage." *New York Times*, January 15, 1973.

Tomasson, Robert E. "Grenade Wrecks Police Car Here." *New York Times*, December 21, 1971.

———. "Man Killed and 2 Policemen Are Wounded in Harlem Gunfight." *New York Times*, April 20, 1971.

Treaster, Joseph B. "Marilyn Buck: A Fugitive and Long a Radical." *New York Times*, October 23, 1981.

Viola, David. "When the Cops Were Spies and the Terrorists Were Everywhere." The Gotham Center for New York History, October 10, 2019.

Waggoner, Walter H. "Chesimard Murder Trial Opens in New Brunswick." *New York Times*, February 16, 1977.

———. "Joanne Chesimard Convicted in Killing of Jersey Trooper." *New York Times*, March 26, 1977.

———. "Neurosurgeon's Testimony Backs Mrs. Chesimard." *New York Times*, March 17, 1977.

Walsh, George M. "Brinks Prosecutors Seek to Bolster Rison Testimony." *Journal-News*, May 18, 1983.

———. "How a Week of Terror Unfolded . . ." *Journal-News*, October 25, 1981.

———. "Prison Break Critique Offered at Brink's Trial." *Journal-News*, May 19, 1983.

———. "Robbery-Murder Nabbed." *Journal-News*, February 13, 1986.

Walsh, James. "Shakur, Buck Get Lengthy Prison Terms." *Journal-News*, August 3, 1988.

Weber, Brandon. "When Native Americans Routed the Ku Klux Klan in the Battle of Hayes Pond." *Progressive*, July 19, 2018.

Weingarten, Christopher R. "I Get Around: The Oral History of 2pac's Digital Underground Years." *Rolling Stone*, April 6, 2017.

DOCUMENTS

"Assata Bulletin," Assata Shakur Defense Committee, March 7, 1977: http://freedomarchives.org/Documents/Finder/DOC513_scans/Assata_Shakur/513.Assata.Bulletin.March7.1977.pdf

Black Liberation Army Communiqué No. 4: http://freedomarchives.org/Documents/Finder/DOC513_scans/BLA/513.BLA.communiques.pdf

Black Liberation Army Communiqué No. 12: http://freedomarchives.org/Documents/Finder/DOC513_scans/BLA/513.BLA.communiques.pdf

Face the Nation Interview with Stokely Carmichael, Chairman of the Student Nonviolent Coordinating Committee, Sunday, June 19, 1966: https://www.crmvet.org/nars/660619_sncc_stokely_ftn.pdf

"FBI Memo from J. Edgar Hoover concerning Garvey" (October 11, 1919), from Robert A. Hill (Ed.), *The Marcus Garvey and Universal Negro Improvement Association Papers, Volume II*, Berkeley and Los Angeles: University of California Press, 1983: https://www-1.gsb.columbia.edu/documents/document_07_04_020_hoover.pdf

"Free Assata Shakur" Communiqué, May 19 Communist Organization: http://freedomarchives.org/Documents/Finder/DOC37_scans/37.May19.Free AssataShakur.flyer.pdf

Memo, J. Edgar Hoover, FBI Director, to Field Offices, August 25, 1967: https://vault.fbi.gov/cointel-pro/cointel-pro-black-extremists/cointelpro-black-extremists-part-01-of

"Mutulu Shakur: A Life of Struggle": https://freedomarchives.org/Documents/Finder/DOC510_scans/New_Afrikan_Prisoners/510.mutulu.shakur.life.struggle.pdf

Odinga, Sekou, Interview in *Can't Jail the Spirit: Political Prisoners in the U.S.: A Collection of Biographies,* Committee to End the Marion Lockdown, 1985: https://www.freedomarchives.org/Documents/Finder/DOC3_scans/3.cant.jail.spirit.1985.pdf

Records & Briefs—New York State Appellate Division, Vol. 220, Library of the New York Law Institute, "Riots, Civil, and Criminal Disorders: Hearings before the United States Senate Committee on Government Operations, Permanent Subcommittee on Investigations, Ninetieth and Ninety-First Congresses," United States: U.S. Government Printing Office, 1969

"Tape from Assata": http://freedomarchives.org/Documents/Finder/DOC513_scans/Assata_Shakur/513.Assata.tape.from.assata.pdf

"Terrorism: A Staff Study," Committee on Internal Security, United States House of Representatives, Ninety-Third Congress, Second Session, August 1, 1974

"The FBI's Covert Action Program to Destroy The Black Panther Party": https://www.hsdl.org/?view&did=479831

United States Congress Senate Committee on Government Operations, Permanent Subcommittee on Investigations, "Riots, Civil, and Criminal Disorders: Hearings before the United States Senate Committee on Government Operations, Permanent Subcommittee on Investigations, Ninetieth and Ninety-First Congresses," United States: U.S. Government Printing Office, 1969

FILM, TELEVISION, AND VIDEO

Donovan, Mia (Dir.), *Dope Is Death,* Eyesteelfilm, March 6, 2020

Lazin, Lauren (Dir.), *Tupac: Resurrection,* Amaru Entertainment, Inc., November 14, 2003

MTV News Tupac interview with Tabitha Soren, October 27, 1995: https://www.youtube.com/watch?v=GpPbYGJRg0Q

"Mutulu Shakur," *American Gangster,* Season 3, Ep. 6, BET, November 27, 2009

Rolando, Gloria (Dir.), *Eyes of the Rainbow,* 1997

"Tupac at Malcolm X Grassroots Movement": https://www.youtube.com
    /watch?v=3m2OUSZ5WR8
Tupac Clinton Correctional Facility prison interview, 1995
"Tupac Shakur 1988 High School Interview," Historic Films Stock Footage
    Archive: https://www.youtube.com/watch?v=v_XT9-C5Qu8
"Tupac Shakur Speaks—National Chairman for the New Afrikan Panther
    Party (1989)": https://www.youtube.com/watch?v=MW8JeFKEAxM

INTERVIEWS WITH THE AUTHOR

Walter Bosque del Rio, July 8, 2021
Richard Fischbein, January 4, 2021
Yaasmyn Fula, June 8 and June 16, 2022
Cyril "Brother Bullwhip" Innis Jr., July 9, 2021
Sekou Odinga, May 3, April 4, and July 13, 2021
Susan Rosenberg, February 24, 2021
Makini Shakur, December 29, 2020
Malik Shakur, July 22, 2021
Mopreme Shakur, November 17, 2020, and January 20, 2022
Cleo Silvers, November 28, 2020
Leila Steinberg, January 24 and February 1, 2022
Bilal Sunni-Ali, December 1, December 8, and December 15, 2020
Watani Tyehimba, January 21 and February 9, 2021
Akinyele Umoja, November 10 and December 17, 2020

INDEX

McCabe, Edward P., 107
McGriff, Kenneth "Supreme," 249
McKenzie, Roland, 73–74
McKiernan, Robert, 160
McLucas, Lonnie, 84
Me Against the World (album), 258
Media County (PA), FBI office heist, 91–92
Meeropol, Abel and Anne, 148
Meglio, John J., 53
Meredith, James, 36
meridians, in traditional Chinese medicine, 121n
"Message to the Grass Roots" (Malcolm X), 23
methadone, 120
Middleton, Pete, 180
Mississippi Summer Project (1964), 34
MMI. *See* Muslim Mosque, Inc.
Mocedes the Mellow (rapper). *See* Shakur, Maurice (Mopreme)
Monster: The Autobiography of an L.A. Gang Member (Monster Kody; Sanyika Shakur), 252
"Monster Kody." *See* Scott, Kody "Monster Kody"
Monte Carlo on the Sea (North Carolina), 146
Moore, Audley "Queen Mother," 44, 101, 109, 196
"Mouse Man." *See* Smith, Dana "Mouse Man"
Muhammad, Elijah, 22–25, 49
Muntaqim, Jalil Abdul, 137
Murphy, Patrick, 130, 160
Murtagh, Judge John, 15, 129
Muslim Mosque, Inc. (MMI), 24
MXGM. *See* Malcolm X Grassroots Movement
Myers, Twymon Ford, 136, 138, 140, 158–60, 170, 181, 186

NAACP. *See* National Association for the Advancement of Colored People
NADA. *See* National Acupuncture Detoxification Association (NADA) protocol
NAIM. *See* New Afrikan Independence Movement
Nanuet Mall robbery, 206–11
Napier, Sam, 87, 128, 134–35, 202
NAPO. *See* New Afrikan People's Organization
Nation of Islam (NOI), 22–24, 49, 108, 256
National Acupuncture Detoxification Association (NADA) protocol, 266–67
National Association for the Advancement of Colored People (NAACP), 35–36, 38, 105
National Black Government Convention, 109
National Coalition for Black Human Rights, 195
National Committee for the Defense of Political Prisoners, 133
National Movement for the Establishment of the 49th State, 108
National Task Force for Cointelpro Litigation and Research, 124, 175, 196, 224, 236
National Urban League, 105
Negroes with Guns (Williams), 47
Nelson, Richard, 159, 166
New Afrikan Independence Movement (NAIM), 107, 110, 120
New Afrikan Panthers, 236–37, 239
New Afrikan People's Organization (NAPO), 237